P9-DFY-143

⊕ RAND McNALLY

The Atlas of
DREAM PLACES

The Atlas of
DREAM
PLACES

A grand tour of
the world's best
loved destinations

⊕ RAND McNALLY

Rand McNally
The Atlas of Dream Places

Published by Rand McNally
in 1995 in the U.S.A.

A Marshall Edition
Conceived, edited, and designed by
Marshall Editions, 170 Piccadilly, London W1V 9DD

Copyright © 1995 Marshall Editions Developments Limited

All rights reserved. No part of this book may be reproduced or utilized
in any form or by any means, electronic or mechanical, including
photocopying, recording, or by any information storage or retrieval
system, without permission in writing from the publishers.

Library of Congress Cataloging in Publication Data

The atlas of dream places : a grand tour of the world's
  best-loved destinations.
        p.   cm
      Includes bibliographical references and index.
      ISBN 0-528-83774-5 (hc)
      1. Geography. 2. Tourist trade.   I. Rand McNally and Company.
  G116.D74 1995
  338.4'791—dc20   95–17381
                                       CIP

Editor   Anne Yelland
Art editor   Frances de Rees
Picture editor   Zilda Tandy
Research   Jolika Feszt, Jon Richards
Index   Kathie Gill
Copy editors   Isabella Raeburn, Maggi McCormick
DTP editors   Mary Pickles, Pennie Jelliff
Editorial director   Sophie Collins
Managing editor   Lindsay McTeague
Production editor   Sorrel Everton
Production   Sarah Hinks

Contributors:
Sophie Campbell 6–9, 26–39, 46–47, 66–75, 127, 138–51,
   163–69, 178–81, 190–93
Antony Mason 11–23, 54–59, 62–65, 76–77, 106–11, 128–37,
   158–61, 176–77, 194–99
Caroline Taggart 24–25, 40–45, 48–53, 61, 82–93, 96–105,
   120–21, 156–57, 182–89
Jennifer Westwood 78–81, 95, 112–19, 122–25, 152–55

Illustrators:
David Atkinson (feature maps)
Sue Sharples (place maps)

Printed and bound in Italy by
New Interlitho SpA, Milan
Originated by Master Image, Hong Kong

Contents

Introduction

The nature of dreams

"There is no place more wonderful than this: there is no place more marvelous than here."

MILAREPA, ON MOUNT KAILAS

Throughout the twentieth century, human beings have become increasingly intrigued by the possibility of traveling through time, either going back to see how our ancestors once lived, or moving forward to see how our descendants will survive. We are filled with limitless curiosity, an insatiable desire to imagine and understand the existence of others.

Places of pilgrimage exert a powerful attraction, drawing believers to their precincts in search of a higher consciousness or the ultimate truth. Tibetan pilgrims pause on the path overlooking the town of Shigatse.

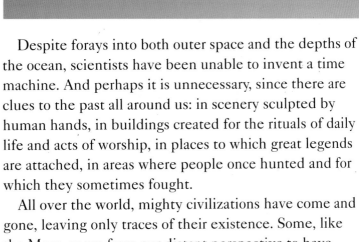

Despite forays into both outer space and the depths of the ocean, scientists have been unable to invent a time machine. And perhaps it is unnecessary, since there are clues to the past all around us: in scenery sculpted by human hands, in buildings created for the rituals of daily life and acts of worship, in places to which great legends are attached, in areas where people once hunted and for which they sometimes fought.

All over the world, mighty civilizations have come and gone, leaving only traces of their existence. Some, like the Maya, seem from our distant perspective to have disappeared in the blink of an eye, as absolutely and inexplicably as the dinosaurs. They have left no clues as to the cause of their demise. Others – such as the Romans or the ancient Greeks – became decadent and weak, barely recognizable as the great world conquerors they had once been. And yet more were overcome, simply absorbed into another, dominant way of life.

"Traveling," said Descartes, "is almost like talking with men of other centuries." This is our great gift. In a

Nara was once the capital of Japan and is today renowned for its ancient artefacts and Buddhist temples, including the Yakashi Temple. A Japanese proverb holds that one can die content having seen the city.

Notre-Dame Cathedral is a window on the past: it has stood in the center of Paris for more than eight centuries and the glass in its rose windows was crafted more than 600 years ago.

physical – if not temporal – sense, we can travel. We can cover vast distances in a short time, visiting lands and cultures which are utterly alien to our experience. Whether great cities of sophistication and beauty – like Paris or Kyoto – remote eyries such as Machu Picchu in Peru, or the staggering achievements of ancient architects and builders, like the Temple of Amun at Karnak, their very stones hold our dreams.

But the substance of a dream comes as much from within as from a place itself. We take the facts we have, the tales we believe, and the evidence we can see, and mold them into an image that may not reflect reality *per se*. It reflects the reality that we want to see. So poets have seized on the "spirit" of a place throughout the ages; such legendary entities as Xanadu and Camelot have come alive through the eyes of writers; quests like the Odyssey and the wanderings of Don Quixote exist through their pens; inveterate travelers such as Marco Polo and Christopher Columbus have left written evidence of what they saw on their journeys. What does it matter if Kathmandu is not Shangri-La? It still has all the mystique and fascination of the hidden mountain kingdom James Hilton wrote about in *Lost Horizon*. It has the spirit of Shangri-La.

Today, as techniques of time-tagging and virtual reality quickly develop, the bare bones of these cultures can be clad in flesh. We can step into another world, in feeling as

"...favoured and sensual, exuding from the banks of its golden river a miasma of perpetual excitement..."

LAURIE LEE, ON SEVILLE

well as in fact. The pages of this book take you on a similar voyage of discovery, building up the layers of history and fable, heroes and villains, events momentous and mundane, often in surroundings of exquisite natural beauty. They describe the places where people – ancient and modern – lived, loved, ate, slept, worked, and worshipped. They recall their legends and their battles, their songs and their sayings.

When James Leigh Hunt wrote his poem "The Nile" in the early nineteenth century, he said of the great river: "It flows through old hushed Egypt and its sands / Like some grave mighty thought, threading a dream...." He recognized that what builds the atmosphere of a place is a tangible feeling of identity which is more than the sum of its parts. This is what we seek here. And, in finding our dreams, we may find that the stones that sing stories of the past also hold the key to the future.

Tranquil lakes reflect rolling hills, lofty trees, and a perfect sky in Britain's Lake District, an area that has inspired generations of writers and artists.

CITIES *of* ROMANCE *and* CREATION

THE WORD CIVILIZATION IS DEFINED BY REFERENCE TO cities, complex webs of streets and buildings, of government, commerce, art and leisure, worship, learning. And cities evoke complex dreams, the reveries of travelers drawn to their famous monuments, and drawn also to wander the very streets where momentous events unfolded, where great figures of the past once walked. Dreams also created these intricate urban landscapes – the dreams and visions of their founders and their architects, and also of the countless citizens who have contributed to the character and appearance of their city, imbuing it with its own unique stamp and flavor. No one knows who laid the foundations of Damascus, perhaps the oldest city on earth, maybe the site of paradise; St. Petersburg, by contrast, was conceived and executed to the glory of a tsar a mere three centuries ago. Farther west are different urban treasures: the cobbled streets of Prague echo to the strains of folk violins, those of Seville resound with flamenco, and those of Venice are "paved" with water. From the quarter of Paris where the world's finest artists produced their masterpieces to that of New Orleans where jazz was born, the romance of each city is unique.

Bridges under streetlights, the moon reflected in a river, and buildings that have witnessed generations of citizens living and loving in good times and bad are the essence of a city. Paris – one of the world's greatest metropolises – is unmistakable.

St. Petersburg

Gem of the northern ice

Even during the summer, there is the hint of a chill in the air, carried on the steady breaths of Arctic breeze which send white clouds scudding over the open spaces of the hinterland. Left to its own devices, Nature would have presented a flat and forlorn, faintly hopeless landscape, where the River Neva grinds its path through a delta of islands at its mouth on the Gulf of Finland, sparkling gently in the pale northern light. Instead there is a miracle: lining the riverbank is the world's most northerly metropolis – a startling confectioner's realm of icing-sugar palaces, bejeweled cathedrals, gilded spires, and panoramic vistas.

St. Petersburg is the product of one man's determination to pull Russia kicking and screaming into the modern world. For Tsar Peter the Great, who reigned between 1682 and 1725, Europe held the keys to the future of his backward country. With St. Petersburg he wanted to create a "window on Europe," a grand port with marine access to the West, as well as a modern and exquisite city to rival Paris and London. He succeeded triumphantly: "The united magnificence of all the cities of Europe could but equal St. Petersburg," gushed the French philosopher Voltaire. But Peter the Great's city is more than the sum of its inspirations: it has a unique atmosphere, a curious mixture of European and Russian – combined with the almost barbaric sense of scale that was the hallmark of the tsars.

Peter was an extraordinary man. He possessed a furious energy, a voracious interest in all manner of things, a vision of how his country

Illuminated against the long, dark nights of the St. Petersburg winter, the golden dome of St. Isaac's Cathedral glows with ethereal beauty – a landmark that can be seen from the countryside beyond the outskirts of the city. While the cathedral's exterior is a sober, Neoclassical statement of imperial grandeur, its interior is like a vast jewelry box of mosaics, painted panels, gilded cartouches, precious icons, and columns of startling green malachite stone from the Ural Mountains.

ST. PETERSBURG

RUSSIA

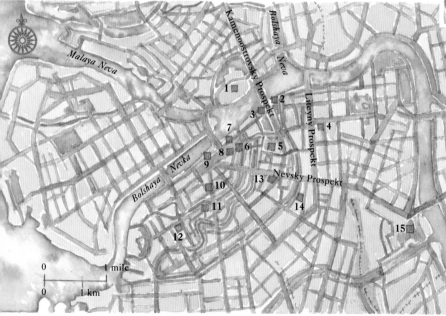

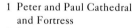

1. Peter and Paul Cathedral and Fortress
2. Summer Palace
3. Marble Palace
4. Cathedral of the Transfiguration
5. Church of the Resurrection
6. General Staff Building
7. Winter Palace (Hermitage)
8. Palace Square
9. Admiralty
10. St. Isaac's Cathedral
11. Yusupov Palace
12. Mariinsky Theatre
13. Kazan Cathedral
14. Beloselsky–Belozevsky Palace
15. Alexander Nevsky Monastery

might be. Yet he was also boorish, prone to uncontrolled fits and to outbursts of savagery and sadism. It was during the Great Northern War (1700–21) with Sweden that he conceived the idea for his new city, planting it on swampy lands at the enemy's doorstep. Work began in 1703, which makes St. Petersburg – for all its appearances – a young city, younger than New York by almost a century.

During the first years of construction, Peter lived in a humble log cabin, preserved today on the north bank of the Neva. The city began to take shape around him – not without enormous abuses to which his autocratic rule gave him access. Some 40,000 laborers were commandeered: serfs, convicts, Swedish prisoners of war, and craftsmen who were forbidden to work elsewhere. The first tasks were to drain the marshes with canals and then to drive thousands of wooden piles into the mud on which to lay the city's foundations. Meanwhile, the massive Peter and Paul Fortress, with its 60-foot (18-m) thick ramparts, was built on Hare Island to protect the infant city. Thousands of workers died of scurvy, dysentery, and typhoid, but were replaced by others press-ganged into the task. Nor was the nobility excused: after 1710, members of the court and the imperial government were obliged to move to St. Petersburg, build palaces there, and people the city. St. Petersburg was made the new national capital in 1712, a calculated insult to Moscow, a city Peter detested.

The style was to be European through and through, and before long it was not just architects and decorators who were arriving in St. Petersburg from all over Europe to make their fortune, but painters, musicians, dance masters, dressmakers, and cooks. In the reign of Catherine the Great (1762–92), St. Petersburg's high society enjoyed a ceaseless round of glittering balls, attended by thousands who paraded through the streets and squares in processions of gilded carriages. The city developed as a center of European culture and in the nineteenth century was host to a string of great composers: Tchaikovsky, Borodin, Mussorgsky, Rimsky-Korsakov. To these were added the sometimes dissident voices of many of the great names of Russian literature, notably Pushkin and Dostoevsky.

Grandeur is a keynote in St. Petersburg: St. Isaac's Cathedral can hold a congregation of 14,000; Kazan Cathedral was the third-largest cathedral in the world when it was built; the Winter Palace boasts more than 1,100 rooms and 117 staircases. Next to it, the needle-thin spire of the Admiralty is at the hub of the city plan, from which broad avenues, or Prospekts, radiate outward over many of the 600 bridges that span the river and a series of concentric canals. The most celebrated avenue, the Nevsky Prospekt, was named after Alexander Nevsky, who defeated the Swedes on the Neva in 1240. With its high-class shops, restaurants, and cafés, richly refurbished in the late nineteenth century in Art Nouveau style, it was once the most elegant commercial street in Russia.

This city plan was symbolic of the highly centralized nature of Russian imperial rule. Following Peter's reforms, nobles were conscripted to serve in the increasingly hierarchical administration, at the pinnacle of which was the royal family. Peter's daughter, the Empress Elizabeth, had an entourage of 24,000 people, all of whom

Russia is one of the great homes of classical ballet, and during the communist period St. Petersburg's Kirov Ballet was among the most celebrated in the world. It still performs in the spectacular nineteenth-century Kirov Theater (now called by its original name, the Mariinsky Theater), in which the audience sit beneath lavish gilded ornament and chandeliers, in chairs upholstered in blue velvet.

Rudolf Nureyev, Natalia Makarova, and Mikhail Baryshnikov were all trained at the Kirov before fleeing to the West.

The southern side of the Winter Palace looks out over the huge Palace Square, the scene of several momentous events in Russian history. The Alexander Column, raised in 1834 as a monument to Tsar Alexander I's victory over Napoleon in 1814, is made from a 148-foot (45-m) high piece of granite – the tallest single carved stone in the world.

The Hermitage was once simply an arm of the Winter Palace, used by Catherine the Great to display her growing collection of paintings, which included works by Titian, Raphael, Rembrandt, and Rubens.

After the Revolution, the private collections of the Russian elite were confiscated, and the Hermitage Museum acquired some 14,000 paintings and 12,000 sculptures, making it one of the world's greatest art collections. It includes, among other treasures, numerous works by the Impressionists and Postimpressionists. In 1946 the Winter Palace itself was adapted to house the collection, but most of the sumptuous staterooms and apartments were left intact.

followed her as she moved back and forth between St. Petersburg and Moscow. The wealthiest Russian families had palaces for the summer, palaces for the winter, hunting lodges, and country retreats, as well as strings of estates, huge private art collections, yachts, stables full of horses, numerous servants, and countless serfs.

In the limited nature of the top of this social pyramid lay the seeds of its destruction. Beneath the froth of St. Petersburg's architecture and social whirl seethed a growing discontent. This spilled over into bloody confrontation periodically in the nineteenth century, until in January 1905 a demonstration by desperate peasant families bearing religious icons, on their way to plead the help of the tsar, was intercepted in the Palace Square by the militia, and some 200 died. In March 1917, the tsar abdicated before a rising storm of discontent and criticisms about the conduct of World War I; then on October 25, the Palace Square was again the scene of a momentous uprising, when the Bolsheviks removed the Provisional Government from the Winter Palace and finally seized power.

St. Petersburg underwent painful decades of transformation. Although it lost the title of capital to Moscow in 1918, it became the most advanced industrial city in the Soviet Union, and its population eventually grew to some five million. The result was massive overcrowding and a proliferation of faceless and seedy suburbs. And the stifling traditions of tsarist bureaucracy and civil abuses persisted beneath the new mask of communism.

The city's name had been changed to Petrograd at the outbreak of World War I in 1914, as the tsar felt that St. Petersburg was too Germanic. Five days after the death of the Bolshevik leader Lenin in 1924, it was renamed Leningrad. The palaces were turned into offices, and the churches into public institutions. The historic center of the city slid into patrician decay, its ocher and orange stucco fading and crumbling through the neglect arising from a genuine distaste for any reminders of the iniquities of pre-Revolutionary days.

Worse was to come. In World War II the German army laid siege to Leningrad from September 1941 to January 1944 – almost 900 days of savage bombardment and blockade, during which some 200,000 people died from injuries, and a further 600,000 from starvation and disease. But with the same determination and energy with which the city had been founded, Leningrad was rebuilt after the war, and in a program of restoration, many of the great imperial palaces were lovingly reconstructed to exacting standards.

In 1991, after the dramatic collapse of communism in the Soviet Union, the people of Leningrad voted to call their city St. Petersburg once more. Today, despite sharing with its fellow Russian cities the problems of coming to terms with a capitalist economy and straitened times, there is a fresh sparkle in St. Petersburg, no longer to be found only in the reflections of the restored palaces and bridges in the canals and the river. It is also visible in the smiles of the shoppers wandering down a revitalized Nevsky Prospekt, of children splashing in the fountains of the Admiralty Gardens on a summer's day, of the street musicians on the bridges, and of grandmothers attending mass in St. Isaac's Cathedral.

The Beloselsky-Belozevsky Palace, off the Nevsky Prospekt, dates from the mid-nineteenth century and is but one of the countless mansions built by the wealthy ruling classes to serve as impressive residences close to court. The predominant style of architecture was a spirited mixture of Neoclassical formality offset by Baroque ornament. After the 1917 Revolution, the Beloselsky-Belozevsky Palace was seized by the state and became the headquarters of the local Communist Party.

Nowhere in St. Petersburg is the exquisite sense of scale, rhythm, and lightness of touch more eloquently expressed than in the Winter Palace. In summer its carefully modulated ranks of columns and windows are reflected in the broad waters of the Neva; but in winter the river remains locked for four months under ice so thick that horse races were staged on it in imperial times.

The glittering onion-shaped domes of the summer residence of Catherine the Great, in the district called Pushkin to the south of the city, strike an uncharacteristically Russian note for St. Petersburg. Like the Winter Palace constructed for Tsarina Elizabeth in the same period, the Catherine Palace was designed by Bartolomeo Rastrelli. Gutted during the Siege of Leningrad of 1941–44, it has since been meticulously restored.

"As we slalomed between potholes I had my first delighted view of pastel-colored buildings: a church painted white with a green trim, a yellow mansion with white columns; then, across the Neva River, a huge green and white palace looking like the most beautiful iced cake. I don't know what I expected, but not this sense of gaiety, light-heartedness."

MARTHA GELLHORN, 1991

Venice

City of canals, domes, and spires

Seen across its sparkling lagoon, Venice lines the horizon like a thin brushstroke of watercolor beneath the intense blue of the Adriatic sky. But as the *vaporetto* ferries from the Lido close in on the city, the shapes harden, forming into penciled spires and domes, their strong shadows crosshatched in the sunlight. What from a distance seemed like a hazy blur crisps into stone miraculously floating on water, bold and solid at its foot, rising to a froth of architectural ornament.

Venice is a place like no other, a city turned on its head, mocking the traditional assumptions of urban planning. The streets are filled with water; the dozens of islands defined by them are crisscrossed by a maze of alleys and pavements, linked by a jigsaw of bridges. The characteristic sounds of this metropolis are footfalls and the chatter of pedestrians, the hum of the motorized ferries, the gruff calls of the gondoliers, and at night, the gentle lapping of waves against the stonework at the water's edge.

Small wonder, then, that Venice is one of the world's most treasured cities, celebrated by countless artists, musicians, and writers, including Byron, Shelley, Proust, Thomas Mann, Henry James, Turner, Monet, Liszt, and Wagner. Today visited by thousands of tourists every year, Venice somehow transcends their onslaught. The city has had time to adapt: for the last 300 years of its 1,500-year history, it has been persistently invaded by visitors, starting with the eighteenth-century European nobles on the Grand Tour. Unlike Rome, Venice could boast no Classical remains, but it had been the

The church of Santa Maria della Salute (St. Mary of Health) was built to honor the city's pledge to the Virgin Mary that a church would be built in her name if she would deliver the city from the plague of 1630–31, which claimed the lives of some 95,000 citizens. In the Festa della Salute, *held on November 21 each year, a procession leaves St. Mark's Square for the church, making its way across the Grand Canal on two temporary bridges constructed over rows of boats.*

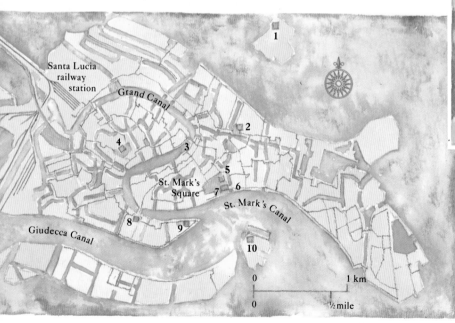

1 San Michele
2 Santi Giovanni e Paolo
3 Rialto Bridge
4 Santa Maria Gloriosa
   dei Frari
5 St. Mark's Basilica
6 Bridge of Sighs
7 Doge's Palace
8 Gallerie dell'Accademia
9 San Giorgio Maggiore
10 Santa Maria della Salute

center of one of the most powerful empires of the Mediterranean and had accumulated an immense wealth of architectural, artistic, and other treasures. Furthermore, Venice was celebrated – and notorious – for its sexual license and for the beauty of its women.

By the peculiar circumstances of the city's social structure, Venetian women were catapulted into what today would be termed a sexual revolution. In order to preserve their wealth, merchant families provided only one son with a suitable – often loveless – marriage to produce legitimate heirs. Other sons were left to play the field, which included married women, "surplus" daughters (many of whom became nuns), and prostitutes (by the late sixteenth century, there were some 11,000 prostitutes in the city, around 13 percent of the population). By the eighteenth century, the moral climate was lax in the extreme. Married women seldom consorted with their husbands, but were attended by a devoted lover, or *cicisbeo*, who pandered to their every whim. This was the world in which the most notorious of amorous rakes – Giacomo Casanova – was raised.

The atmosphere was at its most heated during the Carnival season, which lasted from the end of December to Shrove Tuesday – culminating in a heady final ten days of balls, theater, dancing, and feasting – and was ruled by burlesque *Commedia dell'Arte* characters. Throughout this period, everyone was masked and anonymous. The traditional disguise – for both sexes – was *la bautta*, consisting of a beak-shaped white mask, a black tricorn hat, and a black cloak. No one knew who was with whom, and could only guess at the background, social class, even the sex of any individual. The *frisson* of surprise and scandal was part and parcel of Venetian social life.

Such dangerous, decadent living was relished by the more tearaway Romantics, none more so than the most wayward and fascinating of them all, Lord Byron. But, by his day, this heady lifestyle was coming to an end. Indeed, the licentiousness was perhaps a product of the long decline which set in during the sixteenth century, after which merchant families rested on their laurels and lived off their shrinking capital, sold their heirlooms to visiting lords, and watched their grand old palazzos crumble picturesquely into the canals.

Venice's origins date from the fifth century A.D., when Roman families from mainland northern Italy fled from the invading Huns and took refuge on an archipelago of some 120 muddy islands in the lagoon. They quickly established a solid community based on trade derived from their lucrative saltpans and built homes over the tidal mud flats by driving wooden piles deep into the mud. Although it forged economic and political links with the Byzantines – whose empire covered most of the eastern and southern Mediterranean littoral – Venice remained independent, appointing its first doge in A.D. 697. As the Byzantine Empire declined, Venice moved in to fill the vacuum and by the 1420s dominated Mediterranean trade, and had a virtual monopoly in Europe over the distribution of goods coming out of the Middle East. These included incense and spices, as well as the porcelain, silks, and gems that were traded from the Far East along the Silk Roads. The Rialto area, at the center point of the Grand Canal, was the commercial hub of this great empire.

Amid a feast of music, dancing, opera, theater, side shows, gambling, and partying, masked Venetians enjoyed the fun and indiscretions of the Carnival, which English diarist John Evelyn called "folly and madness." All this came to an end when Napoleon took control of the city in 1797, and the Carnival lay dormant until it was revived in 1979 – albeit in a tamer and more modest form.

The ceiling of St. Mark's Basilica consists of a series of robust arches and three cupolas, smothered in gilded mosaics, testaments to the Byzantine influence that underlies much of the early architecture of Venice. Around the westernmost cupola – the earliest, dating from the twelfth century – are depicted the twelve seated apostles receiving the enlightenment of the Holy Ghost at Pentecost.

Native Venetian Antonio Canaletto painted numerous scenes of Venice, which were eagerly bought by visiting nobles as mementoes of the Grand Tour. In his Commemoration of the Wedding of the Doge and the Sea, *the ornate state barge, the* Bucintoro, *sails in front of the Doge's Palace, surrounded by festive crowds in their gondolas.*

The Bucintoro *was burned on the orders of Napoleon, whose revolutionary armies sought to destroy the Church's grip on society.*

To defend its interests, Venice created the most powerful navy in Europe, a fleet of sleek galleys, which it pitted against rival trading nations, notably the Genoese and the Ottoman Turks. In the east of the city, the supremely efficient shipyard and munitions factory, the Arsenale, could build a warship in just twelve hours.

Throughout this golden age, Venice was sustained by a highly organized populace ruled as a republic – *la serenissima repubblica*, "the most serene republic" – under the elected figurehead, the doge. The splendid Doge's Palace was completed in 1341. The governing senate remained in the hands of a limited number of ruling families, but the fact that they elected the doge prevented any one of them from creating a dynasty of the kind that led to tyranny in other Italian city-states. The people were protected by a degree of democracy and by a network of guilds and *scuole* (charitable confraternities). The result was unrivaled stability, underpinned by economic prosperity.

St. Mark's Basilica, a triumph of Byzantine architecture, was built in the late eleventh century. After a series of fires in the city during the twelfth century, the wooden houses were replaced by stone ones, built on stone foundations laid over the original piles. The wealth of the merchant families was spent on palazzos on the waterfront, fine clothes and jewelry, on the endowment of lavish churches, and on painting – thereby fostering the tradition that in the sixteenth century produced the great artists Giorgione, Titian, Tintoretto, and Veronese. The celebrated Venetian weakness for song was translated into choirs of orphanage children and *castrati*. The world's first public opera house, the Danieli, opened in 1637 with *Proserpina Rapita* by Claudio Monteverdi, a pioneer of the new genre.

The wealth of the state also funded extravagant pageants. The most famous of these was *La Senza* on Ascension Day, during which the doge traveled out into the lagoon in a huge gilded barge, the *Bucintoro*, to perform the ritual wedding between Venice and the Sea. As he tossed a golden ring into the waves, he declared: "With this we wed you, O Sea, in sign of our true and perpetual dominion."

Venice could not help but be reminded that the sea was vital to its prosperity and well-being, an essential part of its very soul. But when the Portuguese navigator Vasco da Gama rounded the Cape of Good Hope and sailed on to India in 1498, the writing was on the wall. The future lay in the sea routes to India and the Far East, and in the Americas. After 1650 Venice was no longer a political force, and it gradually withdrew its tentacles into the safety of its lagoon.

The city's long-cherished isolation from the mainland was broken by the construction of a road and rail link in 1846. In the twentieth century, battered by the wakes of power boats and the digging of artesian wells, Venice was found to be sinking into the mud, its marriage with the sea apparently irretrievably one-sided. A freak tide and disastrous flood in November 1966 dramatically highlighted the city's plight, inspiring an international project to save Venice through the construction of sea defenses and restoration. The signs are that this campaign has been successful, a demonstration that this is one dream place which the world will not easily consign to oblivion.

"Streets covered with water. Please advise," cabled humorist Robert Benchley to his publisher during a visit to Venice in the 1930s. The city's 200 canals are crossed by some 400 bridges, which delineate the boundaries of the island blocks into which the city is divided. These in turn are composed of one or more campi, *or squares, each with its own church and well.*

Gondolas lie at rest at the foot of the Grand Canal, with a view of the island and church of San Giorgio Maggiore in the distance. Gondolas have been made to the same pattern since about 1650 and are painted black following a decree of 1562 to curb a propensity toward lavish ostentation. Traditional details include the bladelike motif, or ferro, *which crowns the prow, brass seahorses on the deck, and the walnut oarlock, or* forcola. *The keel is built slightly off-center to give the gondolier extra leverage on his single oar, which is mounted on the starboard side and which also serves as the rudder. In the eighteenth century, there were 14,000 gondolas; today they number about 500.*

The Orient Express

It is difficult to appreciate today that little more than a century ago, the concept of crossing the border from one country to another while remaining on the same train was innovative, luxurious, and highly saleable. Yet in an era when trains rarely boasted either restaurant cars or restroom facilities, the lavish brainchild of the Belgian entrepreneur Georges Nagelmackers seemed like the stuff of which dreams are made.

The maiden voyage of the Orient Express began in Paris in 1883. In a journey scheduled to take 81 hours and 40 minutes, it crossed four international frontiers, passing through Germany, Austria–Hungary, Bulgaria, and Turkey. The passengers had to change trains only once, after crossing the Danube into Bulgaria, which they did by boat. And at Varna on the Black Sea, they left the train again, so that a boat could carry them to their

ARC DE TRIOMPHE

DUOMO

MEDITERRANEAN SEA

Posters advertised the speed and convenience of the Orient Express.

London

Dover

Calais

Amiens

Seine

Paris

Nancy

Strasbourg

Stuttgart

Rhône

Munich

Danube

Salzburg

Vien

Lausanne

Po

Milan

Verona

Venice

Trieste

Zagre

0   40   80   120 miles

0   100   200 km

journey's end, Constantinople, gateway to Asia and, to nineteenth-century Europeans, byword for the exotic.

From the start, luxury was the keynote. The compartments, or coupés, boasted comfortable chairs, Turkish carpets, and foldaway double beds with silk sheets; the bathrooms were outfitted with Italian marble and offered clean towels, soap, and toilet water, services not provided even in the continent's most expensive hotels. The ladies' lounge was decorated in Louis XV style and might have been transferred wholesale from a French chateau. And the smoking room's leather armchairs and array of books might once have graced a gentlemen's club in London.

The dining room was the last word in opulence, with mahogany and teak panels inlaid with rosewood; carved scrolls and cornices; ceiling paintings; and, perhaps most important for over-indulgent diners, chairs that could be moved away from the table to allow the occupant to relax. Dinner on the first night lasted three hours and included lobster, oysters, caviar, and game, accompanied by champagne and followed by Napoleon brandy and fine Havana cigars.

Yet the Orient Express's exclusive image scarcely outlasted its founder: soon after Nagelmackers's death in 1905, the train began to cater for ordinary tourists. But it never lost its hold on the public imagination.

It was celebrated in fiction, by Agatha Christie and others who dwelt on its sumptuous heyday. And its name passed into the legendary realms of espionage and special agents when two men fell from the train in mysterious circumstances. It regained a measure of its former cachet when ex-royalty chose to travel on board: the ousted Austro–Hungarian emperor Charles hatched his attempt to regain his throne on the train, and Britain's Edward VIII used it to steal away to Vienna after his abdication.

Then, in the 1980s, when all dreams seemed capable of fulfillment, the Orient Express was restored to its former glory. Once again, it is possible to dine lavishly and then sleep in comfort aboard the sumptuous train which crosses the frontiers of Europe without disturbing the repose of its passengers.

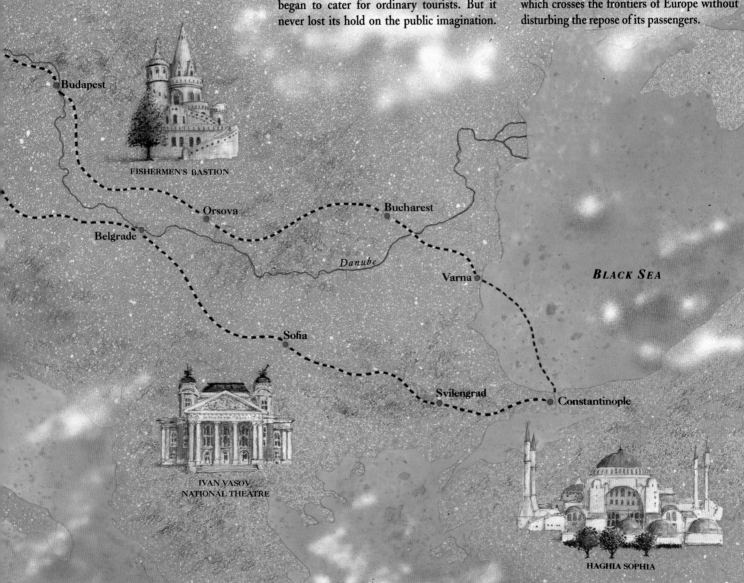

Budapest

FISHERMEN'S BASTION

Orsova

Bucharest

Belgrade

Danube

Varna

BLACK SEA

Sofia

IVAN VASOV NATIONAL THEATRE

Svilengrad

Constantinople

HAGHIA SOPHIA

Damascus

Paradise on earth

Centuries ago, when the Umayyad Mosque of Damascus was a young building, its walls glittered with more than 1 acre (4,000 m²) of mosaics. Thousands upon thousands of tiles transformed the stone surface into a world of streams fringed with willow fronds and flowers and slender trees laden with fruit. Fragments survive today, and some scholars see them as a depiction of Qur'anic paradise, or of the Garden of Eden. Others simply consider them to be a picture of Damascus at the very height of its beauty.

They could well be both, for Damascenes have long considered their city to be the original site of earthly paradise. It lies 2,250 feet (690 m) above sea level in the southwest of what is now Syria, flanked to the north, south, and east by the emptiness of the Syrian Desert and caught up to the west in the foothills of the Anti-Lebanon mountain range. The Barada River (the Abana of the Bible, whose name means "cool waters") tumbles down from these mountains into the warmth and divides into several streams which thread their way through the city. The village of Mezze, at the point of division, is thought to be the site of the Garden of Eden. Adam is believed to have been fashioned by God from the clay of the Barada, and Abel to have been buried by Cain in a cave high on Mount Kassioun, which towers over the city. The rocks, streaked with mineral deposits, ran red with his blood.

This paradisiacal belief runs through Damascene history like a stubborn thread. At the very least, the city deserved the label in the

In the cavernous interior of the Umayyad Mosque, a lone Muslim prays. This is the third most important Islamic site after Mecca and the Dome of the Rock in Jerusalem, and it can comfortably hold thousands of worshippers for daily prayers. The mosque's roof is supported by the original pillars of the Christian Basilica of St. John.

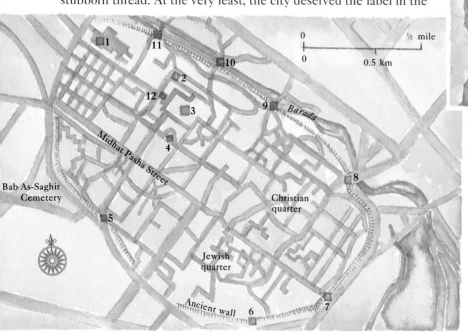

1 Citadel
2 Az-Zahiriyya Madrassa
3 Great Umayyad Mosque
4 El-Azem Palace
5 Gate of Mars
6 Gate of Saturn and St. Paul's Chapel
7 Gate of the Sun
8 Gate of Venus
9 Gate of the Moon
10 Gate of Mercury
11 Gate of Deliverance
12 Western gate of the Temple of Jupiter

metaphorical sense. How must it have looked to the weary caravans emerging from the desert, or to merchants from the Mediterranean coast taking the single treacherous goods route down through the mountains? Lying on its hillside plateau, laced with streams and irrigation systems, drenched with greenery, full of minarets and spires, it was a city that seemed removed from reality. Poised between the cold of the hills and the heat of the desert, between barren sand and infertile mountain soil, Damascus was an oasis in the most glamorous sense of the word.

Today, Damascus – in Arabic, Dimashq, but also known by its French name of Damas, and by its inhabitants as Esh Sham – is a noisy, modern city, transformed by Western building styles and reinforced concrete into a metropolis. Memories of its fabulous past are locked in its southeastern corner, within the yellow walls of the Old City, where the citadel and some of the original gates still stand and traders still hang their wares in the twisted alleys of the souk.

But however modern, and however readily he has exchanged his *galabiyah* for a business suit, any Damascene will assert that his city is the oldest in the world. If Muslim, he will say that it was founded by Demchak, slave of Abraham; if not, he might say that its creator was Uz, great-grandson of Noah, whose descendants were the industrious Arameans. Other contenders for the title of oldest city – San'aa in Yemen, for example, which considers itself to have been founded by Noah's son Shem – are ignored. Damascus is simply the most ancient city on earth.

For once, archaeology bears this out. In the burial mounds known as *tells*, which dot the plain around the city, evidence has been found of a people who settled on the site of Damascus 3,000 years before the Arameans arrived in the thirteenth century B.C. From these beginnings, in a place presumably chosen for its fertility, the city became a stage across which tribes and dynasties passed as the centuries went by – some making their mark, others leaving no trace.

The Egyptians toyed with it for a while, before conceding it to the Ammonites, the first Semitic settlers. The Arameans set up irrigation systems and orchards and a street grid based on the Babylonian model, and brought with them the cult of Haddad, the Thunderer. King David captured the city and then returned it. It was seized and plundered by the Assyrians in 732 B.C., and by the Babylonians, the Persians, and Alexander the Great. Haddad was joined by the sun gods of Persepolis and, when the Romans arrived in 64 B.C., the mighty Jupiter.

From this point, the chronology is clearer, since the Greco-Roman remains – colonnades, foundation stones, or slabs of inscribed rock – beneath the medieval and modern city are sometimes exposed by time. Of the seven mighty Roman gates which pierced the city walls, only one, the Gate of the Sun, remains wholly intact, but the great Temple of Jupiter – and the Christian Basilica of St. John that was built on top of it – still figure in the environs of the Umayyad Mosque.

The Romans brought something else with them in the years before Christ: the insatiable hunger of the West for the luxuries of the East. Emperors and generals craved exotic foods and wines.

A Damascene woman shelters under an arch of the El-Azem Palace, now the Museum of Arts and Popular Traditions. Built in 1749 for the Ottoman governor of Damascus – Assa Pasha el-Azem – the palace includes a fountained courtyard surrounded by striped colonnades of Moorish stone and refreshed by the sound of water.

Christians dispute the authentic site of Saint Paul's blinding on the road to Damascus. Some 3½ miles (6 km) south of the city is a shrine on the supposed spot, and there is another in the Christian cemetery to the east of the city. The sanctuary beneath the Gate of Saturn (above), commemorates the place where Paul is said to have been lowered over the wall in a basket, to escape the Jewish guards.

"...the silent gardens stood blurred green with river mist in whose setting shimmered the city, beautiful as ever, like a pearl in the morning sun"

T.E. LAWRENCE, 1918

Upper-class women clamored for perfumes, silks, and cosmetics. The Roman Empire fused East and West under a single banner, and the already profitable exchange of goods and money became a flood. Damascus was at the hub of this vast market, absorbing the fabulous wealth coming across the desert from the Gulf of Persia, from the Silk Road, and from ships which evaded piracy in the Mediterranean, and pumping it out to meet European demand.

The emperor Julian's description of Rome's eastern capital, "...the city which in very truth belongs to Zeus and is the eye of the whole East – sacred and most mighty Damascus," could have applied with equal truth to its power as a trading city. And perhaps its fabled image was more secular than religious, based on the desire for precious goods – the like of which had rarely been seen in Europe – rather than spiritual craving.

In those days the narrow streets of the city were alive with strange languages, skins of different colors, and outlandish costumes, as merchants brought in incense and myrrh from the Arabian peninsula; jade and silks from China; animals and their skins; tusks, shells, and horns from Africa. Egyptian traders crossed the Sinai Desert with their camels, and Syrians from Palmyra carried goods arriving from the Gulf on the next stage of their journey. From nearby Petra came gold and silver, from India sugar, cotton, and spices. Jars of unguents and oils arrived for the eager hands of Westerners; and Syria itself provided glass, wine, scented woods, golden amber, linen, wool, and rugs. Even today, the name Damascus is synonymous with luxury: full, red Damask roses; thick Damask cloth; dried Damascus plums and dates and figs. The Romans, too, had found paradise on earth.

It was a Roman citizen, in the first years after Christ's death, who brought new fame to Damascus and made it a place of pilgrimage for Christians, which it remains to this day. Paul of Tarsus – Saul in Hebrew – was traveling to the city to extradite radical Christians for trial in Jerusalem. According to the Book of Acts, "It happened that on the road to Damascus, suddenly a light from heaven shone all around him." Blinded, he fell to the ground and heard a voice say "Saul, Saul, why are you persecuting me?" "Who are you, Lord?" he asked. "I am Jesus, whom you are persecuting," said the voice. Paul was led to the house of Judas, in the Street Called Straight, which (now known as Bab Sharqi Street) still exists in the Old City, and was cured of his blindness and baptized by a man named Ananais.

The site of Paul's blinding is a matter of dispute; those looking for more solid evidence of the city's Christian connections can find it, ironically, in the shadow of one of Islam's greatest feats of architecture – the Umayyad Mosque. This huge building, with its striped stone walls and beautiful, spacious interior, arose from the rubble of the Christian Basilica of St. John the Baptist, whose severed head is said to lie beneath the foundations. A shrine to Saint John still remains, much revered, while the mighty columns of the church support a roof decorated with Kufic verse, and the bricks surround a prayer niche which faces south, to Mecca.

Islam reached Damascus around the year A.D. 635, stepping easily into the breach between the city – by then a Byzantine military

Five times a day, Damascus echoes to the sound of the muezzins calling the faithful to prayer from minarets all over the city. Outside the Great Mosque, an elderly pilgrim wearing the white skull cap of the hajj bathes his feet in one of the ornate stone pools before midday prayers.

"Damascus and its limitless desert...its innumerable domes of mosques and palaces reflecting the rays of the setting sun, and the bright blue waters of the several rivers sparkling and disappearing in turn through the streets and gardens"

ALPHONSE DE LAMARTINE, 1832–33

Clearly visible from the exterior, Islamic arches and Christian pillars support the Great Mosque, which towers over the rambling souk in Damascus's citadel. The citadel walls enclose what is now known as the Old City; around it sprawls the modern metropolis with its high-rise buildings and busy traffic.

outpost – and the Byzantine capital of Constantinople. The Umayyads, an aristocratic Meccan family converted early by the Prophet, established a powerful dynasty in Syria, and by the time Caliph Walid succeeded in 705, Damascus was the capital of an empire stretching from Spain to the Indus Valley.

Walid was obsessed with the creation of the new mosque, which he dreamed would be one of the most important Muslim buildings in the world. Lead for the roof and precious metals for the mosaics (which were created by 1,200 skilled Greeks) came from across the empire. Artists were brought from Constantinople. The first minarets in Islamic architecture soared above the city, and one of them – named after Jesus, who was respected as a prophet by Muslims – was believed to be the place where he would alight at the Second Coming. The central Dome of the Eagle stood high above its prayer hall, supported by the old pillars of the Christian basilica. The building took seven years to complete, at enormous cost, although the caliph refused to read the accounts: "We have spent this for God," he said, "and we will not count it."

For a while Damascus reveled in its splendor. It had a beautiful new mosque and an immense goods trade. Pilgrims on the hajj – the journey to Mecca that every devout Muslim hopes to make once in his lifetime – needed provisioning, and Damascus obliged, plundering its orchards and groves for pomegranates, figs, nuts, and olives, and its rich fields for grains and vegetables. But in 750 the Muslim capital was moved to Baghdad, and a shadow fell upon the city. It became lawless, and distinct quarters for Jews, Muslims, and Christians began to evolve. Wealthy houses turned blank walls to the street, hiding their lush courtyards and bubbling fountains from public view.

That the Great Mosque still survives, after more than 1,000 years, is a testament to its strength and to the skill of those who rebuilt it after the depredations of fire in 1069 and the coming of Tamerlane in 1400. The latter, who is said to have torched the building with 30,000 people inside, added insult to injury by taking the city's most skilled artists and craftsmen with him for the rebuilding of Samarkand.

But survive it did, and Damascus underwent brief periods of renaissance under the Turks, Mamluks, and Ottomans. The *khans* (caravanserais with warehousing on the ground floor and rooms for traveling merchants above) and the religious foundations known as madrassas, with their peaceful interiors and cupolas topped with melon-shaped domes, can still be seen in the jumble of the Old City today. The souk still trades from noon to night, albeit on a more modest scale, shaded from the harsh sun by awnings draped across the gaps between buildings.

In 1960, France was forced to relinquish its Syrian protectorate, which it had held for 40 years. Ever since, for the first time in its long history, Syria has been free of all foreign control. But in the great city of Damascus, the evidence of conquerors and their cultures remains, hidden among the ancient fragments of buildings and the modern face of the city. These are the tangible reminders that throughout the ages all men have wanted their share of paradise on earth.

From a minaret rich in Ottoman Turkish decoration, a muezzin calls the Muslim population to prayer. The distinctive rounded arch of contrasting stone stripes, stylized flowers around the inner arch, and geometrical stonework on the balcony reflect the Muslim love of decoration without showing anthropomorphic figures, which are forbidden in Qur'anic law.

In a rare moment of calm in the busy life of the souk, a carpet seller has the opportunity to sit and repair one of his wares. Whatever the value of the merchandise, a prospective buyer is always asked inside and fêted with conversation and thick, black Turkish coffee, in true Middle Eastern style.

The flamboyant peacock and sinuous foliage that decorate a seventeenth-century tile are testament to the astonishing skills of Damascene artists and craftsmen. Small wonder, then, that Tamerlane took hundreds of their ancestors with him to Samarkand, to create a new imperial city among the ruins.

"The sight [of Damascus] is enough to make one cry out with pleasure. For weeks I had been seeking the Orient of legend; at last I had found it!"

ROLAND DORGELES

Vieux Carré
Heart of the Big Easy

Many ghosts inhabit the streets of the small, vivacious section of New Orleans known as the Vieux Carré, or Old Quarter. The voice of Blanche du Bois mingles with the accented French of high-born Creole families; the houses of artists rub shoulders with those of writers; laughter echoes from former brothels and bars; and voodoo queens seem more than just a memory in the streets around the Catholic cathedral of St. Louis. The sugared-almond facades of the two-story "gallery" houses, with their wrought-iron balconies and hanging plants, grow more beautiful with age. The sidewalks still hold the sounds of Fats Domino and Kid Thomas Valentine. This is the heart of the city that William Faulkner described as "a place created for and by voluptuousness, the abashness and unabashed senses."

New Orleans started life as an outpost on the banks of the Mississippi, the key to trade with the interior. The first French explorer, La Salle, passed the site on his way down to the mouth of the river, which he claimed for Louis XIV, the Sun King. The city La Nouvelle Orléans (named after the Duc d'Orléans, regent for the boy king Louis XV) was planned in Paris and founded in 1718 on behalf of the Company of the Indies, which intended to open up Louisiana and make vast fortunes for its French shareholders.

The grid system, which survives in the streets of the Vieux Carré, was laid out in 1721, after floods and fires had repeatedly destroyed

Intricate, lacy wrought-iron balconies line early nineteenth-century houses in the French quarter of New Orleans, showing the influence of French and Spanish architecture. Until the 1820s, the predominant influence in the city was Caribbean rather than European, which earned New Orleans its nickname, the "Big Easy."

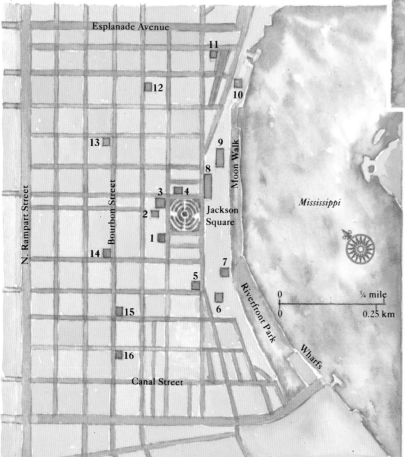

1 Cabildo
2 St. Louis Cathedral
3 Presbytère
4 Pontalba Apartments
5 French Market Inn
6 Jackson Brewery
7 Millhouse Brewhouse
8 Café du Monde
9 French Market
10 Farmers' Market
11 Old U.S. Mint
12 Gallier Mansion
13 Leftie Blacksmith's Shop
14 Inn on Bourbon
15 Old Absinthe Bar
16 Old Absinthe House

the young settlement. Levees were built up- and downriver to protect the city from the might of the Mississippi. The Ursuline Sisters arrived from France, bringing with them orphans and middle-class "casket girls" to marry to the colonists, and building a convent which is today the oldest brick-and-post building in the Mississippi valley.

The Company of the Indies soon lost patience with a place that was subject to natural disasters, disease, and the depredations of Indian tribes. The 7,000 colonists found themselves handed from France to Spain under a secret agreement. Rumors abounded that the French-speaking Acadians – known as Cajuns – who had arrived from Canada were to be sold off as slaves, and that the Spanish were going to renege on the company's debts. The ensuing revolt was quelled by 2,600 Spanish mercenaries; the city passed back to the French and was eventually sold to the American government, which reluctantly bought it in the so-called Louisiana Purchase of 1803 under the shrewd guidance of Thomas Jefferson.

New Orleans might have been tossed continually between France and Spain, but in cultural terms it was unquestionably more Caribbean than European. The old Creole families, New-World-born descendants of European stock (the term later came to include light-skinned African–Americans, who often shared surnames and antecedents with white Creoles), brought colonial influences from the West Indies, coupled with a Latin elegance and sophistication. In many ways, New Orleans was less oppressive for Negros than other Southern cities; mixed marriage was permitted, and when the abolition of slavery came in the nineteenth century, the city had some 750 "free people of color" (freed slaves or mixed-race heirs of white colonists) who were themselves slave owners. Others were carpenters, iron workers, musicians, artists, and businessmen, which gave the city a lively ethnic pedigree.

Refined, Catholic New Orleans was horrified when the Louisiana Purchase handed over the state's 965,000 sq. miles (2.5 million km²) lock, stock, and barrel to the Protestant Yankees, for just $15 million. Things changed fast. The first steamboat, the *New Orleans*, chugged downriver in 1812, ushering in a new era of trade. General Andrew Jackson fought off the British two years later with a ragtag army of Indians, frontiersmen, and pirates (the latter under the Lafitte brothers, who took their pardons and went straight back to piracy). Suddenly New Orleans was where everybody wanted to be.

So appalled were the Creole families by the rough backwoods people who came down the Mississippi on their flatboats, bringing all their possessions and their bad habits, that a no-man's-land was designated between the "Old City" and the new American sector. The strip of land became today's Canal Street, which divides the faded splendor of the Quarter from the grandiose Classical mansions built by Yankee businessmen made rich on river trade.

Cotton poured out of New Orleans to the mills of Europe, and the area's sugar plantations were thriving. The port boomed: in one year, around 950 flatboats and 2,900 steamboats arrived downriver, some of them from as far as 3,000 miles (4,800 km) away. By 1820, the city had a population of more than 40,000. But not everything

New Orleans – and the Vieux Carré in particular – is the home of Dixie (named after the "Dix," or $10 bill used by flatboatmen on the Mississippi). Louis Armstrong used to play in a band on a steamboat, and his successors still play in bars, dance halls, and nightclubs all over the city.

Store owners on Royal Street follow the old Vieux Carré tradition of living over the store. Commerce below and leisure above makes for an easy traffic between the two during siesta hour. The galleries or balconies not only provide shade and somewhere to sit, they protect pedestrians from tropical downpours.

Sleep is abandoned during Mardi Gras, the Lenten celebration which is probably the most famous carnival outside Rio. Groups of people from every walk of life – the krewes – spend months preparing costumes and floats, and competition during the week of revelries around Mardi Gras itself is intense.

The carnival is a family festival: children join in the dancing and feast on "king cakes" with toys hidden inside.

was perfect. The city was caught by a deep bend in the river on one side and by Lake Pontchartrain on the other. It claimed to have more canals than Venice, and it certainly had more rain; floods and mild weather caused massive epidemics of cholera and yellow fever, and whites – now less than half of the population – began to move out to the suburbs. The inhabitants of the Quarter, however, confident that there was nowhere better to live, stayed put.

There is still an extraordinary variety of architecture in the 4,000-foot (1,220-m) by 1,800-foot (550-m) area. One-story Creole cottages, with low windows and pitched roofs, open directly onto the street. Wooden "shotgun" houses, built one room wide to occupy narrow lots, with each room leading back through the next, still stand with their characteristic detailing over the porches and windows. The gallery houses, decorated with ornate wrought ironwork and protected from the weather by overhanging roofs, could be open to the elements during the worst of the summer storms.

The carnival of Mardi Gras ("Fat Tuesday," the last day before Lent) and the riotous carnival celebrations leading up to it, began in the early nineteenth century, but only became official in 1857. In 1827 a parade group of students called the Mystick Krewe of Comus was formed, later followed by the Krewe of Rex. Today there are dozens of krewes, but the "old liners," or upper-class families of the city, can be identified by their allegiance to one of the older groups. The carnival balls and displays begin on Twelfth Night in January, and for several exhausting weeks the revelries lead up to Mardi Gras itself. The streets of the Quarter are festooned with decorations, alive with light and music, and spectators line the upper balconies to watch the processions pass.

Early in the city's history, the colored population had its own celebrations in the Quadroon Ballroom (quadroons were one quarter Negro, octaroons one eighth) on Orleans Street, when mulatto girls were presented by their mothers to become the mistresses of white Creole men. Some people believed that the rituals of Carnival were linked to the ancient practice of voodoo, brought over by West African slaves via Haiti. Certainly the cult was powerful enough in the late eighteenth century to be banned for fear of slave insurrection. One hundred years later, one of its most famous proponents, the beautiful Marie Laveau, presided over sacred rites on St. John's Eve (June 23) and well-attended meetings in Congo Square. Her daughter, also Marie, practiced in high society as well as among the slaves.

New Orleans seceded from the Union in 1861, suffering as much after as during the Civil War. It was never destroyed, but from 1865 to 1877, the city was ruled by the infamous Scallywags (Republican southerners) and Carpetbaggers (Yankees out for their own gain) who between them bled it dry. Its fortunes revived in World War I – the period when jazz was born – and again in World War II, when imports and exports burgeoned and the port again came alive. Today the city is busy, noisy, and not without its problems. But New Orleans is still the "Big Easy," and right at its heart is the Vieux Carré, a piece of Caribbean style, French elegance, and Spanish charm that belongs on American soil.

"Don't you just love those long rainy afternoons in New Orleans when an hour isn't just an hour – but a little piece of eternity dropped into your hands – and who knows what to do with it?"

BLANCHE DUBOIS IN TENNESSEE WILLIAMS'S
A STREETCAR NAMED DESIRE, 1947

Bourbon Street, a magnet for visiting tourists, excels at doing what New Orleans does best: having a good time at its own pace. The sound of Dixie and the smell of fried chicken drift down its length at all times of the day and night.

The name reflects the city's French origins, and its open houses a Caribbean bonhomie.

Far from the noise and bustle of the Mississippi's biggest port, a Colonial stucco mansion sits at the end of a magnificent driveway of oak trees. Many fortunes were made and lost on the river and in the back country – the bayous – shipping cotton, lumber, rice, and sugar. By 1840 New Orleans equaled New York City in the volume of its harbor traffic.

Montmartre
Artists' quarter of Paris

The fame of Montmartre dates from the nineteenth century and the "bohemian" pleasures associated with the lives and works of the artists who made their home in the *quartier*. Situated on the highest point in Paris – the Butte de Montmartre – it was until 100 years ago a self-contained community an hour's trudge uphill through narrow streets from the banks of the Seine 460 feet (140 m) below. The first of its taverns, cabarets, and cafés – and the free and easy reputation that went with them – were established before the Revolution. But in the earliest known painting of Montmartre, a watercolor by Georges Michel dating from around 1800, it is surrounded by tracts of open countryside. And the hill is dotted with the windmills which became such an integral part of its image.

Throughout the nineteenth century, but particularly after 1871, artists and writers, attracted as much by the cheap accommodation as by the unrestricted lifestyle, came to paint Montmartre's windmills and its young women, and to draw inspiration from the nightlife of the Place Pigalle and the views from the Butte itself. By this time, the once-numerous windmills no longer played a vital role in food production, and the three that remained were converted into dance halls and bars, providing cheap entertainment and panoramic views. Such cabarets sprang up all over Montmartre. At the Elysée-Montmartre on Boulevard Rochechouart, admission was 75 centimes.

An early resident, composer Hector Berlioz, embodied the Romantic view that art springs from "direct relation to feeling." As a

Paul Abadie's impressive Romano-Byzantine basilica of Notre-Dame du Sacré-Coeur is second only to the Eiffel Tower as an instantly and universally recognizable symbol of Paris. Much of it was financed by public subscription, with prominent families donating statues or whole chapels. The bell, known as the Savoyarde, was presented by the churches of the duchy of Savoy, and at 19 tons is one of the heaviest in the world.

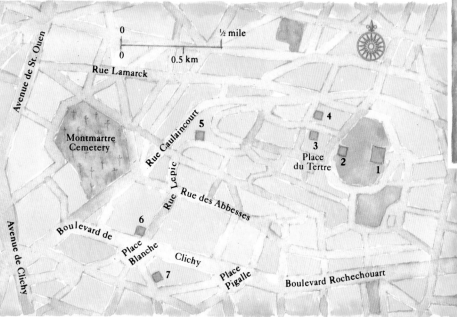

MONTMARTRE □

FRANCE

1 Sacré-Coeur
2 St. Pierre de Montmartre
3 Musée de Montmartre
4 Au Lapin Agile
5 Moulin de la Galette
6 Moulin Rouge
7 Comédie de Paris

young man new to Paris, he fell desperately in love with the Irish Shakespearean actress Harriet Smithson and was driven half-mad by her indifference. Having finally persuaded her to marry him, he became indifferent himself and pursued another lady who had resisted his passion to Italy, with the (unfulfilled) intention of killing her and committing suicide. Perversely, his feelings for Harriet – whom he married but then left – were rekindled by her early death.

The paintings of Pierre Auguste Renoir epitomize the early years of Montmartre's heyday. Already established in a studio nearer the center of Paris, he became an habitué of the Moulin de la Galette in the 1870s and took rooms nearby so that he could work there in the afternoons. Although he recorded the nightlife, Renoir did not dwell on its seedier side – his subjects were of less importance to him than the portrayal of light and nuances of color, and his Montmartre paintings celebrate a golden age, depicting a love of life that became more cynical in the work of later artists.

Immediately following the Franco–Prussian war of 1870–71 came a period of social upheaval, with industrial development changing the long-established structure of society and bringing the urban working classes to greater prominence. Romanticism in the arts gave way to Realism and then to Naturalism, a down-to-earth approach brilliantly evoked in the novels of Montmartre resident Emile Zola.

At the same time, the very reputation that had appealed to the great artists was leading to Montmartre's downfall. Second-rate artists who could not aspire to the talent of their idols emulated their lifestyle instead. And as better roads and transportation made the *quartier* more accessible, Montmartre's exaggerated reputation for erotic entertainment and easy women attracted the bourgeoisie, who came to view the "low life" from a safe distance, or perhaps partake of some of its forbidden fruits. Chief among the attractions were the professional dancers who performed the *chahut*, a precursor of the can-can which showed the dancers' legs in a similarly uninhibited fashion. But there were innocent diversions, too. In 1890, the year after the Moulin Rouge opened, it advertised donkey races and merry-go-rounds, as well as dancing and circuses.

The commercialization of Montmartre did not suit the artists who had sought bohemian seclusion. At about the time of World War I, they began to move out, mostly to Montparnasse, leaving the Place du Tertre by day to the street artists who sell instant portraits and mass-produced sketches of Sacré-Coeur, and by night to the many cafés and restaurants that roll out their awnings to enable customers to dine by moonlight overlooking the city.

But a stone's throw from the Place du Tertre, uphill along the Rue des Saules, or westward along the Rue Lepic, it is still possible to recapture some of the feeling which inspired Berlioz, Renoir, Degas, Utrillo, Van Gogh, Toulouse-Lautrec, Picasso, Modigliani, George Sand, Flaubert, and Zola. The narrow streets and terraced houses of Utrillo's paintings remain. The names of the cabarets linger, although most of them are long gone. The Moulin Rouge is now a cinema; the fabric of the Moulin de la Galette has been restored; of the great cabarets, only the Lapin Agile is still there.

One of the attractions for the artists who moved to Montmartre in the nineteenth century was its inaccessibility. The summit of the Butte is still a stiff climb, although today the Metro and a funicular railroad carry visitors unwilling, or unable, to walk.

"I dwelt for a long time in Montmartre, where one enjoys very pure air, varied prospects, and can behold magnificent views, whether 'having been virtuous,' one likes to see the sunrise which is very beautiful over Paris, or, having less simple tastes, prefers the empurpled colors of sunset."

GÉRARD DE NERVAL, *PROMENADES ET SOUVENIRS* c.1840

Pierre Auguste Renoir's Au Moulin de la Galette *(1876) evokes the pleasures of Montmartre's heyday. From 1875 on, Renoir always chose his models from among the girls he met at the Moulin, claiming that they struck more natural poses than the professional models to whom he had been accustomed.*

The Place du Tertre has long been one of the focal points of life in Montmartre. It is still the workplace of artists, although they now cater largely for tourists, with local views, instant portraits, and silhouettes.

A stroll around the two principal cemeteries evokes the area's lost glories. Many of the artists, writers, and musicians intrinsically associated with Montmartre lie in the Montmartre Cemetery, including the composers Delibes and Offenbach; the novelists Alexandre Dumas *fils*, Stendhal, and the brothers Goncourt; the poet de Vigny; and the actor Louis Jouvet. Zola's monument is perhaps the most poignant: it is dominated by the words "J'accuse," a reference to his open letter in defense of the wrongfully disgraced army officer Alfred Dreyfus. The letter cost Zola a year's exile, and he did not live to see Dreyfus pardoned and his own actions vindicated.

Farther up the hill, tucked away behind Paris's only remaining vineyard, is the much smaller St. Vincent Cemetery, where Harriet Smithson and Utrillo are buried. On the way to St. Vincent, the Musée de Montmartre occupies a house where Renoir, Utrillo, and Dufy all lived at various times.

Not everyone of note deserted Montmartre in 1918. The area that had nurtured the Cubists was no longer grand enough for Picasso, who was successful enough to move into town and set up a studio in the rather more bourgeois Rue de la Boétie, near the Champs-Elysées. But Braque remained, and with him the poet André Breton, founder of the Surrealist movement which took form and substance in Montmartre in the 1920s.

Religion lingers in Montmartre, too. The church of St. Pierre, the third oldest in Paris, is all that remains of the powerful Benedictine convent that once crowned the hill (hence the Place and Rue des Abbesses) and contains the tomb of its twelfth-century founder, Queen Adelaide of Savoy, wife of Louis VI. It also houses four marble columns said to have been part of the Roman temple that once stood on the site.

But the area's best-known religious building is a mere 100 years old. The Basilica of Notre-Dame du Sacré-Coeur was conceived in the wake of France's humiliation in the Franco–Prussian War, with a view to restoring national and Catholic pride – and, coincidentally, to cleaning up the sleazier elements of Montmartre's reputation. Completed in 1910 and consecrated in 1919, Sacré-Coeur is said to have cost 40 million francs.

Admiration of the basilica is by no means universal. From the first, the irreverent Montmartrois christened it "Notre-Dame de la Galette." The Michelin guide grudgingly admits that "the total effect is impressive even if the esthetic appeal is arguable." No one, however, criticizes the view from Sacré-Coeur – the dome adds 272 feet (83 m) to the Butte's height – and by night, seen floodlit from below, the church's white symmetry is dazzling.

Montmartre remains an area of myriad contrasts. Peaceful narrow streets run off seething, garishly lit boulevards. A basilica that is a monument to the faith of thousands of devout working-class Catholics dominates an area whose most famous inhabitants rejected conventional values. Amid the poverty and the squalor, many of France's greatest artists found the inspiration to create their finest work. Somewhere, underneath the layers of commercialization, lies the stuff that dreams are made of.

The Moulin Rouge was one of the three remaining deserted windmills in Montmartre converted into dance halls in the nineteenth century. Here, La Goulue – perhaps the best-known chahuteuse, *subject of many of Toulouse-Lautrec's paintings – and her colleagues performed the scandalous* chahut, *the high-kicking dance whose suggestion of "female availability" brought all Paris flooding in.*

At night the Place du Tertre is dominated by the floodlit brilliance of Sacré-Coeur. The views from the Butte de Montmartre have always attracted both artists and tourists, and now one of its pleasures is dining al fresco with the wonders of one of the most romantic cities in the world stretched out below.

Paris by the Seine

High on the cathedral of Notre-Dame de Paris, on the twin Gothic towers made famous by Victor Hugo's novel *The Hunchback of Notre Dame*, stone gargoyles snarl over the sprawl of Paris as they have done for eight centuries. Far below, the Ile de la Cité, the ancient heart of the metropolis, splits the River Seine in two like a sharp-prowed boat. To the east lies the peaceful Ile St. Louis, with its seventeenth-century hotels and shady avenues; to the south, the Left Bank with its cafés and restaurants; to the northwest, the Tour St. Jacques, once a stopping point for pilgrims on their way to Santiago de Compostela. But the Seine pulls on westward, completing a 6-mile (10-km) stretch through Paris on its way to the sea.

When Julius Caesar arrived in 52 B.C., he christened the small Gallic trading town Lutetia, and during 300 years of Roman rule, the river and its two islands were the city. Trade flourished, buildings mushroomed, reputations grew. Clovis the Frank arrived in A.D. 486, closely followed by Christianity, and richly endowed monasteries appeared on the Left Bank. On the Ile de la Cité the cathedral of St. Etienne, now buried under the foundations of twelfth-century Notre-Dame, was built by Clovis's son.

Through all the changes, the one constant was the Seine. Its two banks developed distinct identities – the Left intellectual, the Right commercial – which are still the same

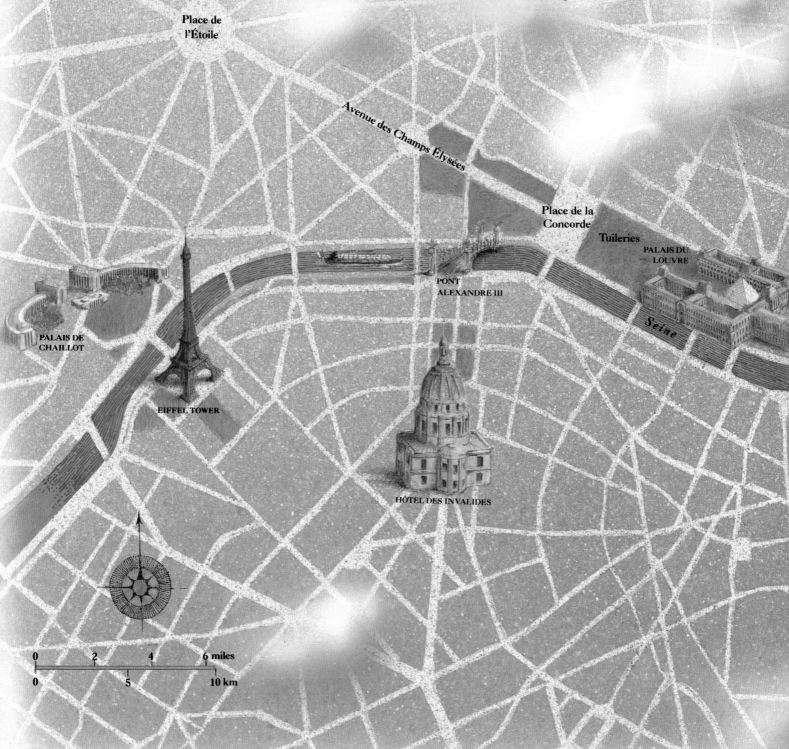

today. The university of the Sorbonne came into being, and as all studies were in Latin, so the Latin Quarter was christened. The watermen formed powerful guilds to control trade. The islands and their surrounding areas teemed with people in cramped, crowded houses and stinking alleyways.

Two of the Left Bank's best-known residents lived at 9 Quai aux Fleurs: the young lovers Abelard and Heloise, teacher and pupil, who were respectively castrated and consigned to a convent for their illegal union. Perhaps they more than anyone have given rise to an image which is overwhelmingly Parisian, that of romance. The lovely bridges that span the Seine – the Pont Neuf, the Pont Louis Philippe, the Pont de Sully – are the haunts of young lovers, who stroll under ornate lamps as the *bâteaux mouches* pleasure boats pass, alive with gaiety and color.

Most of the streets known to Abelard and Heloise were destroyed when Baron Haussmann rebuilt Paris in the nineteenth century. But Notre-Dame, the beautiful Sainte Chapelle with its delicate stained-glass windows, and the Conciergerie (from where Marie Antoinette was led to the guillotine in 1793) survived. So did bridges like the seventeenth-century Pont Neuf – the first Parisian bridge built without houses on each side, so that people could look up and down the Seine – and the *quais* along the river.

These took on a new life, manned by artists and booksellers (with their distinctive green foldaway boxes) instead of boatmen and livestock merchants, and became in their turn the very image of the city. Today, as in the beginning, the legend that is Paris grows and prospers by the River Seine.

Place de la République

ue de Rivoli

SAINTE CHAPELLE

NOTRE-DAME

Ile de la Cité

PONT LOUIS PHILIPPE

Place de la Bastille

Ile St. Louis

atin Quarter

Twilight on the Seine is the time for lovers.

Seville

Vibrant city of endless contrasts

From Columbus to Carmen, from the jubilant flamenco dancers of the spring fair to the somber *nazarenos* who parade the streets during Holy Week, from the glorious Moorish architecture of the Giralda to the magnificent eighteenth-century Maestranza bull ring, Seville is a city of incomparable richness and inexhaustible contrasts. In the early years of the twentieth century, the Sevillan poet Manuel Machado compiled a brief "gazetteer" in verse to describe the eight provinces of Andalusia: Cádiz is salty and bright, and Almería golden. But when he came to his home city, he ran out of words. "Y Sevilla!" the poem ends: no mere line of verse can sum up Seville.

The most important factor in understanding the rich mosaic of modern Seville is the wavering balance of power between Christians and Muslims in the past. The city's Christian traditions date from the first century, and Christianity reigned supreme until the Moorish conquest of 712. Then Islam held sway until 1248, when Ferdinand III recaptured Seville and added it to his Christian kingdom. By that time, the Moorish Almohades, who had made Seville their capital, had left one of the finest legacies in the Western world. The Torre de Oro, Giralda, and Reales Alcázares bear witness to their passion for beautiful architecture and elaborate decoration.

The Reales Alcázares (literally royal citadels) were built on what were probably the ruins of a Roman fortress (Julius Caesar had built

An Almohade creation, the Torre de Oro, or Golden Tower, dates from 1220 and was originally balanced by a silver tower on the opposite bank of the river. Although the golden roof tiles which gave it its name vanished long ago, the tower was used to store some of the hoards of gold and silver which were shipped to Seville from the Americas, and so kept its soubriquet.

SPAIN

□ SEVILLE

1 Macarena Basilica
2 Macarena Gate
3 La Cartuja
4 Casa de Pilatos
5 Giralda
6 Cathedral
7 Reales Alcázares
8 Torre de Oro
9 Plaza de Toros de la Maestranza

the city's walls in 45 B.C.); certainly the first Moorish citadel on the site can be traced back to the eighth century. But it was the Almohades who transformed a mere defensive construction into a palace. Succeeding generations of Christian kings, notably Pedro the Cruel in the fourteenth century, employed the finest *mudéjar* – Moors who stayed on after the reconquest – craftsmen to add to that original and produce the luxurious treasure that still stands today.

The jewel in the Alcázar's sparkling crown is the Hall of the Ambassadors. Here, pink marble columns support horseshoe-shaped arches with richly decorated capitals; black and white glazed tiles adorn the lower part of the walls; the upper part is covered with intricate mosaics; and the whole is topped by a glittering cupola.

For sheer beauty, however, even the Alcázar is cast into shadow by the Casa de Pilatos. It is traditionally believed to have been modeled on the remains of Pilate's house, whose ruins its fifteenth-century creator, the Marquis of Tarifa, had seen in Jerusalem. Although the combination of *mudéjar* and Renaissance architecture make this unlikely, the house does boast a truly gorgeous galleried patio, fine frescoes, delicate plasterwork, and a salon whose ceiling was painted by Francisco Pachego, father-in-law of Velázquez. Outside, the scents of figs and bougainvillea waft across the garden, a welcome oasis of coolness in the heat of the Sevillan summer.

A few minutes' walk from the Alcázar is Seville's great Christian achievement, the cathedral. Built on the site of the Almohades' mosque, it was conceived on such a grand scale "that future generations will think us madmen." Work took more than 100 years – coinciding with the whole of the fifteenth century – but no one who judged the results on size alone could have been disappointed: it is the largest Gothic cathedral in the world. And, although the interior is gloomy, the artistry of the decor is fabulous. The altarpiece and choir are wonderfully intricate, the former adorned with sculpted scenes from the Bible and the latter with wrought-iron grillwork and ebony stalls. The royal chapel boasts a beautiful silver urn containing the remains of Ferdinand III. The cathedral houses some 500 paintings, including one of the few religious works by Goya. And the massive monument to Christopher Columbus is bedecked with four ornate figures.

The cathedral's bell tower, originally the minaret of the mosque which stood on the same site, is the most evocative symbol of Seville, the Giralda. Like the cathedral, it was conceived on a grand scale – the twelfth-century emir Abu Yacub Yusuf ordered a minaret that would surpass all others in beauty. Even today, town planning regulations strictly control the height of buildings in the vicinity so that the tower can be appreciated in all its grandeur.

If Seville owes its richness to any single individual, it could be to Christopher Columbus – or perhaps to Queen Isabella who, in the flush of enthusiasm engendered by the recapture in 1492 of Granada, the last stronghold of the Moors in Spain, sponsored Columbus's first expedition to the New World. He set sail from Huelva, a port on the coast some 75 miles (120 km) southwest of Seville, but subsequent explorers, including Amerigo Vespucci and

Participants in the feria, *or spring fair, enter wholeheartedly into the atmosphere of the "five-day party" which dominates Seville a few weeks after Easter. Even small girls are dressed in the brightly colored, frilly* traje de gitana, *or gypsy costume.*

The Plaza de España in Maria Luisa park is a relic of Seville's first "Expo," the Ibero–American Exhibition of 1929. Decorated with the faces of famous Spaniards, the arcade is now the home of various government offices.

Ferdinand Magellan began their journeys from Seville itself, taking advantage of the deep water harbor of the River Guadalquivir.

More significantly, Columbus's journeys opened up trade with the Americas. In 1503, Isabella established the Casa de Contratación, an exchange house to stimulate and control trade, to the enormous profit of Seville. In the two centuries that followed, gold and jewels beyond measure flowed from the New World up the Guadalquivir and into the pockets of the Sevillans. Madrid became the capital of Spain in 1561, but – it was said – Seville was still capital of the world.

Such a boom could not last, but even after the Casa de Contratación moved to Cádiz in 1717, Seville continued to prosper. In the eighteenth century, its Royal Tobacco Factory was not only the largest employer in Spain – with a work force of 3,000 – but also the nation's second largest building, yielding precedence only to the Escorial outside Madrid. The factory achieved immortality as the workplace of Carmen in Bizet's opera; it is now part of the university.

Seville had a further boom period in the early 1990s with Expo '92, held to mark the 500th anniversary of Columbus's voyage of discovery. The area of La Cartuja, across the Guadalquivir from the city center, was redeveloped with a multimillion peseta investment. In the aftermath of Expo, the area became a public attraction, with all the Spanish pavilions and several of the specialist exhibits remaining in place. A highlight is the navigation pavilion, reflecting the Expo theme and recalling the exploits which made Seville great.

A city for all seasons, Seville is probably at its most vibrant in spring, during the two great festivals of *Semana Santa* (Holy Week) and the *feria*, or fair. Each evening in Holy Week, members of the *cofradías* (brotherhoods) of Seville's many churches emerge onto darkened streets carrying elaborate floats which bear images of Christ and of the virgin to whom their church is dedicated. Each slow-moving procession has its quota of robed and hooded penitents known as *nazarenos*. In the sixteenth century they were scourged as part of their penance, and even today many of the devout are barefoot.

The most famous of the virgins – María Santísima de la Esperanza (Most Holy Mary of Hope) from the Macarena Basilica – is carried in the parade on the Thursday of Holy Week. A Baroque sculpture whose sorrowful face bears a single teardrop, she is not only the most ornate of all the virgins, but she has also been awarded the gold medal of the city, which she wears on a red and gold ribbon around her neck. She is the only one of Seville's virgins to have her own bodyguard – 100 armed citizens dressed in Roman-style breastplates and helmets march alongside her.

The haunting devotional songs known as *saetas* give way, three weeks after Holy Week, to the throbbing, erotic rhythms of flamenco, the "theme tune" of the spring fair. Women and girls of all ages don traditional multicolored, multiflounced dresses, while men wear the flat, broad-brimmed hats and fitted jackets of *caballeros*, or horsemen. Five days of drinking, singing, and dancing culminate in the grand parade of horses and carriages. It is a festival designed for Sevillans, which gives visitors a glimpse of the joy of living that characterizes their flamboyant city.

As much a symbol of Seville as the Eiffel Tower is of Paris, the Giralda was designed as a minaret, but is now the bell tower of the cathedral. Four bronze spheres which used to adorn its roof were lost in an earthquake in the fourteenth century; the present belfry was built in the sixteenth and topped with the giraldilla, *or weather vane, which gives the tower its name.*

The ceiling of the Hall of the Ambassadors in the Reales Alcázares was commissioned in the fourteenth century by Pedro the Cruel, the first Christian king to choose Seville as his capital. Pedro was an early advocate of workers' rights, limiting the power of both the Church and the nobility.

Seville's bullring – the Plaza de Toros de la Maestranza – was built in 1760 in the style of a Roman amphitheater and holds 14,000 spectators. Bullfighting is an integral part of the Sevillan spring and summer, with fights every day from Semana Santa *to the end of the* feria.

Prague

Medieval city of music

Among European capitals, Prague has no rival in beauty. A higgledy-piggledy jumble of terracotta roofs and soft yellow gables, pale blue domes, and countless spires – bristling with turrets, gilded crockets, and orbs – rise above a web of crooked streets. Wrought-iron signs hang over intimate workshops, boutiques, and ancient taverns, lit at night by the soft glow of low-level lighting in conscious imitation of pre-electric days. In the background hover the lavish palaces of princes and kings. It could be the fairytale setting for "The Elves and the Shoemaker." Reality is only marginally less strange: so well preserved is the city's historic center that the Czech film director Miloš Forman chose it as the setting for much of *Amadeus* (1984), a portrait of Mozart – who did some of his best work in Prague and held the city dear.

The unusual beauty of Prague bemuses many visitors: some call it mysterious, others dreamlike, surreal, or bohemian: in fact, the word *bohémien* was coined by the French to describe the casual, anarchic, and artistic lifestyles of gypsies from Bohemia, the kingdom of which Prague was once capital. The otherworldliness of the city is all the more comprehensible in the light of its recent history. For four decades it was hermetically sealed behind the Iron Curtain, mothballed in the grayness of communist society. After Czechoslovakia cast off the Soviet pall in the "Velvet Revolution" at the end of 1989, Western visitors flooded in and found, to their surprise, not a drab monolith of Marxist–Leninist urban planning,

Charles Bridge links the Staré Město (Old Town) on the east bank of the river to the Malá Strana (Lesser Town) on the west. For four centuries the 1,300-foot (400-m) long bridge was the only one across the Vltava and was not only a main artery, but also a processional way for coronations and other state occasions. To the rear the Gothic spires of the Cathedral of St. Vitus rise above the coolly Neoclassical lines of Hradčany Castle.

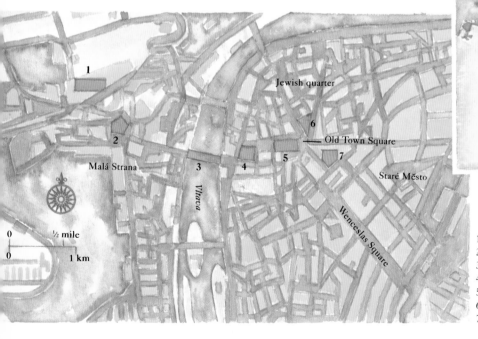

Jewish quarter

Old Town Square

Malá Strana

Staré Město

Vltava

Wenceslas Square

0 — ½ mile
0 — 1 km

□ PRAGUE
CZECH REPUBLIC

1 St. Vitus's Cathedral
2 Church of St. Nicholas
3 Charles Bridge
4 Klementinum
5 Old Town Hall
6 Tyn Church
7 Estates Theater

but a vibrant city of immense charm and with deep historic roots, eager once again to flourish.

To some extent neglect has been Prague's guardian angel. During the eighteenth and nineteenth centuries, it was deliberately treated as a backwater by the Habsburgs who ruled their empire from Vienna. Thus Prague was never the victim of the grandiose rebuilding programs that during the nineteenth century transformed many European capitals – including Paris, Berlin, and Brussels – and its seventeenth- and eighteenth-century heart remained virtually intact.

The calm beauty of the city today, however, cloaks a turbulent past, which on many occasions had found Prague at the crossroads of European history. According to tradition, the city was founded in the ninth century, and religious strife was quickly established as a recurring leitmotif. Paganism was still widespread when in A.D. 929 a young Christian king was assassinated by his heathen brother, Boleslav the Cruel. The murdered king, Wenceslas (or Vaclav), later became patron saint of Bohemia and also the subject of the Christmas carol "Good King Wenceslas," which bears little resemblance to reality.

Over time, Bohemia (corresponding roughly to the modern Czech Republic) was drawn into the Holy Roman Empire. In the early fourteenth century, Prague was made capital of the empire by King Charles of Bohemia, who became Holy Roman Emperor as Charles IV in 1355. He wanted to create a showpiece of Christendom: he founded Charles University, the first in central Europe, and undertook a number of ambitious building projects, including Charles Bridge. Although the foundation stone was laid in 1348, the bridge was not finished until 1400. And the massive remodeling of the Cathedral of St. Vitus commenced by Charles went on over five centuries. It was finally completed in 1929.

Enlightened in some respects, Charles was in others a religious fanatic. He created a host of ostentatious monasteries and convents in Prague, and gathered a huge collection of holy relics, which he displayed in the public squares on an annual Day of Relics for the benefit of thousands of pilgrims who came from far and wide to see them. This sowed the seeds of religious reform, which came to a head under John Huss, a theologian at Charles University. In 1419, four years after Huss was burned at the stake, the "Hussites" seized control of the government. This heralded two centuries of Protestant rule for Prague, which came to an end when the Roman Catholic Habsburg Ferdinand II decided to stamp his authority on the nation.

For nearly 300 years, Prague remained in the firm grip of the Habsburgs, whose first action was to impose the Counter-Reformation. This was led by the Jesuits who built churches, including St. Nicholas's, in ebullient Baroque style. Gentle prosperity helped to fund an energetic building program that included the transformation of the Old Town Square, the renovation of Charles Bridge, and the building of a number of aristocratic palaces on land confiscated from Protestants.

The Protestants were not the only victims of religious discrimination. Prague's large Jewish population was tolerated, but Jews were subjected to all kinds of restrictions and occasional

More than five centuries after its installation, the astronomical clock mounted on the facade of the Old Town Hall is still a major attraction. Not simply a timepiece, it also shows the phases of the moon and sun, and the movements of the stars, and registers the equinoxes and feast days. On the hour, the figure of death turns an hourglass and pulls a bell chord. Figures of the twelve apostles then process through the open hatches above. The lower disk, painted in the nineteenth century, depicts the schedule of seasonal labors for farm workers.

The Old Town Square, a marketplace since the eleventh century, was embellished later by the Gothic Tyn Church (set back from the square) and the fourteenth-century Old Town Hall, with its astronomical clock. Baroque, Rococo, and Neoclassical details add the sparkle of individuality to the pastel-painted facades, ornamented with gables and arches.

The 30 statues of saints which line Charles Bridge were added during the Counter-Reformation, but none the less strike a note of authenticity with their medieval setting. It is said that pious pedestrians once raised their hats to each saint as they passed over the bridge. Among the statues is one of the patron saint of bridges, Saint John Nepomuk, who in 1383 was cast into the Vltava in a sack on the orders of King Wenceslas IV because – so legend recounts – he refused to divulge to the king the contents of the queen's confession.

pogroms. From the twelfth century onward, they were fenced into a ghetto close to the eastern riverbank, to the north of Charles Bridge. Between 1439 and 1787, they had only a small plot of land on which to bury their dead, with the result that, after three and a half centuries, at least 20,000 people had been buried here, in layers up to twelve deep. Today the tightly packed, crooked gravestones, present one of the most remarkable and moving sights of Prague.

In the nineteenth century, the New Town – originally laid out by Charles IV – was developed, and the broad, avenuelike Wenceslas Square, which has become something of a national shrine in this century, laid out. On the collapse of the Austro–Hungarian Empire at the end of World War I, the independent nation of Czechoslovakia emerged, with Prague as its capital. Although the city was overrun and cruelly treated by the Nazis in World War II, it was spared widespread bomb damage. The nation was re-formed after the war, and governed by a coalition led by the communist Klement Gottwald, until he seized absolute power in 1948 and announced the triumph of socialism to the approving masses in the Old Town Square.

Two decades later, the Prague Spring, sailing on the slogan "socialism with a human face" and led by the communist chief Alexander Dubček, was brutally crushed by Soviet tanks. Another two decades passed, until the collapse of Soviet power across eastern Europe emboldened students to demonstrate and, in November 1989, to call for the removal of the communist government. The self-effacing playwright and longterm active opponent of communism, Vaclav Havel, was elected president, and in June 1990 Czechoslovakia held its first free elections in modern history. On January 1, 1993, Slovakia broke away from the Czech Republic, in a separation so amicable as to be dubbed the "Velvet Divorce."

Like the best fairytales, this story has its darker shadows. Prague was the birthplace of Franz Kafka, the author of tales of nightmarish obstruction and metamorphosis, and of bizarre and cruelly witty moral conundrums. Today these shadows may be seen in economic stress, a rise in crime statistics, and an overwhelming influx of tourists. But an aura of good-humored mystery and enchantment still prevails.

And in the background there is always music, from the folksingers and jazz musicians of the oak-paneled cafés, and the myriad performers who bring a fiesta atmosphere to Charles Bridge on a summer's evening, to the concert musicians amid the Jesuit Baroque splendor of the Klementinum. Mozart was feted enthusiastically in Prague; Beethoven, Berlioz, Liszt, Wagner, and Tchaikovsky performed in the magnificent Estates Theater to glittering audiences stacked into the wedding-cake tiers of its balconies. The Czech nation produced its own array of composers, who sought to evoke uniquely Czech themes: Smetana, Dvořák, and Janáček. If any of their works could be singled out as an expression of the sophistication, optimism, and élan of the Czech Republic today, perhaps it is the piece from Smetana's *Má Vlast* (My Country) called "Vltava," evoking in powerful, sweeping, and deeply melodic strains the river that winds its way past the spires of Prague and through the time-honored rhythm of arches beneath Charles Bridge.

Planned in 1653, the Church of St. Nicholas was completed 100 years later. It served the Jesuits for little more than twenty years before their order was suppressed by the pope in 1773, when it became the parish church of the Lesser Town. The Jesuits were obliged to build a tower next to the dome, to replace a watchtower that had previously stood on the site. The result is a peculiar but happy architectural pairing.

The interior of the Church of St. Nicholas is Baroque at its most lavish and exuberant. Four huge, muscular statues of the great Greek Doctors of the Church – who vigorously enforced orthodoxy in the East – underline the architectural message of the church as a whole: the triumph of Catholicism over the heresy of Protestantism. This statue depicts Saint Basil, bishop of Caesarea in the fourth century, known for his sympathy for the poor and as a scourge of the wealthy.

A reassuring sense of history hovers over Prague, caught in the late afternoon light when the noise and bustle of city traffic begins to dim. At the eastern end of Charles Bridge, dainty Baroque spires, domes, and lanterns cluster around the medieval Old Town Bridge Tower, with its trapezoid roof and cones.

ENTANGLED
in
HISTORY

ALL OVER THE WORLD, IN CERTAIN CITIES AND certain buildings, memories of the past are entwined with the present. Monarchs – magnificent or misguided, fabulous or foolhardy – have left their gifts to posterity. Fortresses, palaces, castles, and cathedrals resound with the names of occupants from centuries gone by. Great battles, great romances, and great tragedies have left their mark on the towns and edifices that witnessed their drama. The stupendous palace of the Sun King at Versailles is infinitely removed from Holyroodhouse, where Mary Queen of Scots heard the death knell of her dreams of glory. And the intimate Scandinavian charm of Gripsholm, retreat of the Swedish kings and queens, is a far cry from the drafty prison at Dürnstein, where a faithful minstrel found his master. In Charleston, one of the Deep South's most beautiful cities, one of the ugliest wars in history broke out; and in Poland, a cathedral built to the glory of God became one constant in a nation in turmoil. The stories behind these locations are unique, but all remain inextricably entangled in history.

According to legend, Hohenschwangau in the Bavarian Alps was the home of Lohengrin, the Swan Knight. In the 1830s the castle passed into the hands of the family of Ludwig of Bavaria, who here conceived the fairytale castle of Neuschwanstein, a highlight of the Romantic Road.

Gripsholm

Heart of the Swedish nation

Both a bastion and a royal palace, Gripsholm stands out from its setting on the placid waters of Lake Mälaren like a crudely faceted semiprecious stone in an ancient Nordic crown. Four asymmetric pepperpot towers rise up above the manicured lawns of its pocket-sized island, holding within their gabled clasp a tightly enclosed hexagonal courtyard. A looser chain of dwellings and apartments surrounds a larger courtyard beyond, creating a quaint and artless mishmash of architectural styles that is the hallmark and charm of so much of northern European building of the sixteenth century.

The ruins of an older castle stood on this site when Gustav Eriksson Vasa passed this way in 1520 as he fled from the Danish army under Christian II. It proved a critical moment in Swedish history. From a growing chorus of dissent against the Kalmar Union – a federation of Scandinavian states under the Danish crown – Gustav managed to kindle a sense of Swedish nationalism, leading a successful rebellion which won him the crown of Sweden in 1523, when the Kalmar Union was dissolved.

In 1537 King Gustav Vasa began building a fortified residence of stone at Gripsholm, one of the first of its kind in Sweden. A rough and solemn man of action, Gustav Vasa lived in a wooden cabin while work progressed. His sons were different. Erik considered himself a man of the Renaissance, a poet and a humanist. He invited artists and craftsmen from all over Europe to embellish his nation and searched, in vain, for a foreign princess to marry. In 1560 he was

On the outskirts of the town of Mariefred, which is today served by rail, Gripsholm is still probably best approached by boat – a three-hour trip from Stockholm across the beautiful Lake Mälaren. Floodlit in the cool evenings of the northern spring and fall, or basking in the continuous summer daylight, Gripsholm evokes the pleasant atmosphere of a country house, one which, despite its origins as a fortress, made it a favorite retreat of generations of Swedish royalty.

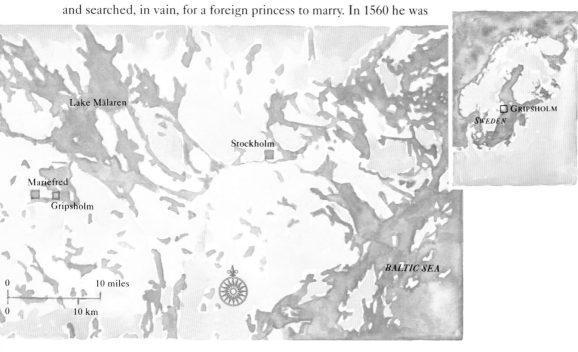

Lake Mälaren

Stockholm

Mariefred

Gripsholm

□ GRIPSHOLM

SWEDEN

BALTIC SEA

0   10 miles

0   10 km

on his way to woo Elizabeth I of England when news reached him of his father's death. He hurried back to Sweden to claim his crown as Erik XIV and ruled for eight years, which were punctuated by a bitter dispute with his half-brothers, Johan and Karl. Johan was imprisoned at Gripsholm, where he lived in some luxury with his wife, a Polish princess, but came to the throne as Johan III in 1568.

Gripsholm's first major transformation took place under Karl, who succeeded as Karl IX in 1599. His bedroom, paneled and decorated in flowery Renaissance style, remains one of the castle's most charming rooms. Under Karl's son, Gustav II Adolf, who reigned from 1611 to 1632, Sweden became a major European power by playing a decisive role in the Thirty Years' War, at the end of which it controlled most of the land surrounding the Baltic. But in 1709 Karl XII tried to march on Moscow and was defeated by the Russians. Sweden was pushed back to the eastern borders of modern Finland.

Through these tumultuous years, Gripsholm slumbered, serving as a dower house for successive royal widows, including Queen Katerina (wife of Karl IX) – for whom an elegant painted bedroom hung with tapestries was created – and Queen Hedvig Eleonora, best known for her remodeling of Drottningholm on the outskirts of Stockholm in the late seventeenth century. But it was Crown Princess Lovisa Ulrika, the extravagant sister of Frederick the Great of Prussia and wife of King Adolf Fredrik, who, almost a century later, ushered in a golden age of Swedish culture, when the arts, architecture, music, and the theater flourished. She stored her growing number of portrait paintings at Gripsholm, thereby laying the foundations for the massive collection of 3,500 portraits of Swedish royalty and leading figures of Swedish public life which is still housed in the castle today.

Princess Lovisa Ulrika's son, Gustav III, built upon his mother's cultural achievements. He came to Gripsholm frequently, and during his reign the castle underwent its second major transformation, when several of the most elegant surviving rooms were installed. The restrained, gilded, Neoclassical grace of the White Hall and the Queen's Wing create a striking, yet harmonious counterpoint to the rugged muscularity of the old fortress which envelops them.

Gustav, a man of culture and learning, promoted all fields of the arts and sciences, and was a passionate enthusiast of the theater. He wrote a number of respected historical plays, including *Gustav Vasa*, *The Valor of Gustav Adolf*, and *Queen Kristina*, extolling the virtues of the country's great former monarchs, and performed with his courtiers in specially built theaters at the royal palaces. One of these is at Gripsholm, a tiny gem squeezed into the upper floor of a tower. But the king's devotion to cultural affairs (during one Christmas, he starred in eight plays) led to the accusation that he was neglecting the country's political life; and in 1792 he was assassinated, an event used by the Italian composer Verdi as the focus of his opera *Un Ballo in Maschera*, first performed in 1859.

In the Napoleonic era, Gripsholm's place at Sweden's cultural heart diminished. Today it is a monument to the birth of the nation and to its past, when on unending summer days kings and queens indulged their love of the arts as an antidote to affairs of state.

The theater at Gripsholm was built for Gustav III by Eric Palmstedt, one of the leading eighteenth-century Swedish architects. Although he solved the problem of fitting it into the confines of a tower by extending the stage backward into the Queen's Wing, all kinds of trompe-l'oeil effects were needed to give it an illusory sense of space. Plays performed by Gustav and his friends were watched by a limited number of courtiers sitting on just four rows of benches and in two tiers of boxes, and by servants who could peer down through concealed, porthole-like openings in the ceiling.

In 1771, the year that he seized the throne of Sweden in a coup d'état, Gustav III was painted, along with his brothers Fredrik Adolf and Karl, by the noted Swedish portraitist Alexander Roslin. Gustav was dubbed "King Charming" by his supporters. With his Danish wife, Queen Sofia Magdalena, he created the most elegant of Gripsholm's interiors. His taste was greatly influenced by a visit to Italy in 1783–84.

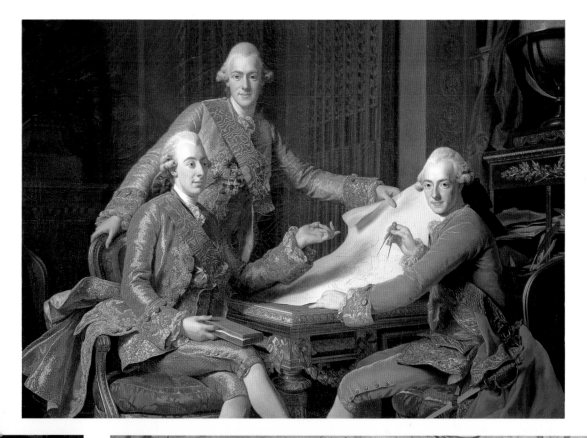

The bedroom of Duke Karl, later King Karl IX, has all the intimate, understated charm of its era, before royal palaces abandoned human scale in the pursuit of grandeur. The wooden panels, bordered by pilasters carved in the Classical style, are painted in imitation of Italian wood inlay, and the white plaster on the ceiling is decorated with light and airy floral patterns. The broad floorboards, low ceiling, and benches lining the walls create an atmosphere of relaxed comfort and warmth.

Charleston
Capital of the Deep South

The very name Charleston calls to mind elegance and a certain Southern way of life: cool white plantation houses set in expansive grounds, the whirling of crinolines in ballrooms, burgeoning trade, rich cottonfields, and an existence as slow as the laziest river.

It was not always so. Long before the English settled the city in 1670, other Europeans had tried to establish themselves in what was then an inhospitable wilderness of salt marshes, swamps, and malarial forest. English explorer Sebastian Cabot visited the coast in the fifteenth century, merely noting its existence before leaving it to the Spanish. A group of French Huguenots arrived in 1562, but the living was so hard and disease so rife that they returned to France within a year, leaving only a fort and the name "Caroline," after their monarch, Charles IX.

When the English settled South Carolina a century later, they established Charles Towne (this time named after Charles II of England) on the west bank of the Ashley River. Some saw the lush vegetation as a potential source of wealth, but according to one chronicler, "Beyond doubt, the flat maritime part is a most unhealthy situation, and the first settlers could scarcely have been cast ashore in any quarter of the globe where they could be exposed to greater hazard from the climate."

Certainly the newcomers quickly found that European grains were unable to survive the subtropical weather, and they soon adapted to trading in natural products. Beaver skins, lumber, and naval supplies –

Elegant whitewashed homes overlook the waterfront in Charleston. In a socially conscious society, such houses, with their wooden balustrades, broad verandas, and palmetto trees, are some of the most desirable in the city, possibly surpassed only by an address "on the Battery" with a view over White Point.

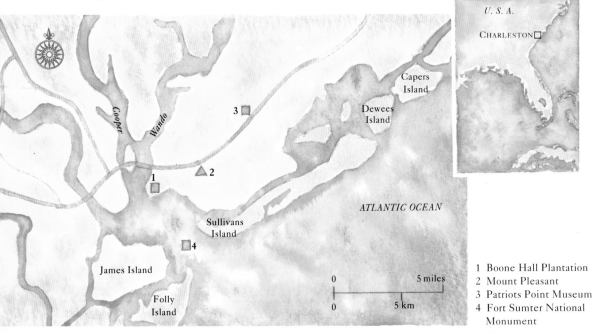

U.S.A.

CHARLESTON □

Capers Island

Dewees Island

ATLANTIC OCEAN

Cooper

Wando

3

2

1

Sullivans Island

4

James Island

Folly Island

| 0 | | 5 miles |
| 0 | | 5 km |

1 Boone Hall Plantation
2 Mount Pleasant
3 Patriots Point Museum
4 Fort Sumter National Monument

such as tar and turpentine (which came from pitch pine trees) – went to England in return for clothes, arms, and ammunition. From the West Indies came rum, sugar, and experienced colonists, many from Barbados, bringing with them the distinctive style of architecture and agriculture that gives the city much of its graceful character.

The administration of the new colony was vested by the king in the Lords Proprietors, a group of English Cavaliers. Under a system of government known as Locke's Constitution, there were eight Proprietors, the eldest of whom was the Palatine, and the Palatine Court sat on behalf of the king. It appointed the governor of the colony and established the noble ranks of baron, cassique, and landgrave, each of which carried substantial endowments of land.

Ten years later, in 1680, the settlement was moved to high ground at the confluence of the Ashley and Cooper rivers and became known as New Charles Towne. More and more people moved there, until eventually it became simply Charles Towne, the focal point of the colony. Although the official creed was the Church of England, freedom of worship was guaranteed, and over the coming decades the city swelled with immigrants: Roundheads and Cavaliers from England, Dissenters from Scotland, Huguenots escaping the Edict of Nantes. Later came Swiss Protestants and Scots Covenanters, along with Irish and German settlers looking for a new life.

In 1693 a new crop, brought from Madagascar by a damaged ship which had docked in Charles Towne harbor, reached the colony. Landgrave Thomas Smith saw its potential, and for the first time rice was planted on the Carolina coast. Its effect was to be enormous. Slaves were imported from the West Indies to help with its cultivation. The population grew rapidly. The Proprietors dismantled the constitution, but soon became unpopular themselves. Under Governor Robert Quarry, pirates were allowed to stop in the city to provision, and by the end of the century, the coast was infested. Eventually, George I agreed with the pleas of the colonists to dismantle Locke's Constitution and took Charles Towne directly under Crown control in 1721. It was the beginning of a long period of success.

Around this time, the governor of Antigua sent some indigo seeds to his daughter in the colony. She grew the plant, extracted the dye, and thus the indigo industry was born. Another newcomer – not to become really significant for another 50 years – was cotton, picked from the seed by hand. Olives and orange trees grew by the coast, hemp, castor oil beans, peanuts, and sugarcane farther inland. Mulberry bushes for silk production grew naturally in the woods; and Dutchmen from the East Indies built irrigation systems for the rice plantations. South Carolina was becoming a land of promise, and Charles Towne was its main trading port.

After the War of Independence (during which Charles Towne was occupied by the British for more than two years), the city changed its name for the last time, to Charleston. After the invention of the saw gin at the end of the eighteenth century, cotton production exploded. A long-staple cotton of superlative quality was grown on the Sea Islands, which spread north and south on both sides of Charleston harbor, forming an inland sea: Edisto Island cotton

When Republican and abolitionist Abraham Lincoln was elected president in 1860, South Carolina seceded from the Union, pitching the country into civil war. The rural southern states fought bitterly to protect their slave-based largely agricultural economy from the industrial north, but after their defeat the 13th Amendment was passed, giving slaves their freedom and the right to vote.

A parade of cadets in traditional uniform at the Citadel Military Academy, founded in 1842, carries with it echoes of Charleston's bellicose history. It was cadets such as these who fired the first shots of the Civil War, as Union ships arrived to relieve Fort Sumter and besiege the city.

On April 12, 1861, the first shots of the Civil War were fired from Fort Sumter, some 3 miles (5 km) southeast of Charleston.

More than 200 cadets from the fort went on to become officers for the Southern cause during the war, which lasted four years and resulted in perhaps one million casualties.

was at one point selling for $2 per pound ($4/kg), while "upland cotton," from the mainland, cost 9 cents per pound (18 cents/kg).

As cotton became increasingly important and eclipsed other exports, the plantation culture really took hold. Following the Barbados example, owners built magnificent mansions for themselves, housing their slaves in the middle of their estates so that they could not communicate with other workers. The city sprouted elegant town houses and paved streets and began to see itself not just as an important trading center, but also as a focal point of Southern culture.

As the ships came and went with bales of cotton, tierces of rice, bushels of corn, and barrels of rosin, Charleston ladies established a complex social system of parties and presentations (the springtime Azalea Festival, with its balls and festival queen, is still a great social event, attended only by selected guests). After the war of 1812 against Britain, when the Battery – a 1,500-foot (457-m) long, 10-foot (3-m) wide stone wall rising straight out of the bay – was built, a Battery address was the desire of every fashionable family. Living "below Broad Street" was (and still is) essential. In White Point Gardens, young ladies strolled with their parasols among the japonicas and wisterias, the tamarisk, magnolia, and opopanax trees, dreaming of young men at the nearby Citadel Military Academy.

These were the golden days of Charleston, when the plantation houses were alive with laughter and music and the streets rang with the sound of carriage wheels. It was a way of life paid for by the labor of slaves. At one point, 350,000 families owned 3 million slaves in the southern states. Supporters of the slave system were keen to point out its benefits. In the words of one, "perhaps nowhere in the world, and at no time in its history, has such an easy, considerate, kind and respectful intercourse subsisted between employer and employee, as between the Southern white man and the Negro."

Such opinions were not shared by the industrial north, which strongly disapproved of slavery and the plantation culture. When abolitionist Abraham Lincoln was elected Republican president in 1860, South Carolina promptly seceded from the Union. The stage was set for civil war. At first the Confederate troops covered themselves in glory. Charleston became the center of Confederate blockade running, and the world's first submarine warfare was introduced in 1863. Two years later, General Sherman destroyed the city of Columbia, and Charleston was evacuated.

The loss of the Civil War spelled the end for "the Mother of the South." Charleston was never the same again. Forced to pay their slaves, many plantation owners went bankrupt. The government broke up the old plantations into 60-acre (24-hectare) plots for the slaves, who now had their freedom and the right to vote, and the whites implemented a system of segregation. At the turn of the century, hurricanes devastated the rice fields. In 1915 the cotton crop was destroyed by boll weevils, while vegetable farming was undermined by the cultivation of the California desert. Hot on the heels of such disasters came the Depression, and many once-great families were forced to sell their homes and their possessions. For the elegant city of Charleston, the Southern dream was over.

The eighteenth-century Magnolia Gardens, noted for its abundant camellias and azaleas, is one of the most popular walking spots in a city renowned for its beautiful flowers and trees. The Charleston of today is a far cry from the swampy, malarial tract of land inhabited by the earliest settlers in the area.

Some 9 miles (15 km) north of the city, Drayton Hall dreams in Palladian splendor among mature subtropical trees and impeccably clipped lawns. Such imposing mansions, perfectly symmetrical and possessed of classical porticoes and columns, reflect the grandeur of the old plantation lifestyle of the privileged few.

Dürnstein

Cage of a lion freed by song

Some 50 miles (80 km) northwest of the Austrian capital Vienna, the River Danube makes its wide, sinuous progress through the low hills of the Wachau region. It passes the heavily wooded medieval houses of the riverside villages, with their narrow streets and onion-tipped church towers, and the cherry orchards of Melk, which in spring litter the water with pink and white blossoms.

In 1854, the young Elizabeth of Wittelsbach traveled downriver from Germany on her way to marry the emperor Franz Joseph in Vienna. Amid all the excitements of the voyage – including celebrations along the route and the arrival of her future husband by barge to escort her into his capital city – she still had time to look out for her first sight of a small village which had been a Danube legend for six centuries. She was waiting for Dürnstein, a hamlet which had earned its place in the history books as the prison of Richard the Lion-Hearted, Plantagenet king of England and sworn enemy of the Austrian archduke Leopold.

Dürnstein's significance dates from an era when Europe was gripped by the fervor of Holy Wars. In the face of increased provocation from the Seljuk Turks, Christian Europe launched the First Crusade, taking Jerusalem in 1099. Just 100 years later, it was recaptured by the legendary Turkish leader Salah al-Din (Saladin). Again Christian armies were mustered, and a great quartet of leaders – Richard I of England, Philip Augustus of France, Leopold of Austria, and Frederick Barbarossa of Germany – set off for the east. Barbarossa

The town that Richard the Lion-Hearted would have seen, as he was hustled through the Kremster Tor (Krems Gate) and up the steep steps to his prison, is still recognizable today. It stands just 720 feet (220 m) above sea level, surrounded by the old Roman vine terraces and dominated by a steep cliff. Here stands the now-ruined castle, another 500 feet (150 m) above the town and a good half hour's walk for the prisoner. In Richard's time, Dürnstein was owned by a trusted Austrian noble, Hadmar von Künstein.

was drowned en route at Antioch. The Crusaders failed to capture Jerusalem and instead besieged and sacked the coastal town of Acre. Leopold hoisted the Austrian colors on the citadel's ramparts, at which an enraged Richard tore them down, shouting that the double eagle of Austria would never take precedence over the lion of England while he lived. His action was to cost him – and England – dearly.

On his way home, Richard was shipwrecked in the Adriatic, coming ashore at Trieste, with a return route which took him through Leopold's territory. At this point, history becomes inextricably entwined with legend, for the king dressed himself and his page as paupers and began the long journey home. One version of the story says that he was recognized while working in the kitchens of an inn; another that his page went to buy food with the king's gloves tucked into his belt. But it is a fact that Richard was arrested at Erdberg, a village outside the walls of Vienna, taken along the Danube and imprisoned in the tower at Dürnstein.

In some respects, Dürnstein has changed little since Richard's day. The monastery and parish church are still standing, along with the medieval graveyard and a fourteenth-century charnel house; and even today the town's gabled inns – known as *Heuriger* – hang bunches of fresh greenery over their doors to advertise the new wine of the year for sale. In this setting, it is easier to believe the part of the tale that has passed into legend. Nobody knew exactly where Richard was imprisoned in Leopold's territory. So his faithful minstrel Blondel set off in search of his master, fruitlessly touring castles and garrisons until he reached Dürnstein. Fanciful pictures depict him playing his lute beneath the castle walls, while singing in the ancient *langue d'oc*: "*Donna, vos beautas | Elas bellas faissos…*" ("Lady, your beauties are so perfect…") only to hear a voice from the tower above continue the song: "*…si bel trop affansia | Ta, de vos, non partrai*" ("…that if it will not offend, I will never leave you"). Thus the loyal Blondel found his master, sending word to England so that the wheels of negotiation could be set in motion for his release.

There is confusion about the provenance of Blondel. There was a contemporary of Richard's, a young man of some distinction, named Blondel del Nesle, but he was a comrade, not a servant. What is beyond doubt is that Richard was taken to Burg Trifels in the Palatinate, where a ransom of 150,000 silver marks was paid for his release. Half of this colossal sum went to Leopold, who was excommunicated by the pope for violence to a Christian Crusader. The other half paid for a new moat around Vienna, the building of the new town of Wiener Neustadt, and the construction of walls around Enns and Hainburg.

The romance of Richard and Blondel's story has tended to obscure the rest of Dürnstein's history. Saint Columba was hanged here on his way to the Holy Land as a pilgrim. And the town was largely destroyed by the Swedes in 1645. Visitors today go to look at the superb Baroque architecture, to climb the Castle Rock, to admire the religious paintings by Matthaus, Merian, and Rudolf von Alt, and to sit in the *Heuriger* and sip wine. Dürnstein is assured of its place on any Danube journey, as a beautiful town with a fascinating story – a subject almost worthy of a song by the minstrel Blondel.

The castle of Melk and surrounding lands were handed over in 1111 to the huge Benedictine abbey – housing a fine library – that dominates the town. Like Dürnstein, Melk is known today for its Baroque buildings and fine wines.

Dürnstein started life as a toll point on the north bank of the Danube, with the original builders of the castle in 1140–45 known, ominously, as "the Robber Barons of Wachau." Some 30 years before Richard's imprisonment in the castle, an Augustinian monastery was built in the town. Later dissolved and rebuilt in the Baroque style – when its church became a parish church – it still dominates the skyline.

Richard the Lion-Hearted became a paragon of bravery and honor, burnished gold by historians. He was, in fact, a brutal and arrogant man whose violent temper frequently landed him in trouble. His fellow crusader and arch-enemy Leopold, widely known as "the Virtuous," was more familiar to his troops as "the Sponge" because of his prodigious drinking habits.

The Romantic Road

Ancient roads wind through the west of Bavaria in southern Germany – roads once trodden by Romans, by Crusader knights, by pilgrims on their way to Rome, by medieval merchants with their tapestries and silken robes. They pass through the gently undulating meadows and vineyards of Franconia, past lakes and over rivers, then slowly begin the rise toward a magnificent crescendo in the forested foot-hills of the Alps. Along their 213 miles (343 km) lies a chain of sleepy medieval towns with crooked streets and half-timbered town halls; stately Baroque palaces and dainty Rococo churches; and fantastical fairytale castles. With enchantment at every turn, the route has been

Rothenburg ob der Tauber.

dubbed in recent years *Die Romantische Straße*, "The Romantic Road."

The road begins in Würzburg, an old trading city which was the seat of the great Schönborn family of prince-bishops. In the eighteenth century, they moved across town, out of their mighty Marienberg fortress into the Residenz, a Baroque masterpiece hailed as one of the architectural wonders of its age. Würzburg is the center of production for the celebrated Franconian wine, still sold in *Bocksbeutel*, traditional squat oval bottles.

Farther south is a trio of walled medieval towns, frozen in time: Rothenburg ob der Tauber, Dinkelsbühl, and Nördlingen im Ries. Clustered inside their walls are charmed medieval worlds of alleys, steps, archways, gables, overhanging stories, and jumbles of red-tiled roofs. Many of these are *Fachwerk* buildings, wood-framed with exposed beams.

Harburg has one of Germany's most famous castles, a beautifully preserved medieval fortress of white walls and red-tiled roofs and turrets. Farther south lies Augsburg, a 2,000-year-old city where broad streets, Romanesque and Gothic churches, and Rococo palaces speak of the tradition of prosperity that once made it the financial center of the Western world. Founded by the Romans in 15 B.C. and named after Emperor Augustus, it was a wealthy trading city in both Roman and medieval times. But it was merchants who really brought it fame.

Families such as the Fuggers, who controlled extensive mineral rights and vast tracts of South America, acquired huge personal wealth and helped to bankroll many of the kingdoms of Europe. Jakob Fugger, the founder of his family's fortunes, was fired with enthusiasm for Renaissance architecture during a visit to Italy and was a key influence in bringing the Renaissance to Germany. In 1523 he built one of Europe's earliest examples of social housing, the Fuggerei, where the old and indigent could live for peppercorn rents in return for saying daily prayers for his soul. The houses are still there, and the residents still say the prayers.

The route south of Augsburg follows the path of the old Via Claudia Augusta, which connected Augsburg to Rome. It rises into the Alpine foothills, a landscape of forests, lakes, and distant peaks. This is the setting for one of the most remarkable German monuments, the fairytale castle at Neuschwanstein, begun in 1869 and completed at the end of the life of Ludwig II of Bavaria. King at the age of nineteen, he was less interested in the affairs of state than in living out a fantasy as a fairytale prince. He led a solitary life, dressing up to enact scenes from the German legends and building ever more ambitious palaces. He also became totally infatuated with the composer Richard Wagner, whose work would never have achieved the scale and scope for which it is celebrated without Ludwig's extravagant patronage.

In the end, Ludwig's cabinet despaired and in 1886 had him certified as insane. Ludwig was imprisoned, but two days later he was found mysteriously drowned in a lake. To the Bavarians he is a hero: not insane but eccentric, living in a dream world. Neuschwanstein remains an evocative testimony to the power of his dream.

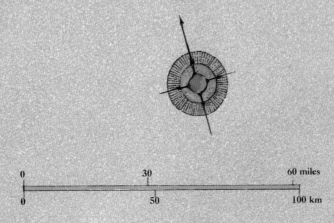

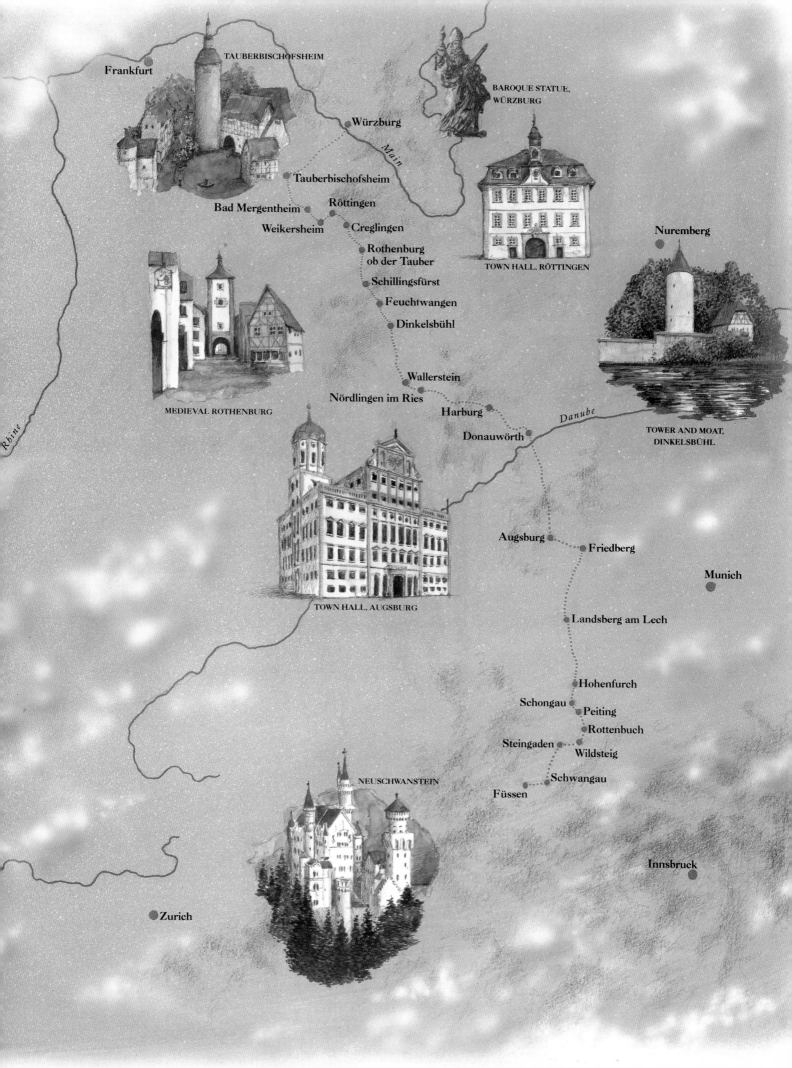

Frankfurt

TAUBERBISCHOFSHEIM

BAROQUE STATUE,
WÜRZBURG

Würzburg

Main

Tauberbischofsheim

Röttingen

Bad Mergentheim

Creglingen

Weikersheim

Rothenburg
ob der Tauber

Schillingsfürst

Feuchtwangen

Dinkelsbühl

TOWN HALL, RÖTTINGEN

Nuremberg

MEDIEVAL ROTHENBURG

Wallerstein

Nördlingen im Ries

Harburg

Danube

Donauwörth

TOWER AND MOAT,
DINKELSBÜHL

Rhine

TOWN HALL, AUGSBURG

Augsburg

Friedberg

Munich

Landsberg am Lech

Hohenfurch

Schongau

Peiting

Rottenbuch

Steingaden

Wildsteig

NEUSCHWANSTEIN

Schwangau

Füssen

Innsbruck

Zurich

Holyroodhouse

Palace of a tragic queen

The romance of the great Renaissance Palace of Holyroodhouse centers on the old towerhouse that forms its historical core and on the passionate, unhappy figure who lived here – Mary, Queen of Scots.

Holyroodhouse has its origins in the abbey of Holyrood, founded in 1128. The abbey's guest houses were frequented by royal visitors, and in time, it became a favorite royal retreat. The palace that exists today began to take shape between 1529 and 1532, when King James V built for himself and his French queen, Mary of Guise, the towerhouse which still stands at the northwestern corner of the palace.

A few days after her birth in December 1542, their daughter Mary succeeded James as ruler of Scotland. She was at the center of intrigue from the first. In 1544, Holyroodhouse was attacked in the "Rough Wooing," Henry VIII's attempt to marry the infant queen to his son Edward. After another assault in 1548, Mary of Guise sent her daughter home. Mary grew up at the glittering French court, with the children of the French king and queen. In 1558, in a splendid ceremony in Notre-Dame Cathedral, she married the heir to the French throne, Francis, who was a year her junior and of whom she grew to be genuinely fond. She danced with his father the king at the celebrations. A dazzling future awaited her.

Later that same year, Elizabeth ascended the English throne, to the dismay of the Catholic French, who deemed the marriage of Henry VIII to her mother Anne Boleyn invalid and Elizabeth illegitimate. The French styled Mary "Dauphiness of France,

Holyrood Abbey was probably named after a relic of the True Cross (or "rood") which found its way here. King James IV of Scotland rebuilt the residential quarters of the abbey in 1501–5, but of his work only a fragment remains.

James V's towerhouse is now embedded in the great Renaissance palace built by King Charles II as the British monarch's official residence in Scotland.

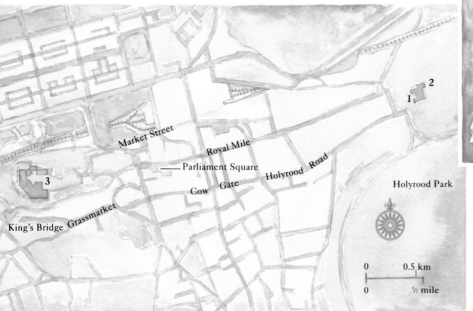

GREAT BRITAIN
EDINBURGH ☐

Market Street
Royal Mile
Parliament Square
Holyrood Road
Cow Gate
Holyrood Park
King's Bridge Grassmarket

0   0.5 km
0   ½ mile

1 Palace of Holyroodhouse
2 Holyrood Abbey
3 Edinburgh Castle

Queen of England and Scotland," but her Guise uncles could not persuade the French to go to war against England on her behalf.

In July 1559, the king of France was killed in a joust: Francis became king and Mary queen. But at the end of 1560, Francis, whose health had never been good, died. Mary, at eighteen, was a widow. Her uncles fell from grace, and in 1561, Mary returned to Scotland, a Catholic in a Protestant land.

She made her home at Holyroodhouse, in her mother's rooms in the towerhouse, known now as Mary Queen of Scots' Bed Chamber and Outer Chamber. With the French throne lost to her, here she dreamed once more of being queen of England. To strengthen her claim, Mary chose as her second husband her cousin Henry Stuart, Lord Darnley (they had a grandmother in common, Henry VIII's sister Margaret Tudor). She had fallen in love with the blonde, beardless youth, by all accounts a fine dancer, while playing nurse when he caught measles.

The Scottish nobility objected; Elizabeth objected; nonetheless Mary and Darnley were married at Holyrood on July 29, 1565. The bride was radiant, and the celebrations lasted four days. But the idyll was shortlived: Mary had married for love and ambition, Darnley for ambition alone. Within a year, disaffected Scottish nobles had manipulated him into authorizing the most savage deed in the palace's history, the murder of Mary's Italian secretary and confidant, David Rizzio. Working Darnley into a state of insane jealousy by saying that Mary and Rizzio were lovers, they made him head of a conspiracy to kill Rizzio and strip Mary of her crown. On March 9, 1566, Rizzio was dragged from his supper with the queen through the Bed Chamber into the Outer Chamber, and killed near the head of the northeastern stairway. He was left lying on the floor in a pool of blood from 56 wounds, one for each of his assassins.

It was the beginning of the end of Mary's dreams. She escaped by feigning reconciliation with Darnley, but never forgave him. And Darnley's dreams of being king of Scotland were dashed when Mary gave birth to their son and her heir in June of that year. (The child was also Elizabeth's heir, and the English queen sent a gold font for his christening.) Darnley was found strangled a mere eight months later in a house outside Edinburgh called Kirk o' Field. The prime suspect was the Earl of Bothwell, the more so since, just three months afterward, having showered him with many of Darnley's jewels and furs, Mary married him at Holyroodhouse. This was too much for the Scots, who forced Mary's abdication in favor of her infant son.

Mary's dignity through nineteen years' imprisonment and, ultimately, at her execution have lent the folly and betrayals of her years at Holyroodhouse a poignancy that has drawn visitors since the 1720s. They were shown a dark stain on the floor and told it was Rizzio's blood, which could not be removed, however often it was scrubbed. By the 1850s, the stain consisted of two blotches, one each side of the line through the doorway, as might be expected from the passage of feet down the centuries. They did not know that the floor level in Mary's rooms had been raised when Holyroodhouse was rebuilt by Charles II. Bound up in the life of one the world's most tragic monarchs, the palace has not lost its power to thrill.

Mary was at supper with Rizzio and others in the northern of the two small "closets" leading off her Bed Chamber (right) on the night of his murder. In one corner is the doorway through which Darnley and the Scottish lords entered and dragged Rizzio out. Mary's initials were added to the wooden ceiling, along with his own, by her son, James VI of Scotland and I of England.

On her marriage to the French dauphin Francis in 1558, when her portrait was painted by François Clouet, Mary was reputed to be the most beautiful woman of her day. She liked music, poetry, and dancing, and the legend of her beauty could be partly attributable to her charisma.

The Darnley Jewel, an enameled gold locket set with precious gemstones, was commissioned by Margaret Douglas, Countess of Lennox, in memory of her husband and of her son, Henry Stuart, Lord Darnley. Although the Earl and Countess of Lennox had promoted their son's marriage to Mary, they blamed her for his death.

The four gold figures on the jewel represent victory, truth, hope, and faith.

"I am the Queen by right of birth, and my place should be there [on the throne]"

MARY, QUEEN OF SCOTS, 1586

Wawel Cathedral
Symbol of Polish sovereignty

Polish history is one of often violent change. In the sixteenth century, the country was a byword for religious tolerance, one of the few in Europe to resist the extremes of Reformation and Counter-Reformation. In the early seventeenth century, it was the continent's largest state, and one of the most enlightened, with a constitutional monarchy and a prosperous economy. Less than 200 years later, Poland had ceased to exist, victim of the ambitions of Prussia, Russia, and the Austro-Hungarian Empire. Its crown jewels were melted down by the Prussians; Austrian soldiers took up residence in its palaces. From 1797 until the Warsaw Pact was dissolved in 1991, Poland knew less than two decades of genuine independence – from 1921 to 1939.

To find a thread of continuity in this tangled history, it is necessary to look to Kraków, capital of Poland from 1040 to 1609, home of the second oldest university in central Europe, and site of Wawel Cathedral and Castle. While the rulers, borders, and very existence of Poland have fluctuated through the centuries, these magnificent buildings on Wawel Hill, overlooking the River Vistula, stand firm as the enduring symbol of all that is Polish. In the words of Pope John Paul II, a former bishop of Kraków, Wawel is "the sanctuary of the nation."

Wawel is the burial place of 41 of the 45 Polish monarchs, and the cathedral contains a shrine to Stanislaw, an early bishop of Kraków who was executed in 1079 for his part in a rebellion against King Boleslaw. The incident forced the king to surrender his throne and

The courtyard of Wawel Castle has three tiers of Florentine arches. The two lower tiers conform to traditional Italian style, but the height of the top tier is a unique adaptation intended to counter-balance the heavy appearance of the pitched roof and overhanging eaves which were essential to withstand the severe northern climate.

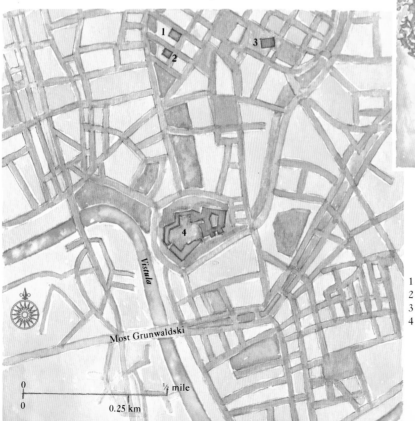

POLAND
KRAKÓW □

1 Collegium Maius
2 University
3 Marieski Church
4 Wawel Cathedral and Castle

Vistula

Most Grunwaldski

0
¼ mile

0
0.25 km

incurred the wrath of both the pope and the Holy Roman Emperor, but it provided Poland with a patron saint.

Most of the cathedral buildings date from the fourteenth century, although the elaborate side chapels were added later. The roof boasts three towers, one of which contains the great Zygmunt Bell, cast in 1520 and still rung on special occasions. It is in the chapels that most of the memorials to the Polish monarchs are to be found, including those of the two kings responsible for the cathedral's creation: Wladyslaw the Short and Kazimierz the Great. Wladyslaw's tomb is of elegant white sandstone, surrounded by effigies of 28 mourning figures; on the other side of the altar, the more flamboyant Kazimierz is commemorated in striking red marble.

The Zygmunt chapel, designed on the orders of King Zygmunt the Old, is the most magnificent of all. Intended by Zygmunt as a mausoleum for his Jagiellon dynasty, which ruled Poland for more than 200 years, it became not only his own memorial, but also that of his son, Zygmunt Augustus, and daughter Anna, the last Jagiellon monarch. The designer was a Florentine, Bartolomeo Berecci, who began work in about 1510. Zygmunt wrote to one of his administrators, "We have seen the Italian and his model of a chapel which he is to build for us and which we like....Take care that he is supplied with as much Hungarian marble as he needs." The result was worth the expense – Berecci's work is a masterpiece of symmetry topped with a golden cupola, the finest piece of Italian Renaissance architecture north of the Alps.

Zygmunt's concern to provide a monument for posterity has a tragic irony. At the time he commissioned the work, he had almost 40 years to live, and he went on to father four children. But his queen, the Milanese Bona Sforza, poisoned her only son's first two wives before either could produce an heir; and although Zygmunt Augustus married again, he was so heartbroken at the loss of his second wife that he refused to consummate his new marriage. His sister Anna succeeded him, but her marriage, when she was over 50, to the prince of Transylvania, heralded a long period of uncertainty for the nation.

The Renaissance Italian influence extends to the castle, too. When Zygmunt the Old returned from his Grand Tour in 1502, he brought with him another Florentine architect, Francesco Fiorentino. Fiorentino was commissioned to restore the royal palace, which had been damaged by fire; the restoration gradually developed into an entirely new design, completed by Berecci after Fiorentino's death. As a result, three tiers of galleries enclose a courtyard that could grace an Italian palazzo. Similarly, the state rooms are a tribute to the work of great Renaissance artists from all over Europe.

What little remains of the Polish crown jewels is kept in the castle, including the most important royal possession of all – the sword of state, or *Szczerbiec*, used since the thirteenth century in the coronation ceremony. The sword found its way to Russia after the partition of 1797, was returned after World War I, and narrowly escaped plunder by the Nazis in World War II. Like Wawel Cathedral itself, it represents the determined spirit of a country that has spent centuries battling against apparently insuperable odds – and triumphed.

Wawel Cathedral and Castle crown Wawel Hill overlooking the Vistula. Tradition has it that a ravenous dragon once lived in a cave below the hill and was slain by the hero Krak, founder of Kraków, who fed it animal skins stuffed with tar and sulfur. Nor is this the only legend associated with Wawel. The cathedral houses a collection of prehistoric bones, including the shinbone of a mammoth and the skull of a hairy rhinoceros. Like the ravens at the Tower of London, their continued presence is reputed to guarantee the cathedral's survival.

The cathedral's beautiful altar cloth was worked in the sixteenth century by a Polish artist, and depicts Jesus, Mary, and Joseph on their flight into Egypt. King Zygmunt Augustus accumulated a magnificent collection of Flemish tapestries, of which some 136 pieces adorn various parts of the castle. Local craftsmen were inspired to copy their style.

In common with much Polish art and design, the cathedral's magnificent Baroque altar owes a great deal stylistically to Italy. The University of Kraków attracted scholars from all over Europe, and the court patronized Italian architects and painters. Many Poles traveled to Italy to complete their studies and brought back Italian ideas and tastes. As a result, Poland has some of the finest Renaissance art and architecture outside Italy, two fine examples being the Gothic Collegium Maius of the university and the mixed styles of the Marieski Church in the market square.

Versailles

Radiant palace of the Sun King

More than 300 years before Disney opened its doors in Europe, another fantasyland glittered on the outskirts of Paris, a world as fabulous, as dazzling, and as far removed from reality as anything modern technology could conjure up. For over a century, while poverty and unrest gripped the rest of France, and the folly and corruption of the aristocracy sowed the seeds of the French Revolution, the French court lived in unimaginable pomp and splendor at Versailles, the dream palace created by Louis XIV, the Sun King.

The story of Versailles is the story of the rise and fall of the Bourbon dynasty, whose monarchs created the most glorious period in France's history, but whose sublime self-belief made them deaf to the cries of their people, cries that soon resounded with bloodlust and vengeance. The Bourbons fell as few monarchs have fallen before or since, victims of their own arrogance as much as of the tide of revolutionary feeling and the guillotine. But while they flourished, they were incomparable.

Versailles is the embodiment of all that was glorious about the Bourbons; it remains a symbol of the glory of France. In creating it, the most absolute of absolute monarchs declared his omnipotence, refusing to let even Nature stand in his way. He insisted on building his palace on the site of his father's modest hunting lodge. It was an extraordinary choice: the ground was marshy and treeless, the air was putrid, and there was no view.

The Fountain of Apollo is one of the masterpieces of sculpture which adorn the gardens at Versailles. The celebrations of Marie Antoinette's wedding to the future Louis XVI in 1770 included the most fabulous spectacle in Versailles' glittering history. Some 200,000 people thronged to witness a display of 20,000 fireworks. The illumination surrounding the Fountain of Apollo was, according to one observer, "far more brilliant than when lighted by the sun in all his splendor."

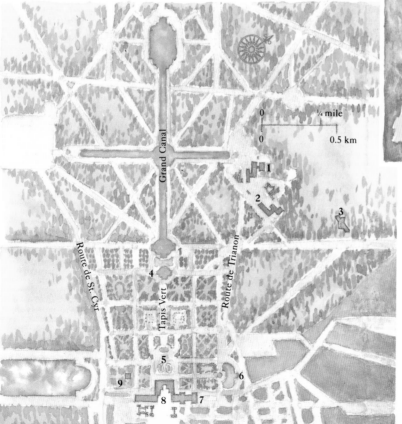

VERSAILLES □

FRANCE

1 Grand Trianon
2 Petit Trianon
3 Hamlet
4 Fountain of Apollo
5 Fountain of Latona
6 Fountain of Neptune
7 Opera House
8 Palace
9 Orangerie

To create a view, Louis set to work on the gardens, employing the great designer André Le Nôtre to landscape the 15,000-acre (6,000-ha) site. Tens of thousands of workmen were brought in to build a canal and ponds, one of which, the Swiss Fountain, is larger than Paris's Place de la Concorde. Thousands of trees and flowers were imported to create a setting fit for the palace that was to come.

Louis counted the cost in neither money nor lives. If Nature had not given Versailles a view, his designers would provide one. If a workman was crushed by a tree, he paid the widow compensation and work continued.

As soon as the gardens were ready to be displayed, and long before the palace itself was completed, Versailles saw its first great fête. The week-long *Plaisirs de l'Ile Enchantée* (Pleasures of the Enchanted Island) in May 1664 included the first performance of Molière's play *La Princesse d'Elide*, written especially for the occasion. There were ballets and jousting – in both of which the king took part – as well as banquets, concerts, and fireworks displays. The evenings were lit by thousands of torches and tens of thousands of candles. Seated on a horse with a golden harness sparkling with jewels, Louis himself led a great procession; a page boy followed him, carrying a shield displaying the sun and the motto "I neither rest nor turn aside." For the first time, in the first public display of the glories of Versailles, Louis compared his own glory to that of the sun. The Sun King was at his zenith.

The palace itself was conceived on an even grander scale than the park. It is impossible to overestimate the splendor of Versailles: everything was magnificent. The two principal architects were Louis Le Vau, responsible for the overall plan, and Jules Hardouin-Mansart, who designed the facade which looks out onto the garden, the chapel, and the fabulous Hall of Mirrors. Charles Le Brun, who had already contributed lavish designs for the fountains and statuary in the garden, was the painter and decorator in charge of the interior. Although there have been many additions and alterations since (including an entire suite of private apartments designed for Louis XV), these three men were responsible for the embodiment of Louis XIV's dream.

Le Vau's task was rendered more difficult by Louis' insistence on keeping the existing buildings intact. The Cour de Marbre, which had been the focal point of Louis XIII's hunting lodge, is still there, a meek corner of the Cour Royale, now dominated by a statue of Louis XIV on horseback. Only those who were sufficiently closely connected to the throne for Louis to address them as *cousin* (relation) were permitted to enter Versailles through this courtyard.

Evidence of Le Brun's genius and Louis' extravagance still pervades the state apartments. The palace abounds with painted ceilings, marble inlay, carved doors, and Gobelin tapestries. On the ceiling of the former throne room, the Sun King attired as Apollo rides a chariot across the heavens. In the chapel, Louis and his queen sat in gilded boxes to hear mass.

The Hall of Mirrors alone could be described as a palace. It is 240 feet (73 m) long, 34 feet (10.5 m) wide, and 40 feet (12.3 m) high.

By 1668 work on the palace was well underway. An artist's impression of that year depicts the king arriving in state at his principal residence. The Cour Royale, the main body of the palace housing the state apartments, and the Tapis Vert, *or "green carpet," which leads from the palace to the Fountain of Apollo and Grand Canal, are clearly visible.*

Louis' title the Sun King derives from his glorious reign, which corresponded with the Golden Age of French art and literature and the political dominance of France in Europe. Louis frequently appeared in plays and masques dressed as the sun god Apollo, and the sun motif recurs throughout the decoration of the palace.

Seventeen arched windows overlook the park. The reflection of the view through them is caught by seventeen mirrors of identical size on the wall opposite. Red marble pilasters line the walls, and marble statues fill the many niches. Light from seventeen huge crystal chandeliers and many smaller ones once filled the room with radiance.

Versailles was more than simply a palace: it was a world within a world. The palace was home to 5,000 courtiers and attendants, with perhaps three times that number housed in the town that grew up around the center of court. The stables accommodated 2,000 carriages and 2,500 horses. Through Versailles – his dream, his monument, his contribution to posterity – Louis was determined that future generations should know of his greatness.

Yet Louis' motives were not entirely vainglorious. King from the age of four, he was only nine years old when the nobles and Paris Parlement (a powerful law court) rose against the crown in 1648. The damage caused to France by the civil war known as the Fronde, during which Louis himself suffered poverty and humiliation, affected him deeply. He sincerely believed that the road to peace lay in running the country himself, stripping his nobles of the power to rise against him, or one another. Only if he kept them idly at court, lavishly entertained but under his eye, could France enjoy peace and prosperity. As an economic policy, it was to prove disastrous for the rest of France, but it made Versailles glitter all the more.

Life at Versailles became less opulent after Louis' second marriage, to the deeply religious Madame de Maintenon. Fireworks, ballets, and bawdy comedies were replaced by *"appartements,"* regular evening receptions in the Hall of Mirrors, where the usual rigid protocol was relaxed, refreshments were provided, and music, dancing, and cards were the sole entertainments. The palace was open to the public, and people thronged to admire the gardens, the fine collection of paintings, and the royal family eating dinner.

For those occasions when he wanted to escape the formalities of court, Louis had a smaller palace in the park. The Trianon – now the Grand Trianon – had originally been a simple retreat he could share with his mistress, but he had it rebuilt as a miniature Versailles, with terraces, fountains, and marble decor almost as sumptuous as that of the great palace – it even had its own Room of Mirrors. The gardens of the Trianon, however, were a refreshing contrast to the formality of the park: the contents of two million flowerpots provided a constant dazzling array of color and fragrance.

It was during the reign of Louis' successor, his great-grandson Louis XV, that the third palace of Versailles was built. The Petit Trianon – designed by Jacques-Ange Gabriel as a retreat for the king and his powerful mistress, Madame de Pompadour – is on an altogether more modest scale. Although Madame de Pompadour died before it was completed, Louis established his new mistress, Madame du Barry, there and spent many hours in the tranquillity and comparative simplicity of both house and garden.

The Petit Trianon provided Marie Antoinette, too, with a retreat. Brought from Austria at the age of fourteen to marry the dauphin (later Louis XVI), she hated the rigid etiquette of Versailles. Within

"Only imagine the effect of a hundred thousand candles in that wonderful suite of rooms. When I entered, I thought that the whole palace was on fire, for sunshine at the height of summer is not half so dazzling."

UNKNOWN VISITOR, ON THE HALL OF MIRRORS

The cozy cottages and fertile vegetable gardens of the hamlet were the product of Marie Antoinette's misguided attempts to reconstruct the simple life. One of the eight houses was set aside for her exclusive use, but its simple exterior was belied by the elegant tapestries and carved marble mantelpieces within.

Garden designer André Le Nôtre was able to embellish the grounds of Versailles with the Grand Canal in addition to myriad fountains thanks to the new technology of the seventeenth century – the discovery of the laws of atmospheric pressure. The fountains' bases were lavishly carved with cherubs created by the decorator Charles Le Brun, cherubs which were gilded afresh every year to guarantee that that they never lost their luster.

Queen at the age of eighteen, Marie Antoinette found in the Petit Trianon a refuge from the court she feared and detested. She laid out an "English garden" in its grounds, with thousands of daffodils and tulips, irises and hyacinths, and flowering shrubs, and replaced Louis XV's hothouses with lawns, a meandering stream, and a Chinese pagoda.

a year of becoming queen, she persuaded Louis to put her in sole charge of the Petit Trianon: even her husband had to await an invitation to visit her there. She held fêtes in the illuminated gardens and had her own theater built, with a Classical facade and gilded interior. Here she performed in amateur theatricals, choosing peasant roles in pastoral comedies extolling the simple life.

Marie Antoinette's love of make-believe led her to extend the English garden she had laid out at the Trianon to create *le hameau* (the hamlet). Set around the existing lake, the hamlet consisted of eight cottages, each with its own vegetable garden, and a farm, mill, bakery, and dairy. Here, well-fed cows grazed, peasants brought their corn to be ground, and the queen made butter. The hamlet was a source of delight to Marie Antoinette, but given the genuine poverty around her, her idyllic imitation of the simple life was considered tastelessly extravagant.

Such extravagance had been typical of Versailles in Louis XIV's day, but while he had reveled in its magnificence, it sat less comfortably on the shoulders of his successors and, indeed, became a financial millstone. Under the Sun King, Versailles had been "open to the public"; both Louis XV, awkward and aloof in public, and Louis XVI, shy, scholarly, and utterly out of touch with his times, shunned contact with their subjects. Marie Antoinette, the poignantly young queen in a foreign land, should have been able to win the love of her adopted people, but although charming with her intimates, she was childishly selfish and took no interest in anyone beyond her own circle. Her character was to contribute to her downfall.

While the queen amused herself playing milkmaid, the Revolution that had been festering in Paris came to a head with the storming of the Bastille on July 14, 1789. (Louis XVI's diary for that day reads "Rien": a keen sportsman, he had been unable to hunt, so had nothing to record.) Three months later, the demands of the people traveled the 12 miles (20 km) to the other world that was Versailles. Angry mobs, the majority of them women, marched from the capital on October 4. The palace was invaded, royal guards murdered, and the king and queen escorted back to Paris as prisoners. Louis XVI lived for little more than three years, Marie Antoinette for four, as prisoners of the populace who had come to hate them, before being guillotined. The kings of France never held court at Versailles again.

The palace survived the Revolution almost intact, although much of its furniture and portable wealth was transferred to the Louvre. Half a century later, Louis Philippe, the Citizen King, decided to turn the neglected palace into a monument to the glories of France. But nineteenth-century taste did not always appreciate the fashions of the preceding 200 years. Louis Philippe spent 23 million francs of his own fortune on "improvements," which involved the destruction of much that had been delightful about the house. Many of the finest eighteenth-century interiors are no more. But what remains is still magnificent, the incomparable legacy of the Sun King, the gift to posterity of which he had dreamed when Versailles was still a noxious marsh an inconvenient distance from town.

Every detail received the architects' and decorators' attentions. The gilded panels of the organ contribute to the lavish white and gold decoration of the chapel, dedicated to Saint Louis. Louis XIV attended mass here every day while he was in residence.

The Hall of Mirrors is Versailles' glory of glories, basking in natural and reflected light. In Louis XIV's time, the gallery boasted Savonnerie carpets, white and gold brocade curtains, and silver furniture of the most intricate workmanship; on the grandest ceremonial occasions, the king presided from a silver throne set on a dais at one end of the gallery.

The great Salle de Spectacle, *or Opera House, was completed for the celebrations of the marriage of Marie Antoinette and the future Louis XVI in 1770. In the interests of economy, the design was executed in wood, then painted pink and green to resemble marble and enriched with gilding.*

Above the royal box was a chandelier 8 feet (2.5 m) high which held 300 pendants; seventeen half-chandeliers, each reflected in its own mirror in the manner of the Hall of Mirrors, lit the remainder of the colonnade. Elsewhere, light was provided by fourteen chandeliers, each 5 feet (1.5 m) high and containing 96 pendants.

PARADISE FOUND

*I*N THE WESTERN HEMISPHERE, NOTIONS OF PARADISE have been enduringly shaped by the Romantics. For them, the "sublime" in Nature had to do with scenes on a more-than-human scale which also contained an element of terror: colossal mountains, beetling precipices, giddying chasms, wild seas that carved huge caves – like Fingal's Cave on Staffa – and great waterfalls such as Victoria Falls. But they preferred a landscape abandoned long ago to one that was merely empty. Visitors might never have admired the barren Egyptian desert but for the tumbled heads of pharaohs, the parched mountain terraces of Greece without their broken marble pillars, or the Bay of Naples were it not for the excavated ruins of Pompeii and Herculaneum. To wild grandeur and antiquity were added images of an idealized countryside as at Grasmere, and in the twentieth century the notion of a personal heaven untouched by human hand. Medieval Europeans would not envy such paradises. Theirs was a safe, orderly place, the wilderness firmly excluded and Nature tamed. The original, after all, was a *paradeisos*, a place where God and man could walk together in the cool of the day – a place such as Mount Kailas, spiritual focus of millions of Hindus, Buddhists, and Jains.

Nature untamed by human hand is nowhere more apparent than at the world's great waterfalls, including the majestic Victoria Falls. Here, the roar of water is deafening, the lush greenery dazzling, and the soft hues of rainbows crystallize, then recede once more into the omnipresent mist.

Grasmere

Lake-strewn land of inspiration

In 1769, a year before the birth of Grasmere's most illustrious resident – William Wordsworth – the poet Thomas Gray wrote of this village in the heart of Britain's Lake District, "No flaring gentleman's-house nor garden-walls break in upon the repose of this little unsuspected paradise, but all is peace." For the author of a nineteenth-century guidebook to the Lake District – as for millions of visitors before and since – the glory of Grasmere and its environs lay in the perennial contrast between tranquil lakes and frowning peaks, "the water's face untroubled and the island-hillock severe in outline, pensive and lonely." In the 1950s, the great fell-walker Alfred Wainwright singled out the "crystal clear" waters of the River Rothay as it meandered around the parish churchyard of St. Oswald's, where it "lingers often, loth to leave an enchanting individuality for the anonymity of the lake."

To the north of Grasmere looms Helm Crag, whose strangely shaped peaks give it the nickname of the Lion and the Lamb. Even today from Helm Crag – at 1,299 feet (396 m) a mere hillock compared to the greater challenges of Helvellyn and Scafell – the view of barely inhabited country seems boundless. Grasmere village huddles in the valley below. From Loughrigg Terrace, south of the lake, the Vale of Grasmere is more obviously populated, but beyond and beyond stretch the unchanging fells. It is by turns an inspiring and a humbling sight: to revel in such beauty is also to shudder at the insignificance of human beings.

Grasmere is less than 1 mile (1.5 km) long and half as wide, yet the lake and its surroundings have inspired generations of poets, artists, and writers. Legend has it that Welsh and, perhaps, Norse bards were extolling the area's beauty in pre-medieval times. In the early nineteenth century, its best-known resident, William Wordsworth, called Grasmere "the loveliest spot that man ever found," and, 100 years later, the author of a classic guidebook to the Lake District observed that "it is rarely that so much beauty is crowded into so little ground."

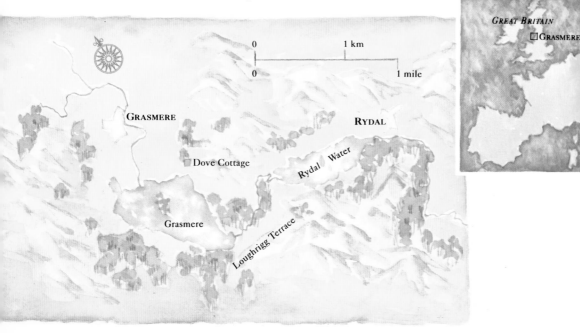

By many standards, the Lake District is small. The National Park, established in 1951, is no more than 25 miles (40 km) from west to east and 30 miles (50 km) north to south. Its highest peak, Scafell Pike, is a mere 3,210 feet (978 m), and only two others top 3,000 feet (910 m). At ground level, the twentieth century and its groups of tourists have taken their toll. Only in the depths of winter is there any vestige of the tranquillity which Wordsworth knew – and he was complaining about overcrowding in 1799.

Although poets without number have lived in or visited the Lake District and been moved to express their admiration in verse, Grasmere owes its fame to the nineteenth-century "Lake Poets" – Wordsworth, Samuel Taylor Coleridge, and Robert Southey – who made Lakeland the literary center of England for half a century. Of the three, Wordsworth was the only native of the northwest, born at Cockermouth; he introduced Coleridge to the Lakes in the course of a walking tour in 1799. It was during this journey that Wordsworth discovered and rented Dove Cottage, where he lived with his sister Dorothy (and from 1802 his wife Mary, though she was an infinitely less important figure in his literary life) until 1808.

Shortly after the Wordsworths moved to Grasmere, Coleridge took a grander house, Greta Hall, 13 miles (21 km) away in Keswick. With his marriage failing, he proceeded to spend the greater part of the next three years at Dove Cottage. In the meantime, he conveniently persuaded his brother-in-law Southey to join him at Greta Hall and to look after the family that he was neglecting.

Coleridge was a man of extremes, given to wild enthusiasms. Predictably, he fell passionately in love with the Lake District. In the course of his first visit, he wrote to Dorothy Wordsworth, "You can feel what I cannot express for myself – how deeply I have been impressed by a world of scenery absolutely new to me. At Rydal and Grasmere I received I think the deepest delight, yet Hawes Water thro' many a varying view kept my eyes dim with tears."

When his precarious health permitted, Coleridge was an indefatigable, even foolhardy, walker. On his frequent journeys from Greta Hall to Dove Cottage, he climbed Helvellyn – one of the area's most formidable peaks – on the way, arriving in Grasmere long after dark. He was one of the first Englishmen to indulge in mountain walking for pleasure and in 1802 undertook a solitary nine-day walk covering more than 100 miles (160 km) and involving ascents and descents of some 3,000 feet (910 m). In the course of what he called his "circumcursion," he became the first known person to climb Scafell Pike. It is entirely in character that he should have written a passionate love letter while he sat on the peak, and that on his descent he chose a short cut that involved scrambling over rocks rather than sticking to the path.

But it is Wordsworth whom Grasmere really celebrates, and who brought most celebrity to the town and its surroundings. Although he lived in Dove Cottage for less than ten years, he made his home in Lakeland for the rest of his life, moving to nearby Allan Bank after the birth of his third child (Dorothy wrote of the luxury of them each having their own room); then briefly to the old vicarage

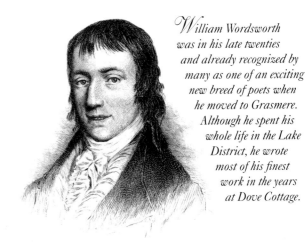

William Wordsworth was in his late twenties and already recognized by many as one of an exciting new breed of poets when he moved to Grasmere. Although he spent his whole life in the Lake District, he wrote most of his finest work in the years at Dove Cottage.

Dove Cottage – once an inn called the Dove and Olive Branch – in Wordsworth's day was simply "the cottage" at Town End, on the main road to Ambleside. Too small for the visiting coaches, that road is today beaten flat by the feet of every literary pilgrim to the Lakes.

The future Poet Laureate Robert Southey moved to Keswick in 1803 and spent the rest of his life there, becoming a leading figure of the literary establishment and turning Greta Hall into a haven for aspiring young poets, including Shelley, long after Coleridge had abandoned the Lakes to wander Europe and settle in London. Southey is buried at Great Crosthwaite.

Looking west from Eskdale, toward Wastdale, the view takes in the remains of the Roman fort at Hardknott. "Well worth the notice of the Traveller who is not afraid of fatigue," wrote Wordsworth in his guidebook, adding that "no part of the country is more distinguished by sublimity."

in Grasmere where, after the death of two of his children, he found the proximity of their graves too much to bear; and finally to Rydal Mount, where he spent his last 37 years.

It was during the years at Dove Cottage that Dorothy kept her *Journals* and Wordsworth wrote many of his best-loved poems. These facts are not unconnected – Dorothy's fascination with the minutiae of nature and her acute powers of observation were a source of inspiration to her beloved brother. Wordsworth did not deny Dorothy's role as his muse: "She gave me eyes, she gave me ears." Brother and sister, with Coleridge and other friends, found plenty of time for walking and enjoying their surroundings, with Dorothy recording what she saw. Each season had its charms: she speaks of snow "as soft as a down cushion"; of "snowdrops that are afraid to pop their white heads quite out"; in March "the wind blew briskly, and the lake was covered all over with bright silver waves, that were there each the twinkling of an eye, then others rose up and took their place as fast as they went away"; in June "the sky…was of a chastened yet rich yellow, fading into pale blue, and streaked and scattered over with steady islands of purple, melting away into shades of pink."

And, most famously of all, she wrote on April 15, 1802, "I never saw daffodils so beautiful.…They grew among the mossy stones about and about them; some rested their heads upon these stones as on a pillow for weariness; and the rest tossed and reeled and danced, and seemed as if they verily laughed with the wind, that blew upon them over the lake; they looked so gay, ever glancing, ever changing." Two years later, in "Daffodils," William wrote: "Ten thousand saw I at a glance, / Tossing their heads in sprightly dance / The waves beside them danced; but they / Out-did the sparkling waves in glee," surely drawing on his sister's record.

Wordsworth's joy in his native land is evident not only in his poetry, but also in the *Guide to the Lakes* which first appeared in 1810, and which he revised a number of times over the next 25 years. On the surface a typical guidebook full of advice about inns and routes, it has poetry even in its prose. A quietly eloquent passage recommends the visitor to rent a boat for a ride around Grasmere: "This circular Vale, in the solemnity of a fine evening, will make from the bosom of the Lake, an impression that will be scarcely ever effaced." And the text is interspersed with poetry inspired by the sights he describes.

His enthusiasm for Lakeland remained with Wordsworth throughout his life: he last climbed Helvellyn in 1840, at the age of 70. Alfred Wainwright was still walking the unchanging fells in his 80s. It was Wainwright who, in answer to the question "Why does a man climb mountains?," penned the words: "It may be, and for most walkers it will be, quite simply a deep love of the hills, a love that has grown over the years, whatever motive first took him there: a feeling that these hills are friends, tried and trusted friends, always there when needed."

The poet would have echoed him. Grasmere, for Wordsworth and for every generation since, was and is always there when needed.

"What happy fortune were it here to live! And, if a thought of dying, if a thought Of mortal separation could intrude With paradise before him, here to die!"

WILLIAM WORDSWORTH, ON HIS FIRST VIEW OF GRASMERE

Wordsworth wrote of the River Brathay at Langdale: "Behold! Beneath our feet, a little lowly Vale, A lowly Vale, and yet uplifted high Among the mountains; even as if the spot Had been, from the eldest time by wish of theirs, So placed, to be shut out from all the world!"

In his Guide to the Lakes, *Wordsworth quotes the reaction of a friend "which may not be uninteresting to painters" to the view north over Fairfield and Hart crags from Rydal Fell, one of the ridges above Grasmere. "I observed," says he, "the beautiful effect of the drifted snow upon the mountains, and the perfect tone of colour."*

Victoria Falls

The smoke that thunders

On a clear day, the spray is visible from 40 miles (65 km) away. Closer to Victoria Falls, the noise has been likened to the roar of 10,000 giants or, less fancifully, a herd of stampeding zebra. A little nearer is a thin strip of rainforest – a lush green curtain after vast stretches of savanna. Then, and only then, are the falls visible. David Livingstone, reputedly the first European to witness their splendor, named them after the British queen; more imaginatively, the Kalolo-Lozi people refer to them as "the smoke that thunders." According to Livingstone, the summit of the spray seemed to mingle with the clouds, becoming darker and more smokelike as it climbed.

Upriver, the Zambezi flows unhurriedly southward. For some 750 miles (1,200 km), its peace is broken only by one small waterfall and a few rapids. But as it approaches the Zimbabwean border, it seems "as if nature has played a joke on the river." Almost without warning, the gentle Zambezi plunges some 350 feet (108 m) into a seething whirlpool of dazzling white foam, forming the most spectacular waterfalls on earth.

The falls are more than 5,600 feet (1,700 m) wide, spanning the entire breadth of the river. In the flood season, some 2.3 million gallons (9 million liters) of water pour over them every second. The spray can rise as high as 1,000 feet (300 m) into the air and covers the surrounding land with an endless delicate shower of rain, enough to furnish Victoria Falls with its own private rainforest.

Unsurprisingly, Victoria Falls are the subject of legend: one native people was too much in awe of them to venture near, while another made sacrifices to their ancestors within sight of one of the rainbows that dance in the spray.

The falls are probably best seen at dawn or dusk, when the variety of colors – from soft pinks to bright reds and oranges – is breathtaking.

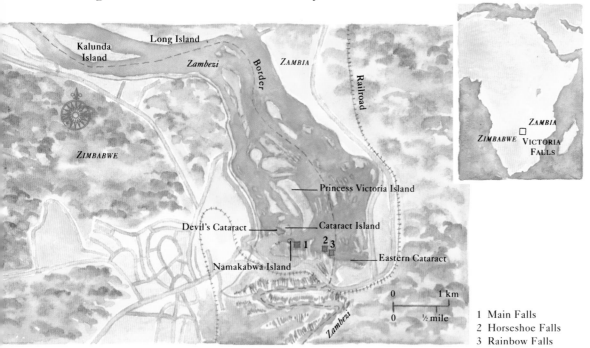

1 Main Falls
2 Horseshoe Falls
3 Rainbow Falls

Five distinct sheets of water make up the falls: the Devil's Cataract, Main Falls, Horseshoe Falls, Rainbow Falls, and the Eastern Cataract, which can almost dry up when the river is low. Below the Eastern Cataract, the water plummets into a narrow chasm and turns at right angles into the bottleneck known as the Boiling Pot. All five owe their existence to a period of massive volcanic activity all over southern Africa some 150 million years ago, which covered the land with a layer of lava 1,000 feet (300 m) thick. As this cooled, it cracked, leaving a hard layer of basalt veined with great fissures. Over millions of years, these fissures, running both east–west and north–south, were filled with limestone, which is much easier for water to carve its way through.

So the Zambezi gouged a course through one of the fissures, its width restricted by the harder layers of basalt on both sides. Then at a point about 60 miles (100 km) south of the present falls, it tumbled 820 feet (250 m) into a valley created by a fault in the lava bed, to form the first falls in the area. The constant rush of water over millions of years has eroded these falls, leaving a series of rapids and a mass of white water in what is now Batoka Gorge. But just above this, the river found both another fault into which it could fall and a north–south fissure into which it could spread.

This process has occurred eight times in the last half million years and will be repeated over the millennia as long as there is water in the riverbed. The Devil's Cataract is the weakest section of the current falls; here the water seethes and rages as it battles against its confinement. The barrier stands firm, but one day it will give way. Then the current falls will cease to exist, the water will seek out another weak spot farther upriver and new falls will form yet again.

The most spectacular way to see Victoria Falls is from the air, but even from ground level, the sheer power of the water is awe-inspiring. The spray is so dense as to be opaque. As long as the sun is shining, rainbows drift in and out of view. At dawn and dusk, the water turns a glorious coral pink. Small wonder, then, that the normally staid Livingstone was moved to eloquence: "On sights as beautiful as this Angels in their flight must have gazed," he wrote.

Although Livingstone's name has become synonymous with the falls, and a statue to him stands close to the Devil's Cataract, the bridge across the river owes its existence to the vision of another colorful figure from colonial history, Cecil Rhodes. His dream was of a rail line running unbroken from the Cape of Good Hope to Cairo, preferably all on British territory. He personally decided that a bridge should be built across the second gorge, just below the Eastern Cataract. Rhodes died in 1902, three years before this part of his project was completed, but the bridge he envisaged links the modern states of Zambia and Zimbabwe by both road and rail.

Rhodes's intention was that passengers on the train should appreciate the beauty of Victoria Falls and feel the spray as they passed. Since then, hundreds of thousands of people have shared his vision. Although the falls constantly rage against their surroundings, the breathtaking spectacle on the Zambezi will be there for thousands of years to come.

The Horseshoe Falls are in the center of the five sections of Victoria Falls to the east of the Main Falls. The Main Falls lie to the east of Namakabwa Island, formerly known as Livingstone Island. The explorer is said to have been taken to the island by canoe to get a clear view of the falls.

So moved was Livingstone by what he saw here that he carved his initials and the date into a tree trunk – the only occasion in all his travels that he indulged himself in this way.

Livingstone's Travels

David Livingstone was the perfect Victorian hero. A charismatic Christian missionary traveling into the depths of an unknown continent, he survived immense personal hardships in pursuit of his lonely battle against the evils of slavery. He was a meticulous geographer, but his writing also conveys his passion for Africa – the vast skies and magnificent landscapes, the constant presence of wild animals, and the peaceful villages inhabited by people whose lives and ways he shared and with whom he often forged deep and lasting bonds.

He was born in 1813. His family was poor, and as a child he worked in a cotton mill, but he attended night classes and qualified as doctor. In 1840 he joined the Missionary Society and was sent to a station in Bechuanaland (Botswana), run by Robert Moffat, whose daughter Mary became Livingstone's wife. In 1849, in the course of his missionary and exploratory travels, he came face to face with the slave trade. Run by Arab traders on the east coast, notably from Zanzibar, this was inflicting untold misery on countless African villages. He vowed to make its eradication his life's work.

Mary accompanied her husband on these early travels, but in 1852 returned to Scotland with their four children. David determined to render the slave trade unnecessary by setting up a center for "christianity, commerce and civilization" on the inland shores of the Zambezi, and he set off along the river. By canoe and overland, he crossed the African continent from Luanda to Quelimane, passing and naming Victoria Falls on the way. He failed to find a navigable route, but returned to England a hero in 1856.

In March 1858, with Mary and six other Europeans, he returned to Africa on behalf of the Royal Geographical Society to lead a paddle-steamer expedition up the Zambezi. The trip gave him another opportunity to fulfill his dream, but it was not a success. The Zambezi was blocked by rapids, and attempts to find a route via the Ruvuma failed. Then, in 1862, Mary died of fever. But Livingstone only returned to England in 1864, after becoming the first European to see Lake Nyasa.

The circumstances of his last expedition suited him better. Traveling overland with a hand-picked group of African guides and porters, as well as Indian sepoys, he aimed to find the source of the Nile. Again he ran into difficulties: he became ill, his supplies were stolen, and he was abandoned by most of his team. For three years, nothing was heard of him. Eventually, an expedition to discover his fate was mounted by the *New York Herald*, led by the young journalist Henry Morton Stanley. On November 10, 1871, after a ten-month journey, he found Livingstone, sick and feeble, living in the village of Ujiji. "Dr. Livingstone, I presume?" asked Stanley. "Yes," was the reply.

Livingstone recovered his strength, and he and Stanley explored the northern shore of Lake Tanganyika. They discovered that this was not – as had been thought – the source of the Nile. But Livingstone was deaf to Stanley's plea to return home with him.

Seven months later he set out again, but on the banks of Lake Bangweulu, his body could take no more. He stayed, almost bedridden, in the village of Chief Chitambo for eight months. On May 1, 1873, he was found dead, kneeling – as if in prayer – by his bed.

Then began his extraordinary final journey. His faithful companions, Chuma and Susi, embalmed his body and carried it 1,000 miles (1,600 km) to the coast to be shipped home. Livingstone was finally laid to rest, amid great public emotion, in Westminster Abbey.

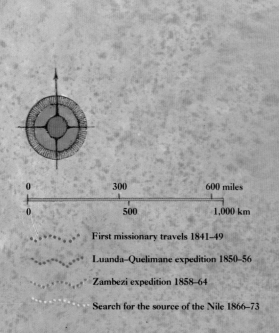

0	300	600 miles
0	500	1,000 km

··········· First missionary travels 1841–49

············ Luanda–Quelimane expedition 1850–56

············ Zambezi expedition 1858–64

············ Search for the source of the Nile 1866–73

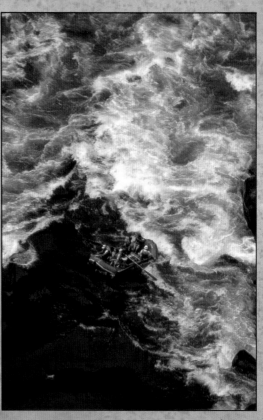

Rapids on the Zambezi still make navigation hazardous.

ATLANTIC OCEAN

UJIJI

Congo

Lake
Victoria

MOUNT KILIMANJARO

Nyangwe

Ujiji

Tabora

Zanzibar

Lualaba

Lake
Tanganyika

Lake
Mweru

uanda

Mikindani

Cuanza

Ruvuma

Lake
Bangweulu

Lugenda

VICTORIA FALLS

Chitambo

Lake
Nyasa

Moçambique

Zambezi

Sesheke

Quelimane

Linyanti

THE MA ROBERT STEAMER

Lake
Ngami

Lmpopo

Kolobeng

INDIAN OCEAN

Mabotsa

Kuruman

TABLE MOUNTAIN

Cape Town

Port Elizabeth

Mount Kailas

Precious snow mountain

For millions of Hindus, Buddhists, Jains, and native Tibetan Bon-po, there is no greater dream place than Mount Kailas. Set on the roof of the world, in the mountain fastnesses of southwestern Tibet, it rises to an ice-capped peak at 22,028 feet (6,714 m). To Tibetan Buddhists, who call it Kang Tise or Kang Rinpoche (precious snow mountain), it is the realm of the gods, of Demchog and Dorje Pangmo, who symbolize the combination of compassion and wisdom essential for the achievement of nirvana, the ultimate spiritual enlightenment. To Hindus, it is the mythical Mount Meru, the cosmic mountain at the center of the universe, whose four sides point to the four cardinal points, and from whose flanks flow four great rivers. It is the abode of Shiva, the Creator and Destroyer, and Parvati, his consort.

As in a dream, the frontiers between myth and reality blur at Mount Kailas. Centuries of religious reverence imbue natural phenomena with the power of symbolism. The peak's very shape – an even, four-sided pyramid – seems to be partly an artless wonder of Nature, partly the artifice of a divine hand. Its sides are indeed oriented toward the cardinal points. And four major rivers do flow from its flanks, for in the immediate vicinity are the sources of the Indus, the Sutlej, the Brahmaputra, and the Karnali, a tributary of the Ganges.

Since time immemorial, Mount Kailas has been the focus of pilgrimage. Hindus cross the high passes over the Himalayas to follow the circuit around the mountain and to bathe in the holy waters of

Mount Kailas is the centerpiece in a landscape of awesome grandeur, which alters like a prism in the varying light conditions of the changing hour and weather. The main pilgrimage season lasts from May to September, but even in these summer months, the nights are bitterly cold and the higher parts of the route may be showered with snow. Yet the monks in neighboring monasteries, and the hermits who in the past lived for years in tiny cell-like caves, are perhaps the only ones who have come to know the full range of the mountain's many moods.

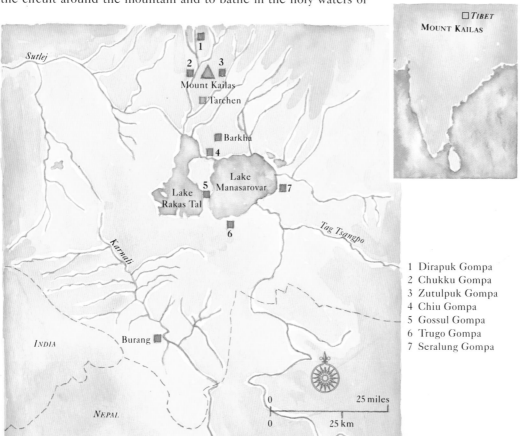

1 Dirapuk Gompa
2 Chukku Gompa
3 Zutulpuk Gompa
4 Chiu Gompa
5 Gossul Gompa
6 Trugo Gompa
7 Seralung Gompa

Lake Manasarovar, a sheet of pure blue water south of Mount Kailas, where Shiva is said to float in his incarnation as a white swan.

Pilgrims come from far and wide and include men, women, the aged, infants. They arrive in the backs of trucks, on foot, with their yaks, some after months, if not years, of travel and pilgrimage through a string of holy sites. But Mount Kailas is the ultimate goal. The circuit, or *kora*, around Mount Kailas is 32 miles (51 km) long, starting from the old wool-trading town of Tarchen. Tibetans like to complete the circuit in a single day, a demanding walk of at least twelve hours. Westerners, unused to physical exertion at these altitudes, take three or four days, resting at the series of small monasteries, or *gompas*, that line the route. Buddhists move clock-wise around the well-trodden path. Their circumambulation is a holy ritual, called *parikrama*. A circuit around Mount Kailas has special value: all sins are erased; it is a form of rebirth in this life-time. Those who complete 108 circuits (a holy number), in the correct frame of mind, are said to attain nirvana.

They set out in a festival spirit well before dawn, walking to the rhythm of muttered mantras. The most famous of these is *Om mani padme hum* (Hail, o jewel in the lotus), cherished as much for the meditative resonance of its sounds as for its meaning. The route is dotted with small shrines, such as the boxlike domed monuments called *chortens*, and cairns of loose stones, many inscribed with prayers. At each of these, the pilgrims break off from the route and walk around the shrine, offering special mantras.

Four points along the route – including the first sight of the peak – are deemed especially holy. At these pilgrims prostrate themselves, lying on the ground so that eight points of their bodies touch the earth: the knees, stomach, chest, mouth, forehead, and hands. The very devout complete the entire circuit like this, stepping forward only to the position on the ground reached by their outstretched hands – a task that takes about two weeks and some 20,000 prostrations.

At many of the holy sites, pilgrims leave behind mementos: offerings of money, written prayers, portraits of themselves, and colorful prayer flags which are said to recite the mantras inscribed upon them every time they flutter in the wind. Every right-minded action can bring merit; every feature of the landscape, enhanced by the clear light and thin air, is imbued with mystic power.

The culmination of the *parikrama* is the 2,500-foot (762-m) ascent from Dirapuk Gompa to the Dolma La pass at 18,536 feet (5,650 m). The presiding god is the female deity Dolma, "she who helps cross," the savior and redeemer, but pilgrims must first pass through Swiwa Tal (the place of death). Here they perform rituals which allow them to contemplate their own deaths, before moving on to enjoy the great elation and sense of release – both physical and spiritual – experienced at the summit. This is the place of rebirth, where all sins are washed away. Then, the long descent takes pilgrims past an emerald-green lake to a grassy plain and a dramatic canyon of multicolored mineral rocks, illuminated by the golden light of the lowering sun – a spectacular reminder of the oneness of Nature and the human quest for spiritual enlightenment.

A pole marks the Dolma Stone at the highest point of the pilgrimage route around Mount Kailas. This is where the goddess Dolma is believed to have shown Gotsangpa – the first pilgrim – the path, and then left him and transformed herself into 21 wolves. Pilgrims, on reaching this point, are said to attain rebirth, an achievement marked by rituals, prayers, and joyous celebratory snacks. They leave offerings of food, coins, photographs, and strips of clothing on the stone, and take home pieces of the prayer flags as sacred amulets.

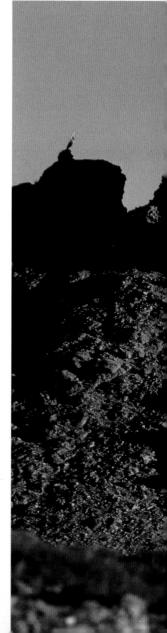

The ice-capped peak of Mount Kailas looms over Chiu Gompa, a monastery on the shores of Lake Manasarovar. The clear, thin air gives a remarkable visual clarity to all features of this remote and near-barren landscape, and confounds the perception of distance. Mount Kailas is in fact some 15 miles (24 km) from Chiu Gompa. The monastery is a stopping point for pilgrims making the 50-mile (80-km) pilgrimage around the lake, which is seen as the complement to Mount Kailas and an embodiment of the forces of light.

Precious snow mountain

"An immense peace fills
the heart of the pilgrim, making him immune
to personal concerns, because, as in a dream,
he feels one with his vision."

LAMA ANAGIRIKA GOVINDA, 1950

Bay of Naples
Birthplace of European culture

There are few places where past and present walk so magically hand in hand as the Bay of Naples. Here, a landscape that might seem merely picturesque is rendered luminous by the dreams and aspirations of a people which vanished long ago.

Curving for some 20 miles (32 km) from Cape Miseno in the north to Punta Campanella, the bay takes a semicircular bite out of the Tyrrhenian Sea, and its blue waters are backed by steep, volcanic hills of rugged beauty. The area has long drawn visitors who are surrounded by proof that the spell it casts over modern tourists is much the same spell by which it enchanted the Romans nearly twenty centuries ago.

They, too, loved its broad prospects and fresh air. The ruling classes, forced to spend part of their year in Rome, were glad to escape here in the heat of summer, and the bay became the play-ground of the wealthy, a Roman Riviera. Cool, spacious, luxurious villas overlooking the sea lined the coast at Baiae (Baia), Neapolis (Naples), and Surrentum (Sorrento).

The Baia of today is a small seaside resort; the Baiae of yesterday was a famous spa which developed around thermal springs. The ruins of its grandiose villas and temples, which were built from the first to the fourth centuries A.D., lie inland. It was the retreat of emperors and nobles, although – regardless of their name – it is doubtful if Nero ever took his ease in the Stufe di Nerone, natural thermal grottoes at the side of the mountain overlooking nearby

The currently dormant peak of Mount Vesuvius dominates the bay and the town of Vico Equense. Described by the German poet Goethe as the "peak of Hell rising out of Paradise," Vesuvius last underwent a period of volcanic activity in 1944. Today, some two million people live on and around its fertile lower slopes – which are covered with vineyards and orchards.

1 Grotta Azzurra
2 Mount Solaro
3 Faraglioni

Lake Lucrino. It is certain, however, that the orator Cicero thought so well of the bay that he had villas dotted along it, at Cumae (Cuma), Puteoli (Pozzuoli), and Pompeii.

Rounding the coast past Naples, Castellammare di Stabia is now an industrial town, but also a tourist center with thermal baths – a reminder that this was ancient Stabiae, where the natural historian Pliny the Elder had his villa. Like Herculaneum and Pompeii, it was destroyed by the massive eruption of Vesuvius in A.D. 79, but unlike them, Stabiae was rebuilt almost immediately because of its magnificent setting and the health-giving mineral springs that made it an ideal country retreat.

The island of Capri, closing the eastern end of the bay, was the resort of emperors. Augustus had a villa here, and Tiberius built a dozen. The remains of one, the Villa Iovis, stand in splendid isolation on the island's northeastern tip. The vista across the bay and the site's seclusion are doubtless the reasons why the old, paranoid, cruel, and (according to rumor) debauched emperor chose it, rather than the fact that the headland provided him with a sheer cliff, the notorious Salto di Tiberio (Tiberius's leap), off which to hurl ex-lovers who, if they survived the fall, were reputedly beaten to death with oars by waiting sailors.

It is more likely to be true that the Grotta di Matermania, a coastal cavern a little farther south, once resounded to cymbals clashed in honor of Kybele, the Magna Mater (great mother). But the Caprese are proud rather than critical of Tiberius, who put their island on the map, and he is invoked again at the most famous of its semi-underwater caves, the Grotta Azzurra (blue grotto), a vaulted cavern filled with a marvelous blue light, the effect of sunshine entering the cave through water. Accessible only by boat and rediscovered as recently as 1826, it was certainly known to the Romans, as the broken statues and pedestals that have been found inside prove. It is less easy to put any faith in the tales of today's boatmen who claim that Tiberius descended to this magnificent underwater swimming pool from the now-ruined Villa Damecuta via a secret passage (in truth a drain), and that in his day the grotto was the scene of orgies.

The history and legends of these ancient cities of the bay have retained their resonance because they have become part of the fabric of European culture. Today the center of Naples is a vivid, lively place of narrow lanes, residential buildings, and markets. Underground, however, lies the more mysterious Naples on which the city is founded, a network of tunnels, grottoes, and wells dating from the Greek and Roman periods.

Eight centuries before the birth of Christ, Greek colonists from Rhodes founded a settlement here which they named Parthenope, after one of the sirens. In ancient myth, these were half-women, half-birds, famous for their singing, who inhabited an islet off southern Italy where their seductive voices lured sailors onto the rocks. The voyager Odysseus encountered them, but stopped his crew's ears with wax and had himself lashed to the mast so that he could listen to their song in safety.

Painted on the walls of the Villa dei Misteri in Pompeii is a cycle of frescoes depicting the rites, or "mysteries," of Dionysus, which gave the house its name. A luxurious suburban villa built in the second century B.C. – before the Romans took over Pompeii – the house was later extended.

The entrance to the cave of the Sibyl of Cumae is a rock-hewn gallery some 350 feet (107 m) long, illuminated by shafts which let in light. These may well have created the acoustic effect noted by Virgil, who described the cave as "Having a hundred mouths, with rushing voices / Carrying the responses of the Sibyl." The Sibyl herself sat hidden in a vaulted chamber at the far end.

The circumstances of its "burial" contributed to the preservation at Herculaneum of the wooden frames of houses and furniture, in addition to clothes and food. The mud and lava that blanketed the town also kept its remains safe from looters and vandals.

Excavation began in 1738, but has frequently been interrupted, and even today the site has not been fully explored.

"...the wide blue stillness of the sleeping sea, the swish of its quiet swell making long slow folds in the silky water..."

HECTOR BERLIOZ, *c.*1832

The sirens themselves were doomed to die if ever a ship sailed by and its crew did not fall victim, so when Odysseus escaped, they killed themselves. Parthenope's body was washed up on the site where later her town was built and, according to the geographer Strabo (who died in A.D. 25), visitors to Parthenope, renamed Neapolis, were taken to see her tomb. The church of San Giovanni Maggiore was later built over it; a marble slab bearing the inscription "Parthenope" was reputedly found during repairs and built into a wall with the siren's name facing inward.

Greek settlers in the bay probably brought the cult of the sirens with them, and they were revered at several places along the coast. In time they came to be shown with fishtails and are almost certainly the ancestors of the mermaids which people medieval myths and legends. Consequently, tiny islets in the bay near Sorrento are pointed out to English-speaking visitors today as "the Isles of the Mermaids," and boatmen take tourists from the Marina Piccola at Sorrento to the Grotta delle Sirene, or "cave of the mermaids," where the sirens allegedly sang their songs. Another claimant to this honor, however, is the "rock of the sirens" near the Marina Piccola on Capri, between the beaches of Pennauto and Mulo.

Shortly before 750 B.C., other Greek settlers founded Cumae, at the northwestern tip of the bay. There they built an acropolis on a rocky outcrop with a wide view of the sea and on its heights placed a temple, now known as the Temple of Jupiter. Lower down was the Temple of Apollo, and the cave of his oracle, the Sibyl of Cumae, revered throughout the Greek world from perhaps the sixth century B.C.

Although in the heyday of the Roman Empire her tomb was shown to visitors, the Sibyl was probably not one person, but a series of priestesses who entered into a trancelike state and uttered prophecies that were believed to come from the gods. Legend, however, said she was a woman from the East who granted her sexual favors to Apollo in return for as many years of life as there were grains in a handful of dust. The grains numbered 1,000, but the Sibyl forgot to ask for eternal youth and became so shriveled with age that finally she was hung up in a bottle at Cumae. When children asked her what she desired, she always answered "I want to die."

Virgil, the Roman poet who spent the last years of his life in Naples, wove the Sibyl's cave and other features of the Cumaean landscape into the *Aeneid*. In this epic poem, Aeneas, revered by Romans as the founder of their race, consults the Sibyl about his destiny and is led by her to the underworld, whose entrance was said to lie near Lake Avernus. This is modern Lago Averno, near Pozzuoli, which is today changed by volcanic activity and development; in Virgil's time it was surrounded by gloomy woods.

The Bay of Naples presents an intensely archaic and mythic landscape, dominated by one of the most famous volcanoes in the world – Vesuvius, active for at least 300,000 years, but now dormant. From its crater on a clear day, the whole of the bay is visible, sweeping in a sickle-shaped curve from the islands of Ischia and Procida at its western end, past Pozzuoli and Naples, and down the Sorrentine peninsula to Capri.

The view from the Marina Grande, Sorrento, across the bay to Naples and the so-called Isles of the Mermaids brought the Roman smart set here. A vast cave near the little harbor of Piccolo Sant' Angelo, called the Baths of Diana, was supposedly the scene of pagan rites.

"[Neapolis] long cherished the language and manners of a Grecian colony; and the choice of Virgil had ennobled this elegant retreat, which attracted the lovers of repose and study from the noise, the smoke, and the laborious opulence of Rome"

EDWARD GIBBON, 1776–88

Antoni di dipi Joli's View of Naples with the Castel Nuovo *records the bay in former times. The Castel Nuovo, or "new fortress," founded in 1279, was so-called to distinguish it from the older Castel dell' Ovo. The pale, picturesque Castel dell' Ovo sits on its own island, the Megaride, where according to legend the siren Parthenope was washed up. Naples was built between the Megaride and Pizzofalcone (falcon's beak).*

It is not the only primeval feature of the bay, which has nineteen volcanic craters in an area of around 25 square miles (64 km²). One of the more surreal landscapes is that of the Phlegraean Fields (known today as the Campi Flegri) between Agnano and Cuma. In ancient times, these were known as "the burning fields," for good reason, since the now-dead craters were then alive with spurts of fire and wisps of steam. The smell of sulfur still hangs over the dead crater of the Agnano volcano, where modern thermal baths sit beside ancient Roman steam baths.

Near Pozzuoli lies the crater of Solfatara, the volcano which inspired Dante's vision of the Inferno. It is almost extinct, its last flickers of life manifesting themselves in the mud volcanoes and sulfurous vapors which pour through cracks in the ground. Pozzuoli itself was originally named Puteoli (the stink) because of the smell of its thermal springs. The Romans nevertheless flocked here to soak and steam, and afterward go and watch the gladiators. Summer visitors today sit where they sat, in the semicircular tiers of the amphitheater of Flavius, which held up to 20,000 spectators, to watch less bloodthirsty open-air theater.

The sailors of many nations putting into the busy port of Puteoli were doubtless impressed by the feat of engineering represented by the Crypta Neapolitana, a road tunnel between Puteoli and Neapolis half a mile (710 m) long and lit by candles. Today's technologically blasé tourists are more taken aback by the fearful raw energy of natural forces and the evidence of bradyseism (the rise and fall of land due to volcanic activity) provided by the pillars – half submerged in the sea – of the so-called Serapeum, actually a marketplace built in the first century A.D. The land level in the oldest part of Pozzuoli rose by nearly 7 feet (2 m) in two years (1982–84), necessitating the evacuation of 30,000 people.

Precautions on this scale were not possible in A.D. 79, when on August 24 and 25 the towns of Pompeii and Herculaneum were buried by the eruption of Vesuvius. The citizens of Pompeii died under a hail of hot cinders as they tried desperately to escape or were smothered by drifting ash in the cellars in which they had taken refuge. Several people hid their treasures, expecting to return, but others – including the person who scrawled "Sodom and Gomorrah" on the wall – recognized it as the end, total destruction wrought by the angry gods.

The homes of these people are more evocative than their public buildings, particularly in Herculaneum, the less industrialized and commercial of the two towns. Since it was nearer to Vesuvius than was Pompeii, it was not smothered in ash but blanketed deep in lava and mud which, by penetrating every crevice and excluding the air, preserved the houses with their wall paintings and furniture better than at Pompeii. Among its many marvels is the Villa dei Papiri, in which a collection of fragile papyrus documents – the library of the scholarly Lucius Calpurnius Piso – though carbonized, miraculously survived. The houses of Herculaneum give an uncanny sense of a living community having just stepped out for a moment. Here the past, arrested in time, is truly alive.

From Mount Solaro – at 1,932 feet (589 m) the highest point on the island – the view to the town of Capri and the trio of rocks known as the Faraglioni gives an indication of the island's rugged beauty.

Today the island is one of Italy's major centers of tourism, but fishing and agriculture are also important, with olives, grapes, and citrus fruits among its major products.

Naples's glass-domed Galleria Umberto I arcade stands opposite the San Carlo Theater, Italy's oldest opera house. Singing is an ancient art in Naples: Nero made his debut here at the annual music festival in A.D. 64 and was in full cry when an earthquake struck. The audience escaped just before the theater collapsed.

The Villa Iovis, on Mount Tiberio, is one of three ruined villas identified as having been built or occupied by the emperor Tiberius, who from fear of intrigue spent his last years on Capri. Four great cisterns, an open-air gallery, thermal baths, and private rooms remain, but not his observatory.

As befitted the emperor, these villas were filled with treasure and objets d'art, in addition to a retinue of servants, entertainers, astrologers, and musicians.

ATLANTIC OCEAN

The skyline of Florence, one of the treasures of the
Grand Tour.

Dover

Calais

NOTRE - DAME

Paris

Orléans

Seine

Rhône

GUILLOTIÈRE BRIDGE

Lyon

Nîmes

Avignon

Cannes

Marseille

PONT DU GARD

Rhine

Tagus

Madrid

MEDITERRANEAN SEA

0	100	200	300	400 mi
0	200	400	600 km	

The Grand Tour

In the seventeenth and eighteenth centuries, before the French Revolution and subsequent Napoleonic wars made travel on the continent of Europe hazardous, any young man of good family completed his education with the journey of a lifetime: his grand tour. The tour was essentially a British concept – although young Dutchmen, Germans, and others also made similar trips – and the itinerary was flexible, but few brought up in northern climes omitted Paris and the major Italian cities.

The young gentleman traveled in the care of a tutor, who bore letters of introduction designed to gain him entrée into polite society wherever he went. The recipient felt obliged to respond: in 1725, the British envoy in Florence complained of the number of tourists he had to entertain.

Facilities were not always reliable, and the notorious British suspicion of "abroad" frequently surfaced: one tutor wrote of his charge that his "whole fear when he first landed was that he should be starved. At dinner he always asked if we knew where to get a supper, and at supper if we were sure of our breakfast."

Almost all tours made their first major stop in Paris, where the sights were splendid, and for the privileged a visit to the court at Versailles was essential. Many went on to Italy via Lyon and Geneva. Those who did not wish to cross the Alps traveled farther south through France and took a ship from Marseille or Nice to Genoa, but poor roads made this an uncomfortable trip.

In Italy the principal destinations were Florence, Venice, Rome, and Naples, of which Rome was the most important. Anyone with any pretensions to education was well read in the classics, and here courses in antiquities were available to supplement the art and architecture on display. Here, too, was the Vasa d'Oro, one of the continent's most luxurious hotels, reputed to have "silken hangings, soft beds and cloth of gold."

The excavations of Herculaneum and Pompeii, begun in 1738 and 1748 respectively, drew many classical scholars to Naples – although here, as in Paris, the social life was also alluring. Sir William Hamilton, husband of Nelson's Emma and envoy from 1764 to 1800, was renowned for his hospitality.

A handful of northern and eastern European cities were deemed worth a visit. Hanover's popularity rocketed after its elector became King George I of England in 1714; before then, Dresden and later Berlin were the most sought-after destinations in what is now Germany. Prague sometimes merited a brief stopover, as did the magnificent imperial capital of Vienna, after an early eighteenth-century spate of building.

But the focus remained France and Italy. Here culture and entertainment combined to provide a young gentleman with "polish," that nebulous quality which smoothed his passage through the rest of his life.

Berlin

Dresden

Prague

Heidelberg

Venice

Padua

Po

Bologna

Pisa

Siena

Florence

DUOMO

DOGE'S PALACE

Tiber

Rome

COLOSSEUM

Naples

Fingal's Cave

Cathedral carved by giants

Of Fingal's Cave on the island of Staffa in the Inner Hebrides, the Romantic poet John Keats wrote "Suppose, now, the giants…had taken a whole mass of…columns and bound them together…then with immense axes had made a cavern…black, with a lurking gloom of purple therein. For solemnity and grandeur it far surpasses the finest cathedral." He was not alone in comparing the cave to a cathedral, not simply because of its columns but also because it evokes the kind of religious awe that stupendous works of Nature can inspire. Keats was one of a line of writers and artists who found in Fingal's Cave something that answered the spirit of the Romantic movement – that beauty tinged with savagery that had previously been found by travelers on the Grand Tour in the high Alpine passes or the wild crags of the Pyrenees.

As far as educated Europe was concerned, Staffa, whose name means "Pillar Island," was "discovered" on August 13, 1772, by the botanist Joseph Banks, who had headed the team of scientists accompanying Captain Cook on his first round-the-world voyage. Now, forced to shelter in the Sound of Mull, he heard of an island not far away with columns of rock like those of the Giant's Causeway. Afire with curiosity, Banks went the next day and subsequently wrote of Staffa as "one of the greatest natural curiosities in the world."

Banks's revelations excited interest not only among scientists, but also in literary circles. In the nineteenth century, many famous writers came to see the island – and sometimes failed to do so. Dr.

Fingal's Cave, some 226 feet (69 m) deep and with an entrance 227 feet (69.2 m) high, was carved by the sea. Fractured columns which form a rough natural walkway above high-water mark allow visitors to penetrate far inside the cave, where size, sound, and color combine to leave a lasting impression.

STAFFA

Meall nan Gambna

Fingal's Cave

1
2
3
4
5
6

0   ½ mile

0   0.5 km

STAFFA

GREAT BRITAIN

1 Goat Cave
2 Clamshell Cave
3 Am Buachaille
4 The Causeway
5 Boat Cave
6 Caves

Johnson, on a tour in 1773, reached Mull on October 14, but was prevented from landing on Staffa by high seas. Others were luckier: Sir Walter Scott declared that Fingal's Cave, unlike many celebrated sights, "exceeded, in my mind, every description I had heard of it."

Keats's image of giants as the builders of the cave echoed folk tradition. In Banks's day, it was already known by the name of the Dark Age hero called Fionn Mac Cumhaill in modern Irish. He became the most popular Gaelic folk hero on both sides of the Irish Sea, invoked in the Highlands in the eighteenth-century cattle blessing *An Saodachadh* (the driving): "The safeguard of Fionn Mac Cumhaill be yours...." Perhaps herdsmen brought his name to Staffa, which they visited each year for the *àiridhean*, or summer grazings, hence such landmarks as Meall nan Gambna, "the hill of the heifers" – the highest point on Staffa – and Am Buachaille, "the herdsman," an islet of twisted basaltic columns near the cave.

It was the titanic scale of the cave that suggested Fionn, for in the imaginations of the Gaels, he and his war band, the Fenians, were giants. According to Hector Boece writing in 1531: "Fynmak-coule...was...xvii cubitis [up to 31 feet (9.3 m)] of hicht...". In Ireland, hilltops and mountain ledges are known by variations on *Suí Finn*, "Fionn's seat," and the gigantic warriors asleep inside the hill of Tomnahurich, Highland, were believed to be Fionn and his Fenians.

In both Ireland and Scotland, Fionn (who came to be known as Fingal in Scotland) was connected with ancient forts, large boulders, standing stones, and megalithic tombs. Dr. Johnson was shown a square stone said to be Fingal's table in a cave on Mull and two standing stones at Lower Kilchattan, on Colonsay, are known as Fingal's limpet hammers. But Fionn was particularly associated with the marvels of the Giant's Causeway and Staffa. Irish bards related that the Giant's Causeway once reached right across the sea, placed there by the giants of Scotland and Ireland so they could visit one another. The Scottish giant Fir Ruadh (the red man) came across the Giant's Causeway to challenge Fionn, but was frightened off by a trick. On Staffa not only Fingal's Cave, but also Fingal's chair, a shallow niche in the columns beside the causeway, is shown to visitors, who need only to sit in it to have their wishes fulfilled.

Fionn and his son Oisín, under the names Fingal and Ossian, were the main characters in James Macpherson's "Ossianic" poems of the 1760s, which he claimed were translations of Gaelic originals, but which were eventually exposed as forgeries. The resulting furore over the poems focused the attention of literary Europe on the Gaelic west and, together with the extraordinary spectacle described by Banks, drew the Romantic poets and novelists to Fingal's Cave.

But the person who made it world famous was a musician – Felix Mendelssohn – who, with a friend named Klingemann, set out on August 7, 1829, aboard the newly introduced paddle-steamer service to sail around Mull, calling at Iona and Staffa. As it had been for Dr. Johnson, the weather was dreadful and the seas rough, but the sights and sounds of the cave had a profound impression on the twenty-year-old Mendelssohn. He was then and there inspired with the majestic theme which later became the *Hebrides Overture*.

Re-erected in Strathpeffer, Highland, the Pictish Eagle Stone dates from the seventh or eighth century A.D. Its Gaelic name was Clach am Tiompain *(the sounding stone) from the noise it was reputed to make. According to legend, it was used by Fingal to cover Fingal's Well, a rock-cut cistern in nearby Knock Farril Fort.*

For visitors today, the Cyclopean pillars of Staffa, encompassed by angry seas, conjure visions of almost unimaginable antiquity and immeasurable force. Now uninhabited, the island bears witness to cataclysmic events some 60 million years ago, when subterranean volcanic activity found a vent along a line from Skye to Ireland, the effects of which can be seen at their most dramatic in Staffa and in the Giant's Causeway in County Antrim, Ulster.

An acquarelle by Carl Gustav Carus faithfully reproduces the wonders of Fingal's Cave. Carus was but one of many artists to immortalize the cave. In 1830, J.M.W. Turner produced a sketch for Sir Walter Scott's Lord of the Isles, *in which the author observed that the cave, "high as the roof of a cathedral, and running deep into the rock, eternally swept by a deep and swelling sea, and paved, as it were, with ruddy marble, baffles all description."*

Felix Mendelssohn's visit to Staffa in 1829 inspired the Hebrides Overture, *popularly known as "Fingal's Cave." The overture was first performed in London in 1832.*

FROM THE MISTS
of the
PAST

The GREAT FEATS OF ARCHITECTURE AND ENGINEERING accomplished by past civilizations prompt the question why. Why build cities or temples in such extraordinary places? Why risk lives and expend such enormous amounts of effort in their creation? Why labor to make them places of such beauty?

The answer is that people build to make a statement. They fly in the face of time, unable to believe that their creation – or indeed their very culture – will not exist forever. The builders of Petra, or Borobodur, the Maya who founded Chichén Itzá, and the Incas who made Cuzco their capital could no more imagine the decline of their civilizations than it is possible to imagine a world without Paris or New York. When the Greeks built Soúnion to the glory of Poseidon and the Egyptians the Temple of Amun at Karnak, both empires were at their zeniths. The energy of such people is a testament to their stubborn belief in humanity, as well as in their gods. And their buildings – whether ruined or intact – are bridges between their world and that of today: a voice from the mists of the past.

The pyramids of Egypt are among the most evocative symbols of a bygone age, built more than 4,000 years ago as tombs for the pharaohs. The contents of the pyramids are a window on a past world, where the fabulously wealthy were buried with all their earthly possessions to ease their way into the afterlife.

Petra

Rose-red city half as old as time

Lost cities cast a spell of their own. For 700 years Petra was lost to Western knowledge, existing only in oblique and tantalizing references by authors of Classical antiquity. It is now a deserted ruin, tucked away in the arid mountain fastnesses of southern Jordan, but – lost no more – more than 1,000 visitors come to it every day. Yet it still holds its mystique: the grand and stately facades carved out of rock, and the cool, empty chambers that lie behind them, beg to tell their tale, but remain bound to silence by the almost total absence of historical records and by the dislocation of an oral history that has run into the sands of time.

The first European to set eyes on Petra in modern times was the Swiss explorer Johann Ludwig Burckhardt, whose dream was to cross the Sahara from east to west with an Arab trading caravan. In the early nineteenth century, the Arab world was intensely suspicious of, and hostile to, Europeans. To achieve his goal, Burckhardt planned to travel as an Arab – and to do this convincingly, he needed to immerse himself in Arab culture. He spent two years in England learning the language, then sailed for Aleppo in Syria, to continue his studies. On route, he adopted Arab dress and took the name Sheikh Ibrahim Ibn Abd Allah. From then on, except in the company of his most intimate friends, he spoke only Arabic.

In Aleppo he prepared himself for the journey ahead by making short excursions to local places of interest, such as Palmyra, the old Roman trading city. He soon discovered the dangers of travel in the

The ornate Palace Tomb, so-called because its facade recalls the architecture of Roman palaces, forms one of a group of monuments set on higher ground above the floor of Wadi Mousa. The scale of the larger tombs suggests that they may also have had a function as temples. The truth may never be known; any contents that might provide a clue were pillaged centuries ago.

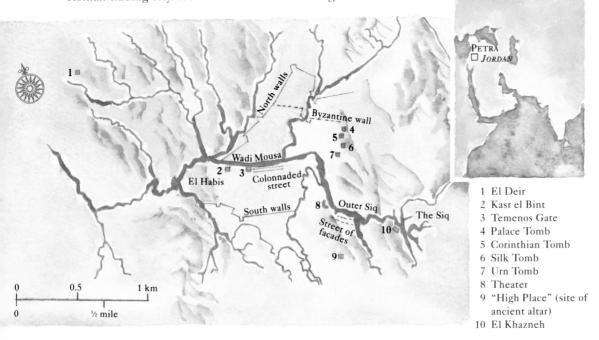

PETRA
☐ JORDAN

1 El Deir
2 Kasr el Bint
3 Temenos Gate
4 Palace Tomb
5 Corinthian Tomb
6 Silk Tomb
7 Urn Tomb
8 Theater
9 "High Place" (site of ancient altar)
10 El Khazneh

region, which was plagued by tribal warfare and by violent brigands who preyed upon trading caravans. Nonetheless, he began the first stage of his dream journey, overland from Aleppo to Cairo. In August 1812, to the south of the Dead Sea, he heard talk of "antiquities" in the valley of Wadi Mousa (a dry watercourse, named after Moses) and decided to investigate. For the price of two old horseshoes, he employed a guide for the day, claiming that he wanted to sacrifice a goat at the nearby altar of Aaron (brother of Moses and a Muslim patriarch). To have admitted that he was interested in ruins would have been fatal. They were pre-Islamic, infidel constructions; and anyone interested in them was deemed to be looking for treasure.

So it was that on August 22, 1812, Burckhardt was guided down the Siq (Arabic for "pass"), the narrow canyon leading into Wadi Mousa. Barely 7 feet (2 m) wide in places, it winds through the rocks for 1¼ miles (2 km), with the precipitous cliffs on each side reaching up some 330 feet (100 m). Here, any stranger cannot help feeling an overwhelming sensation of defenselessness and vulnerability: there can hardly be a more dramatic and intimidating entrance to a city.

Burckhardt noticed signs of ancient construction along the way. His expectations rising, he followed the final curve in the canyon to be presented with an astounding sight. Framed in the cleft of rock at the foot of the Siq, positioned deliberately to impress the visitor, stood a Classical facade in near-perfect condition. But this was no ordinary building, for instead of being constructed of blocks of stone, it had been carved out of a rock face. This was El Khazneh al Faraoun, "the pharaoh's treasury," in fact, probably a tomb, but the popular name refers to the treasures which the ruins were deemed to conceal. Behind the facade is Petra's biggest chamber, a 72-foot (22-m) cube.

He hurried on, noting the myriad tombs, dwellings, and other chambers which had been hollowed out of the cliff faces, some elaborately carved, others plain and functional. Passing the large open-air theater, with its semicircle of 33 rows of stone seats, he reached what he recognized as the old center of the city, a jumble of broken columns, leading to a ruined temple, Kasr el Bint Faraoun, "the palace of the pharaoh's daughter." Burckhardt's obvious excitement at what he saw aroused the suspicions of his guide, and fearing he might be unmasked, he performed his sacrifice and left the valley. He guessed that the place he had discovered must be the lost city of Petra.

Burckhardt never made his African journey. He waited for three years in Cairo for a suitable caravan before dying of dysentery in 1817, aged just 32. However, news of his discoveries at Petra spread, and the "lost city" soon became one of the most exalted destinations for determined travelers. Two English naval officers, disguised as Arabs, visited it in 1818, followed by, among others, the French aristocrat and writer Léon de Laborde, the intrepid English traveler Harriet Martineau, and the writer and artist Edward Lear. Their reports and paintings only served to enhance Petra's reputation as a city of dreams. Its true history remained elusive, but gradually some pieces of the jigsaw began to fit together.

Petra had once been a thriving trading center, the capital city of the Nabataeans, formerly a nomadic Bedouin tribe. In the fourth century

"I stop at the dirtiest caravanserai, use the floor as my mattress and my coat as a blanket, eat with camel drivers, and brush my horse myself, but I see and hear things which remain unknown to him who travels in comfort."

JOHANN LUDWIG BURCKHARDT

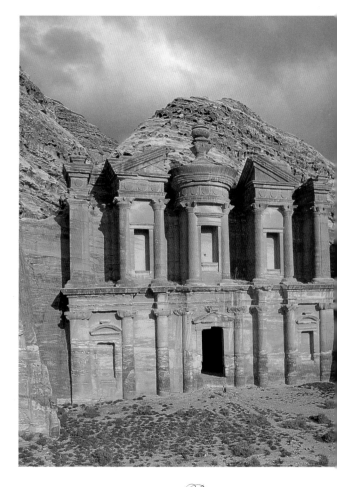

Burckhardt never set eyes on one of the grandest monuments of Petra, El Deir, which stands alone northwest of the city center. Its name, meaning monastery, derives from the tradition that, in the distant past, it was occupied by Christian hermits.

Part of the magic of a visit to Petra, as it was 2,000 years ago, is the journey through the narrow passageway of the Siq. Stepping from its shadows into the light of the desert sun, visitors are greeted by the golden-pink facade of El Khazneh.

B.C., they had begun to settle the valley – which lay at the crossroads between two major trading routes, one running east–west between the Gulf and the Mediterranean, and the other north–south down the Syrian Rift Valley between the Dead and Red seas. Along these routes came frankincense and myrrh, spices, gemstones, gold, ivory, copper, and iron. Petra, accessed by the Siq and other defensible gorges, offered a place to rest and water the camels and a secure market.

Renowned for their honesty, the Nabataeans exploited this lucrative trade, providing a safe passage in return for levies and later taking an active part in it as traders themselves. It made them powerful enough to extend their kingdom to Damascus and Philadelphia (Amman) to the north and Gaza to the west, and to come to the attention of Pompey, who in 64 B.C. was set upon extending the Roman Empire in the Middle East. The Nabataeans bought him off, but by the first century A.D., their kingdom was surrounded by Roman territory. Petra reached its zenith between 50 B.C. and A.D. 70 – when St. Paul was in Damascus, the Nabataeans were its rulers. A few decades later, as trade and power began to slip away, King Rabbel II moved his capital from Petra to Bostra in Syria, and on his death in A.D. 106 the Romans took over, seemingly without a fight.

Throughout the 200 or so years when Petra was at its most prosperous, ever grander buildings were erected in the city. The vast tombs, such as El Khazneh and the row of "Royal Tombs" (the Palace Tomb, the Corinthian Tomb, the Silk Tomb, and the Urn Tomb), show the influences of Assyrian, Phoenician, Greek, and Roman architecture, testaments to the breadth of Petra's trading contacts. The Romans developed the center of the city, erecting the gateway and colonnade to provide a shaded approach through the market to the *temenos*, the sacred precinct containing the Kasr el Bint. Excavations have revealed the remains of the Nymphaeum, an elaborate public fountain supplied by complex pipework and channels leading down from the hills. All this would have been surrounded by enough stone and wood dwellings to hold a population of 20,000, but the houses have all gone, leaving only the sepulchers of the dead to posterity.

The city remained prosperous for about a century after the Romans took over, but they then built a paved trade route that crossed from Tyre, via Palmyra to the River Euphrates, connecting the Mediterranean to the Persian Gulf and the Silk Road. It drained Petra's lifeblood, and gradually the city was forsaken. Crusaders came to the region at the start of the twelfth century, but were cleared out of virtually the entire kingdom of Jerusalem in 1189; from then on, Petra was occupied only by visiting herdsmen who made winter homes in the deserted chambers and used the caves for storage.

Apart from the tourists and the cluster of stalls selling souvenirs and refreshments, Petra remains the same as it has been for over a millennium. As evening falls, an ancient calm returns to the valley. The high crests of the surrounding crags turn golden with the setting sun, throwing the narrow valley into cool, inky shadow and releasing the bitter-sweet fragrances of animal dung and warm rock. Its secrets intact, Petra sinks back into timelessness.

The British watercolorist and traveler David Roberts visited Petra in 1839 and made a number of romantic but largely faithful studies of the ruins. Like Burckhardt, he traveled dressed as an Arab, but arrived with a host of guides and a caravan of 21 camels. This view may have had special appeal to Roberts, who began his career as a set-painter at the Drury Lane Theatre in London. In the foreground is the theater, which was enlarged by the Romans to accommodate 3,000 people – but remains dwarfed by the massive natural backdrop of rock.

Colonnades line the marketplace, once the busy hub of the city. The columns, erected in the Roman period, probably supported a roof to give shade. They provided a stately approach to the temenos, *the sacred sanctuary, which contains the only major free-standing building in Petra, Kasr el Bint, a temple to the fertility god Dusares.*

Architecturally less impressive than its neighbors – the Urn Tomb and the Corinthian Tomb – the Silk Tomb is strikingly adorned by the curious natural stripes in the rock which are reminiscent of shot silk.

Petra's interiors have attracted less attention than its exteriors, which have earned it the appellation "rose-red city." It is, however, a city of myriad hues, changing through the day as the sun makes its way across the sky. Edward Lear's cook, Giorgio, using the imagery of his trade, remarked "O master, we have come to a world where everything is made of chocolate, ham, curry-powder, and salmon."

Soúnion

Quintessence of ancient Greece

A dozen slender, weather-beaten columns rise up from this rocky promontory – a lonely outpost of the Classical world commanding a heartstopping view of the coast and islands, and of the deep-blue sea where sleek galleys once left their spume-flecked wakes.

In ancient times this elegant temple was a landmark to mariners sailing out of Piraeus, the port of Athens – a sight to signal farewell to their home province of Attica as they headed into the Aegean, or to welcome them home on their return. To many travelers today, the temple encapsulates the magic of ancient Greece: beautifully executed architecture, an exquisite sense of location and sympathy to landscape, and the mystery of civilizations buried by time. So moved was Lord Byron by the beauty of Soúnion that he called it a place "to sing and die," and carved his name into one of the columns.

Cape Soúnion is the southernmost point of Attica, the province which surrounds Athens. The landscape to the southeast of the city is one of gentle hills covered by fertile fields and olive groves rich in wildflowers in spring, and punctuated by red-tiled farmhouses and shadowy pines. The coast is famous for its beaches of golden sand, popular with Athenians escaping the heat of the city. Toward Soúnion, however, the hills become more barren, and in summer the grasses, gorse, and thistles become crisp and fragrant in the scorching sun.

On the tip of Cape Soúnion, 200 feet (60 m) above the lapping waves, the Greeks decided to build a temple to their sea god,

The shadows and hues of Soúnion's creamy-white columns change throughout the day and are at their most bewitching at dawn and dusk. Re-erected in modern times, these columns present one of the most evocative sights of ancient Greece – yet in its heyday, solid walls within the columns, which enclosed a shrine to Poseidon, would have given the temple a far less ethereal silhouette.

Athens
Piraeus

Keratea

Lávrion

Soúnion

AEGEAN SEA

Áyois Yeóryios

0   10 miles

0   10 km

GREECE
SOÚNION

Poseidon. The site may have long been sacred to Poseidon. Legend suggests that a temple was built here to appease him after Athens had chosen Athene as its patron goddess in his place. According to the myth, this honor was settled by a contest between Athene and Poseidon: whoever brought the most beneficial gift to the people of Attica would be selected as patron. Poseidon banged his trident on the ground and conjured up a horse (he was also the god of horses). But Athene produced an olive tree and was declared the winner.

The first known temple at Soúnion was built in about 490 B.C., in the early years of the Persian Wars, when Athens was assembling a navy to fend off its attackers and needed all the goodwill it could invoke. The silver mines of Lávrion – to the west of Soúnion – helped to fund both the navy and the temple. But before construction could be completed, the temple was destroyed by the Persians. In 480 B.C., their vast army of 400,000 men and fleet of 800 ships were thwarted by a small band of Spartans at the pass of Thermopylae and by storms at sea. In a fit of pique, the Persians laid waste to much of Attica, including Athens. At Soúnion they knocked down the temple and overturned the statues, scarring the face of a huge *kouros* – the stylized statue of a naked youth – now in Athens's Archaeological Museum. The outrage to Poseidon, however, may have been their downfall: shortly afterward, west of Soúnion, the Persian fleet was delivered a crushing blow by the Greek navy at Salamis.

By the middle of the fifth century B.C., Athens had entered its Golden Age, during which its most famous building, the Parthenon, was erected. At about this time, work began again at Soúnion. The temple of Poseidon was built in the Classic Greek style, with ranks of Doric columns of local marble lining a platform around the inner chamber – the *naos* – which served as a shrine to the god. The temple was decorated with fine relief carvings, some of which have survived. They include part of the frieze that adorned the exterior of the *naos*, featuring Lapiths and centaurs, as well as the exploits of the Attic hero Theseus, by some accounts the son of Poseidon.

The Peloponnesian War (431–404 B.C.) against Sparta brought the Golden Age of Athens to a close. During this period, Athens fortified the temple at Soúnion – a valuable lookout post – with eleven towers and walls 10 feet (3 m) thick. Then, in the second century B.C., slaves from the silver mines at Lávrion revolted and took over the temple, and when Greece fell into the hands of the Romans after 146 B.C., it became the haunt of pirates. When Pausanias – the author of the world's first travel guide, *Hellados Periēgēsis* (Description of Greece) – began his journey in Attica in the latter half of the second century A.D., he passed Cape Soúnion but did not linger.

More than sixteen centuries later, Cape Soúnion was still a dangerous place. On one of his many visits to the temple, Byron was attacked by a band of pirates. Today tourists invade the site every afternoon, on day trips from Athens. But at the beginning and end of the day, when the columns are caught in the softening rays of a low sun, or on clear nights in the silver light of the moon, the ruins take on the kind of meditative calm appropriate to an ancient temple in one of the world's most enchanting locations.

The temple at Soúnion, overlooking the vital shipping lanes into Athens, was dedicated to Poseidon, the brother of Zeus and lord of the sea. He is portrayed (as in this bronze head dating from the fifth century B.C.) as a figure of dignity, but was also capable of ill-tempered violence, which could arouse storms and cause earthquakes.

Mariners had one of the best views of the elegant columns of the temple, seen from below and set against the rocky headland on which it is perched. As they passed, they could invoke the goodwill and protection of Poseidon, or express their thanks to him for their safe deliverance.

A temple to Athene once stood below the temple of Poseidon on the promontory, but in the second century B.C., it was dismantled and re-erected in Athens.

Cuzco

Golden city of the Incas

In the late fifteenth century, while medieval Europe squabbled and fought over territory and looked at the rest of the world with avaricious eyes, an empire on the far side of the globe was reaching its spectacular zenith. From a capital city high in the cordillera of the Andes, it stretched across Peru, Bolivia, Chile, Ecuador, and northern Argentina, covering some 350,000 sq. miles (900,000 km^2) of mountains, jungles, and rivers and supporting a population of some twelve million people. It was called Tawantinsuyu, "four quarters of the earth," and its capital city was Cuzco, the "navel of the world." It is today remembered as the semi-legendary empire of the Incas.

By 1500 the greatest territorial entity in the history of South America had just over 30 years left before the arrival of Francisco Pizarro and his conquistadors. And it is only thanks to post-conquest Spanish and *cholo* (mixed blood) chroniclers that there is any written evidence of its existence. The Incas wrote nothing down, and even their oral history was carefully constructed to fit a strict imperial image, concentrating on the wealth and efficiency of the empire and the power of the emperor himself.

Legends ascribe the founding of Cuzco to Manco Capac, son of the Sun God and the first Inca, in about 1100. But archaeologists believe that the Incas simply became the most powerful of the many Andean tribes, gradually moving toward the valuable fertile valleys around the Urubamba River. From 1438 onward, under the

Half an hour's walk from Cuzco, the huge stone walls of the fortress at Sacsayhuaman form a natural grandstand. During the Inti Raymi *festival, on and around June 24, dancers and musicians from the surrounding villages converge on Cuzco for days of festivities and* chicha *(maize beer) drinking to celebrate the winter solstice and the return of the sun.*

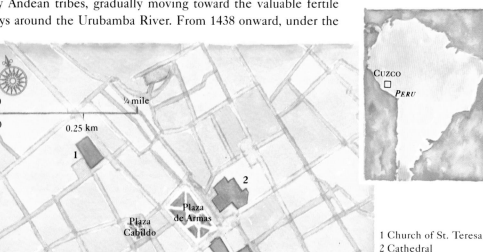

1 Church of St. Teresa
2 Cathedral
3 La Compania
4 House of the Chosen Women (Church of Santa Catalina)
5 Temple of the Sun (Church of Santo Domingo)
6 La Merced
7 Church and Monastery of St. Francis

Inca Pachacuti (literally "mover of the earth"), the empire began to expand aggressively, as the Incas conquered chieftains and demanded allegiance as they went.

Situated at 11,152 feet (3,399 m) above sea level in a naturally fortified area of great fertility, Cuzco was the spiritual heart of the empire and home of the emperor. Each Inca (the word "Inca" means "emperor," but is now used as a collective noun for his subjects) married his sister and set up his own royal corporation known as a *panaca*. Some of the palaces of the *panacas* still stand in Cuzco; others are buried under Spanish buildings, but it was from here that the lines of power radiated outward across the growing imperial territory. When the Inca died, his sons, wives, and concubines continued in his *panaca*, but the power passed to the corporation with the new Inca at its head.

Under Pachacuti, Cuzco became a center of complex ceremonies and extraordinary wealth. He transformed his capital city: the valley floor was flattened, agricultural terraces were built, and irrigation systems formed. Hostile tribes were subjugated simply by uprooting them and moving them into Cuzco's sphere of influence, while their land was given to loyal Inca subjects. Defiance meant the confiscation of lands and the destruction of people; their skulls were made into cups for *chicha* (maize beer) and their skins into drums.

A new street plan was devised for the capital based, symbolically, on the shape of the great mountain predator, the puma, with the mighty three-tiered fortress of Sacsayhuaman as its head. Pachacuti developed a state religion around the worship of Viracocha (the Ancient One), who figured in one of the creation myths as the maker of men and is believed by some to be Kontiki, who sailed to Polynesia on a boat of reeds. The greatest shrine to Viracocha was the Temple of the Sun, built of perfectly fitting mortarless masonry – an Inca trademark – strong enough to withstand the earthquakes common to the area, and measuring 1,000 feet (300 m) in circumference.

Spectacular rituals revolved around the temple, the interior of which was covered in sheets of beaten gold. At its center was a huge image of the Sun God, a human face on a disk surrounded by golden rays. Around that were idols representing Apu Illapu, the Rain Giver; Mama-Kilya, the Moon Mother; and other deities in the pantheon, as well as shrines to the Pleiades, Venus, lightning, and rainbows.

Most magnificent of all was the Coricancha, a garden of solid gold divided into four to represent the quarters of the empire and containing life-size golden models of each area's crops, vegetation, and animals. There were said to be golden ears of corn, golden llamas, even a golden herdsboy with a golden staff. The truth will never be known: the conquistadors simply recorded the weight of gold plundered – some 3,500 pounds (1,600 kg) – and sent it back to Spain.

The Incas controlled their empire by two means: the construction of a colossal system of paved and stepped roads, which penetrated every corner of their territory; and the invention of the *quipu*, a system that used knotted strings with which to record numerical information, a variation on the abacus. Messengers known as *chasquis*, legendary for their running speed, could cross the empire in a matter

"The city is the greatest and finest ever seen in this country, or anywhere in the Indies."

FRANCISCO PIZARRO, CONQUISTADOR, *c.*1531

The red Spanish roofs and Baroque church towers of the Inca capital of Cuzco lie in a valley in the Andean cordillera which has been partly flattened. Said to have been based on the shape of a puma, with Sacsayhuaman at its head and the great square of Huayaca Pata at its heart, Cuzco was the empire's administrative center and the home of the Sapa Inca – the emperor – himself.

Revealed by an earthquake in 1950, the smooth stones of the Coricancha make a perfect, mortarless curve beneath the walls of the Spanish church of Santo Domingo. Once the "golden garden" of the Temple of the Sun, the Coricancha was filled with golden figurines of crops and animals. All were sent to Spain to be melted down.

The 1950 earthquake was the second in Cuzco's history – the first occurred exactly three centuries earlier. On both occasions, the colonial buildings collapsed and the supporting Inca stonework survived.

of days with messages from outlying districts or with *quipus* containing information about population figures, crop yields, and taxes collected. Some taxes were levied in the form of tithes – food, livestock, or precious metals – while the rest were paid in work days; able-bodied men fought, built roads, or erected public buildings free of charge.

This was the Cuzco the Spanish heard about in their feverish search for South American gold. A city of great architectural beauty and elaborate ceremonial, at the center of a vast and powerful empire. A city, most importantly, possessed of such fabulous wealth that it could fill Spanish ships with gold and silver. Unaware of their impending doom, the Inca Atahualpa and his subjects went about their daily lives in the capital. Each day, the temple priests – diviners, doctors, confessors, and sorcerers – roasted maize cobs on the fire as a sacrifice to the Sun. And each day, the Chosen Women wove a new Inca's poncho of finest vicuña wool, to be burned daily. On the first day of each lunar month, 30 priests sacrificed 100 pure white llamas in Huayaca Pata, the great square of Cuzco.

The Incas greeted the Spanish newcomers as friends and showed them around Cuzco, allowing them to see the lie of the land and the wealth that could be plundered. Atahualpa was tricked into a meeting and imprisoned, far from his loyal supporters. He agreed to pay a ransom for his release, promising to fill a room the size of his cell – roughly 3,100 cu. feet (88 m³) – once over with gold and twice with silver. Although his offer was accepted and treasure-laden llamas set out for Cuzco, Atahualpa was murdered and the precious metals sent to Seville for smelting. Thus began a new era in Cuzco's history.

Today in Cuzco's paved and cobbled streets, the influence of the conquistadors is still clearly visible. The massive, inward-sloping Inca stonework ends at a height of about 6 feet (1.8 m) and is topped by the brick walls and balconied upper floors of the Spanish houses, with their shallow tiled roofs and shuttered windows. Local people say that the Spanish were unable to destroy the massive lower layers of Inca masonry and had to use them for foundation stones instead. In Hatunrumiyoc, or "the street of the great stone", a base block with twelve carved angles fits exactly into its mighty neighbors.

The Temple of the Sun, too, was partly demolished. Above the surviving curved wall of the Coricancha soars the church and monastery of Santo Domingo, its monks replacing the 400 temple attendants, priests, and priestesses of Inca times. In the Great Square, Cuzco Cathedral stands on the site of a former great Inca's palace. The House of the Chosen Women and the *panacas* of the nobility became mansions and headquarters of the colonial administrators, and the city became famous for some of the best examples of High Baroque architecture in South America.

Cuzco is once again a focal point – of Peruvian cultural pride. Visitors walk the streets, admiring the masonry, wondering at the ostentation of the Spanish churches, trying to imagine the Great Square on sacrificial days, when blood and *chicha* flowed into the river. Every year, thousands of hikers head up the valley of the Urubamba, to walk the Inca Trail, and the winter solstice festival of *Inti Raymi* is celebrated among the great stones of Sacsayhuaman each June 24.

"It seemed like an unbelievable dream.... What could this place be?

HIRAM BINGHAM, 1911

Quecha women, wearing their distinctive flat hats of coarse homespun stuffed with straw, sit beside surviving Inca masonry at the village of Chincheros, in the province of Cuzco, weaving the bold, decorative textiles for which the area is famous. That Quecha is still the lingua franca in many areas that were part of the empire more than four centuries ago is a tribute to the immense power and influence of the Incas.

A woman leads her llamas across the plain in front of Sacsayhuaman, where three tiers of mighty Inca stonework once guarded the city of Cuzco like rows of teeth. Theories abound as to how the Incas, using only manpower, pulleys, and wood, could have maneuvered carved stones weighing up to 360 tons into position and fitted them so precisely to their neighbors that even today it is impossible to insert a knife blade between them.

The Inca Trail

In 1911, deep in the Peruvian jungle and several days' walk from the town of Cuzco, American explorer Hiram Bingham stepped out of the trees to be faced by a white stone gateway, buried beneath dense foliage. Beyond it he could see walls, buildings, and temples, scattered over a ridge connecting the bowl of jungle to a soaring mountain peak. He could scarcely believe his good fortune: he had discovered Vilcabamba, last home of the Incas.

Bingham was in fact mistaken. Vilcabamba lies 60 miles (100 km) away to the west; nor was his "discovery" of any surprise to the local Indian population. But he had found Machu Picchu, or "ancient peak," a site of great importance to the Incas, fantastically situated in the center of Peru. The world's imagination was gripped.

Over the next few years, Bingham and his colleagues uncovered more ruins and the remains of a paved imperial highway, which has become known to modern travelers as the Inca Trail. The Incas controlled their vast empire by means of good roads and excellent communications, and the trail, which loops and winds through deep gorges and over mountain passes, was used by supply trains of llamas, the legendary Inca runners (or *chasquis*), and – illicitly – by smugglers trying to avoid imperial taxes.

Today, walkers climb off the zigzagging train from Cuzco at a spot known as Kilometer 88, or start farther down the so-called Sacred Valley of the Urubamba River at the Inca ruins of Ollantaytambo. Here trapezoid doorways,

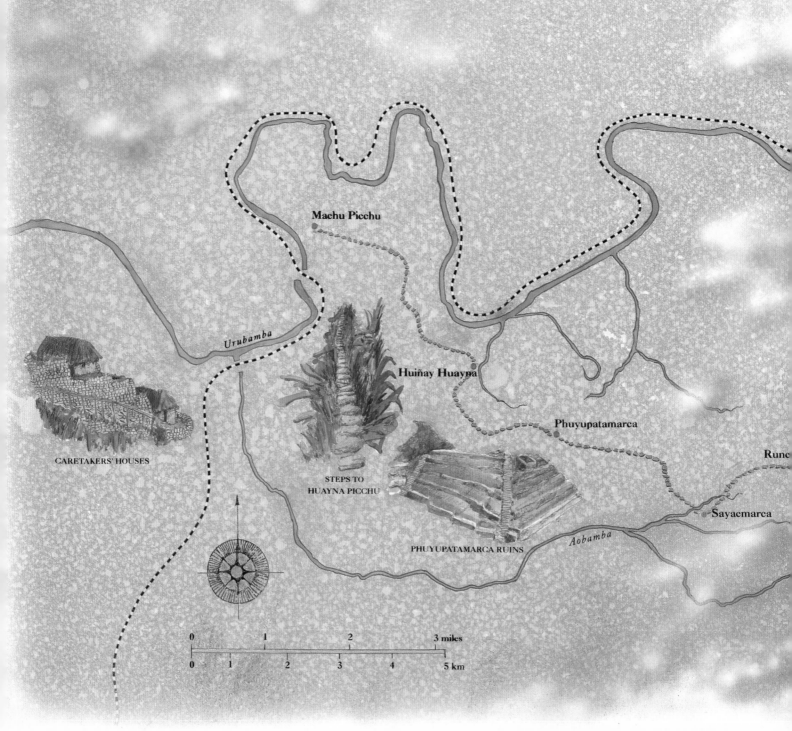

Machu Picchu

Urubamba

CARETAKERS' HOUSES

Huiñay Huayna

STEPS TO
HUAYNA PICCHU

Phuyupatamarca

Runc

Sayacmarca

PHUYUPATAMARCA RUINS

Aobamba

0		1		2		3 miles
0	1	2	3	4		5 km

buildings strong enough to resist earth tremors, and stone compounds separated by narrow alleyways give a foretaste of the layout of Machu Picchu, three days' hard uphill walk along the Urubamba gorge.

Ruins dot the length of the trail; some of them are temple sites, others are control points, supply bases, or the travelers' lodgings known as *tambos*. Recent research suggests that Machu Picchu was the focal point of an entire region, perhaps the fiefdom of a relative of the Incas, which had already fallen into disrepair before the advent of the Spanish. This would explain why the European conquerors – who were originally welcomed by the Incas – never knew of its existence.

All the passes along the trail offer superb views. But from the third, at 13,000 feet (4,000 m), there is the breathtaking sight of the Sacred Valley and of the ritual baths and agricultural terracing of Phuyupatamarca, or "cloud level town." One of the many functions suggested for the region is that of coca supplier to the Incas and, in particular, their priests, who chewed the leaves as a narcotic. Certainly Machu Picchu itself has hundreds of terraces contouring the hills.

But the vista that everybody waits to see is from the very top of the trail, through the Intipunku, or Gate of the Sun. The path hugs the hillside, turns the corner, and there below lies Machu Picchu, now cleared and white, in the towering shadow of Huayna Picchu, or "young peak." This was the view that the *chasquis* saw in the sixteenth century, as they ran into the city carrying their knotted string messages, and that Bingham and his men looked back on as they worked their way home along the Inca Trail, then still overgrown and obscured by collapsed masonry. It is a view that no one forgets.

STONE BRIDGE OVER THE CARABAYA

Corihuachina

Llactapata

Urubamba

Carabaya

Ollantaytambo

STOREHOUSES

Caretaker's cottage, Machu Picchu, at the end of the Inca Trail.

Borobodur

Temple of serene stone buddhas

Early mornings on the Kedu plateau in south-central Java begin with a dense mist, which lies over the paddy fields and forests like a shroud. Far above it, and above the birds which skim the treetops, sharp eyes might catch sight of a dark shape, dotted with cones, which rises out of the cleared jungle like a pyramid. A closer look reveals a series of circular stone platforms, each with its own ring of bell-shaped stupas, diminishing in size as they ascend to a simple stone summit. This is the monument of Borobodur, towering over the mist and trees as it has done for more than 1,000 years.

Set in a wide valley, surrounded by volcanoes and separated from its neighboring regions by a mountain range, Borobodur is isolated both geographically and spiritually. It is one of a handful of surviving Buddhist structures in a country which has strong animist and Hindu roots and has been predominantly Muslim for nearly four centuries. Every village has its mosque, and for the Kedu farmers who turn toward Mecca five times a day, Borobodur serves as a strange reminder of earlier rulers and their beliefs.

Anthropological finds, such as Java Man and the Surakarta skulls, show that there have been people in Java for millennia. In the centuries before Christ, Java's indigenous population was probably swollen by waves of immigrants from the Malay peninsula, who brought with them a set of early animistic beliefs. Then, around the first and second centuries A.D., Indian influences began to reach Javanese shores. Hinduism and Buddhism arrived in equal measure,

As it has done for more than 1,000 years, one of the statues of the infinite Dhyani Buddha sits in its broken stupa, looking out across the lush valley that surrounds the monument of Borobodur. All 72 buddhas on the highest circular terraces are in the sila *position, sitting with crossed legs and hands raised at chest height, deep in meditation.*

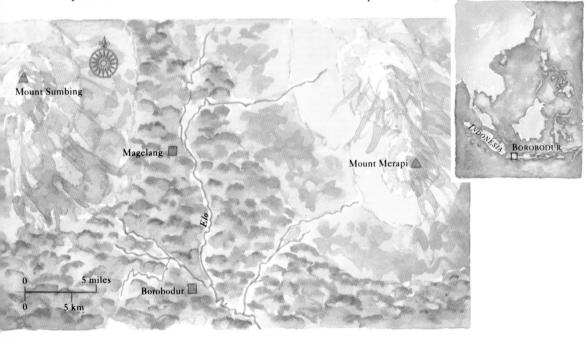

and for 1,500 years there was a constant shifting between the two as different princes vied for power. The oldest edifices in Java, the temples of the Dieng plateau, date from the seventh century and are Hindu. Just 100 years later, the powerful Sailendra dynasty brought Buddhism to the fore. Each religion was syncretic, absorbing elements of those that had gone before, and some historians believe that Borobodur started life as a Hindu shrine in around A.D. 780 before being converted to a stupa in 792.

Whatever his religion, any devout Javanese king was expected to protect holy sites and to promote learning and the performance of religious rituals. The Kedu plateau, with its fertile volcanic soil and large population, was the perfect place for a powerful Sailendra king to create a shrine, which could be built using free feudal labor.

Borobodur is one of the great achievements of Buddhist architecture, not only because of its size, but also because of its extraordinary unity of expression. It has never been added to, cluttered with outbuildings, or surrounded by the noise and houses of a city. Its black andesite stone has weathered to a gentle, uniform gray. Centuries of abandonment under Muslim rule have given it a dreamlike quality, which is emphasized by its physical isolation.

To build Borobodur, the jungle had to be felled, the land cleared, and the mighty temple mound built and flattened, ready to support a stone plinth 400 feet (120 m) square and 15 feet (4.5 m) high. The first five terraces, which were square, supported three circular terraces topped by a solid-walled stone stupa. Each retaining wall was pierced by a straight flight of steps, giving access to all the terraces, so that pilgrims could walk around the stupa clockwise in the accepted Buddhist fashion.

The Buddhism which reached Java in the first century A.D. was Mahayana Buddhism, which holds that belief is enough to bring all mankind to enlightenment and therefore to nirvana. The Gautama Buddha preached that man must follow the "middle way" to eliminate desire and therefore suffering, evolving through a series of rebirths to achieve supreme enlightenment. Borobodur is a tangible symbol of this journey. Its metaphysical meaning is not hard to grasp. The walls of the terraces are covered in exquisitely detailed bas reliefs, past which the pilgrim must walk. The lowest two depict the struggles of man and his good and bad deeds in daily life. The middle level deals with events in the life of Buddha, starting with his enlightenment under a pipal tree (which came to be known as the Bo – enlightenment – tree) in northern India, as well as scenes from the *jataka* stories of his previous lives. The upper levels depict philosophical themes taken from the Mahayana scriptures, and there, just as human preoccupations must be abandoned to attain nirvana, the relief carvings cease abruptly and give way to the three unadorned circular terraces.

On these terraces are situated Borobodur's most distinctive feature: 72 bell-shaped stupas, each of carved stone latticework, which house 72 seated buddhas that stare serenely out across the valley. Some are headless, long since vandalized, others are missing the tops of their stupas, but nothing can take away the atmosphere

An aerial view of one of the world's greatest religious structures shows the metaphysical significance of Borobodur. Pilgrims follow a clockwise route around the lower, square terraces, which are decorated with carvings of earthly preoccupations, the lives of Buddha, and interpretations of Mahayana scripture. The austere upper terraces, with their seated buddhas, represent the eventual attainment of nirvana.

"*Rich beyond power of description in ornament, yet highly monumental; Baroque and Classical; exuberant and restrained; fragile and massive; severe yet full of mystery; it is the incarnation of the inevitable and eternal, beyond earthly understanding. It is the universe itself symbolized in carven stone.*"

JAN POORTENAAR, 1928

Thousands of blocks of volcanic andesite adorn the lower levels of Borobodur. Several hundred depict the life of the Gautama Buddha, who was born in Nepal in the fifth or sixth century B.C. and achieved enlightenment under the Bo tree in northern India. The sculptures represent an extraordinary feat of restoration over the past 90 years by Dutch, English, and Indonesian archaeologists and engineers.

of tranquillity that pervades the upper levels. The statues are of the infinite, ethereal Dhyani Buddha, each one in the *sila* position.

Local tradition claims that Mount Tidar, to the north of Borobodur, was used by the gods to nail Java to the center of the earth and stop it from shifting in the sea. Another popular belief is that the builder of Borobodur is enshrined in the mountains where he watches over his creation to keep it safe. But during the dark years, only a century after it was built, when the Hindu Majapahit empire was in the ascendant, murkier rumors swirled about the gigantic stupa. It was said that the Sailendra king had buried his builders in the temple, and that a visiting prince had died after looking upon the "thousand statues of Borobodur."

In fact, the ashes of the builders were enshrined in the structure after their death, and stone statues were carved, representing them as gods for posterity. But by now Borobodur had been overtaken by time and temporal matters; the Majapahits gave way to the first Muslim rulers, who built up mighty courts to the south and east of the Kedu plateau, in the rival cities of Yogyakarta and Surakarta. When the Dutch arrived, the tussle for power began in earnest. Borobodur, marooned on its distant plateau, sank quietly beneath the encroaching jungle and all but disappeared from view.

There it would have lain forgotten, had it not been for the arrival of Thomas Stamford Raffles, keen to uphold the interests of the British East India Company against the Dutch on Batavia, as Java was then known. Well informed in local matters and aware of the monument's existence, he commissioned H.C. Cornelis to investigate its condition in 1814. Under Kedu's resident administrator and with the help of local villagers, probably the direct descendants of its builders, Borobodur emerged from the jungle in 1835. The main stupa was opened, but it was empty. Some 50 years later, as the clearing work continued, it was found that the lower levels of bas reliefs had been hidden behind stone walls, possibly erected to buttress the crumbling temple mound.

Restoration began under Theodorus van Erp during the final period of Dutch colonial rule, but Borobodur had to wait until 1973 and a UNESCO-funded program before attaining something of its former glory. At a cost of $25 million over a period of ten years, 2 million cu. feet (57,000 m³) of stone were dismantled, labeled, cleaned, and replaced; and 27,000 sq. feet (2,500 m²) of bas reliefs were photographed, restored, and returned to their original positions. A large park was cleared around the monument to protect it from vandals and to keep the jungle at bay.

The first thing that modern visitors notice is the atmosphere of peace and calm. And then that, unlike almost every other Buddhist holy place in the world, there are relatively few worshippers. The local people are almost all Muslim, and the monument has no relics to attract Buddhist pilgrims from abroad. There are no monks with plates of offerings, no flowers strewn before a shrine, no chanting, incense, or gongs. It is almost possible to believe that Borobodur, conceived as one, built as one, and surviving as one, has itself attained enlightenment, and is no longer a monument of this world.

Borobodur's pinnacles tower over the fertile landscape of the Kedu plateau, surrounded by fields of rice, tobacco plants, and sugarcane, interrupted only by stands of virgin jungle and the distant volcanic peaks of mounts Sumbing, Merbabu, and Merapi.

An overwhelming majority of the farmers who plant the crops and till the fields are Muslim, and Borobodur stands as a reminder of their distant Buddhist past.

Close up, the stone buddhas of Borobodur exude tranquillity. Carved on the spot by skilled artists brought in during the period of construction, they are made from the dark volcanic stone used for the entire edifice. Many of the statues' heads and bell-like stupas have been destroyed over the centuries by religious vandals, making restoration a formidable task.

"...the fructifying touch of heaven; when tranquil love descends in waves of contentment, unspeakable satisfaction"

JOHAN SCHELTEMA, 1912

Luxor
City of palaces

The huge-pillared temple of Karnak on the banks of the Nile is one of the most awe-inspiring religious buildings on earth. From here, an avenue lined with sphinxes ran south to Luxor. The ancient name for this place was Thebes, which embraced present-day Karnak and Luxor and, across the Nile in western Thebes, the tombs and mortuary temples of the pharaohs in the Valleys of the Kings and Queens. The heart of Egypt from 2100 to 750 B.C., Thebes embodied a central tenet of Egyptian religion. On the river's east bank, the direction of sunrise, stood the city of the living, home of the kings. On its west, the direction of sunset, was their necropolis. The Nile between was both the river that gave Egypt life and the mythological river sailed in his barque by the sun god Re as he descended to the underworld each night.

Egyptian spirituality is at its most powerful at Thebes. Even the titanic images of kings and the carvings of battles fought and won are there not from mere vainglory, but to contribute to the city's role as a symbol of the mysteries of existence. These mysteries were celebrated in the cult of Amun. During the Middle Kingdom (*c.* 2040–1782 B.C.), when Thebes was the capital of Egypt, Re – previously the supreme state deity – was merged with the ram-headed local god Amun, to become Amun-Re, king of the gods.

Originally linked with fecundity, Amun was identified with the ruling dynasty both as its progenitor and in the person of his human incarnation, the king. Karnak was his state temple, where the deity's

Amenhotep III, who reigned from 1390 to 1353 B.C. during the eighteenth dynasty, built major portions of the temple of Luxor and the third pylon, or gateway, and a statue of the sacred scarab beetle at the temple of Karnak. In addition, he was responsible for the funerary temple that bore his name in western Thebes. Of this, only the huge colossi remain.

LUXOR □

EGYPT

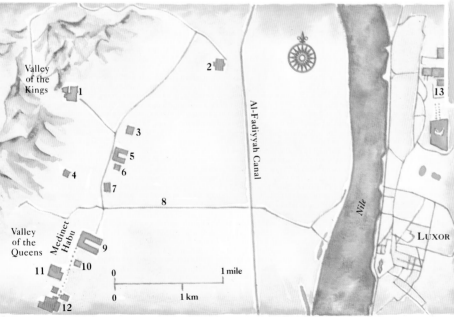

1 Temple of Hatshepsut
2 Temple of Seti
3 Temple of Tuthmosis III
4 Temple of Ptolemy IV
5 Ramesseum
6 Temple of Tuthmosis IV
7 Temple of Meneptah
8 Colossi of Amenhotep III
9 Temple and Palace of Ramses III
10 Temple of Thoth
11 Temple of Ramses III
12 Palace of Amenhotep III
13 Great Temple of Amun, Karnak

image lived with his wife Mut and their child Khonsu. Here were kept the Triad's sacred barques, model ships on which their images rode.

The vast temple is roofless now; gone are the orchestrated movements from light to dark, profane to sacred, as processions passed from the blaze of the Egyptian sun through the gathering gloom of inner courts, forbidden to the public, to the blackness of the windowless sanctuary holding the god's monolithic shrine. Amun was omnipresent, simultaneously here and in his celestial home, and when the priests came daily to anoint him and offer sacrifice, they cried as they threw back the shrine's doors: "The Gates of Heaven are open."

Amun means "the hidden one," and for their glimpse of the god, ordinary Egyptians had to wait for the great festivals when the statues of the Triad were brought out in their barques. Every year, when the Nile overflowed its banks, came the festival of Opet, when Amun of Karnak visited Amun of Luxor in his temple. The four-week-long festival comes to life in reliefs at Luxor in which Tutankhamun is shown offering sacrifice before the barques of the Triad at Karnak. Priests raised the boats shoulder high on poles and carried them out of the temple through the third pylon, where flying streamers fluttered from huge flagstaffs. Preceded by musicians, they went down to the quay whence barges bore the images upriver. The barques arrived at Luxor, and the priests hoisted them and carried them into the temple.

The procession entered through the first pylon, built by Ramses II in the thirteenth century B.C. and flanked by two colossal statues of him. Just inside is the triple shrine where the barques rested. The procession then continued through the Hypostyle Hall – lined on three sides by double rows of columns representing papyrus reeds – and made its way through a forest of stone pillars symbolizing burgeoning vegetation, along a colonnade, and across a court to the shrines reserved for the barques of Mut and Khonsu. The barque of Amun proceeded through an offering hall into the sanctuary, beyond which lay the *ipet* (private rooms) surrounding the four-columned holy of holies. Here stood Amun of Luxor on his pedestal.

The remoteness of this sanctuary may reflect the secret nature of Amun and of the rites performed here. The festival's true purpose is unknown, but it revolved around the procreative powers of Amun, and of his earthly embodiment, the king, and may have included a sacred marriage which took place in the *ipet*. Theologically, Amun of Luxor paired with the queen; in practice the king was her partner.

But Amun was more than a god of increase. Amun of Luxor periodically crossed the Nile to western Thebes to visit another Amun at Medinet Habu. This site is now dominated by the mortuary temple of Ramses III, but originally only a pillared cloister surrounded the barque shrine of Amun, with a sanctuary behind. This so-called Small Temple was concerned with life, death, and renewal. When Amun of Luxor came here, he was believed to undergo a series of changes which made him at once his own grandfather, father, and son.

Thebes's day passed, as did Egypt's native kings, but the Small Temple devoted to the hidden lord of the cycle of existence kept its religious significance into Roman times, long after the monumental funerary temple of Ramses III had ceased to function.

Ram-headed crio-sphinxes, symbolizing the power of the ram-headed Theban god Amun, line the route between the temple of Karnak and the rectangular quay built by Ramses II from which the river barge bearing the sacred barque of Amun departed for Luxor or western Thebes.

Reliefs in the arcade at the temple of Luxor show the sacred barques being both towed, against the current, to Luxor by tugboats and pulled by soldiers, courtiers, and singers lining the riverbank and heaving on ropes.

The 2-mile (3-km) avenue of sphinxes led southward from the south gate of the temple of Karnak to Luxor's temples and royal and aristocratic dwellings. These impressive buildings gave the area its name, since Luxor in Arabic means "city of palaces."

In contrast to the secular buildings at Luxor and Karnak, which were intended to last only a lifetime and were made of mud bricks, the religious edifices were conceived for all eternity. Constructed of granite from Aswan, limestone from Tura near Cairo, and sandstone from several sites along the Nile, parts of the temples here have stood for more than four millennia.

A Nile Journey

Egypt, where a strong scent of the exotic overlays the attractions of antiquity, has lured Westerners from the earliest days of mass tourism. By 1875 Thomas Cook's Nile steamers were catering for 180 people at a time; but the truly luxurious cruises of the 1920s and '30s allowed a handful of the very rich to relax in glass-encased observation lounges, cooled by whirring fans and ministered to by attentive servants. On the way, the boat moored long enough for passengers to make short excursions to pyramids and temples, but they always returned in time to dress for dinner.

Cruises could begin at Aswan and head downstream toward Cairo. The first major stop was Luxor, on the site of the ancient capital, Thebes. Here an enthusiast might choose to stay longer, for in addition to the temples of Luxor and Thebes themselves, the great Temple of Amun at Karnak and the Valley of the Kings – burial place of the pharaohs – are within easy reach. Among the tombs of the Valley of the Kings was that of Tutankhamun, unique in that its treasures remained largely intact until modern times.

Karnak is one of the great sites of Egypt, its temple almost overpowering in size and intricacy. It is approached by the Avenue of the Sphinxes, of which only a segment remains, but whose 2-mile (3-km) length was once entirely lined with sphinxes, each with a statue of the self-aggrandizing pharaoh Ramses II between its paws. The pink granite obelisk of Queen Hatshepsut and the Festival Hall of Tuthmosis III, with its star-studded ceiling supported on 52 pillars, are other wondrous survivors of the ancient world.

From Luxor, the Nile threads its way northward to al-Amarnah, where the pharaoh Akhenaten built his doomed capital, Akhetaten. The city was inhabited for a mere eleven years; after the pharaoh's death in 1362 B.C., the court returned to Thebes.

Just before the journey's end lies Giza, home of the most famous monuments of all – the Great Pyramid and the Sphinx. About 3,500 years old, 450 feet (137 m) high, and 745 feet (227 m) square at the base, the Great Pyramid of Khufu, or Cheops, was built of some two and a half million blocks of red granite, each weighing about 2.5 tons, quarried in Aswan and brought to the site by boat. Even the burial chamber is carved from red granite. The Greek historian Herodotus estimated that the construction must have required a workforce of 100,000 men.

The Sphinx, or "terrible one," 260 feet (80 m) long and 72 feet (22 m) high, dates from the same period. Although much of her face has worn away, the enigmatic smile is still clearly visible, reminding observers of the time when this mythical lionlike creature with a human head was said to kill all those who could not answer her riddle.

And so to Cairo, in the early 1920s still the comfortable capital of a British protectorate. Here, the intrepid travelers were able to conclude their magical journey as they had begun it – absorbing the colorful atmosphere without the slightest risk of discomfort.

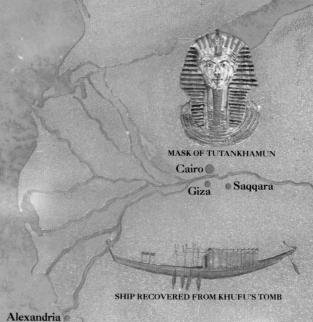

MASK OF TUTANKHAMUN

Cairo

Giza Saqqara

SHIP RECOVERED FROM KHUFU'S TOMB

Alexandria

MEDITERRANEAN SEA

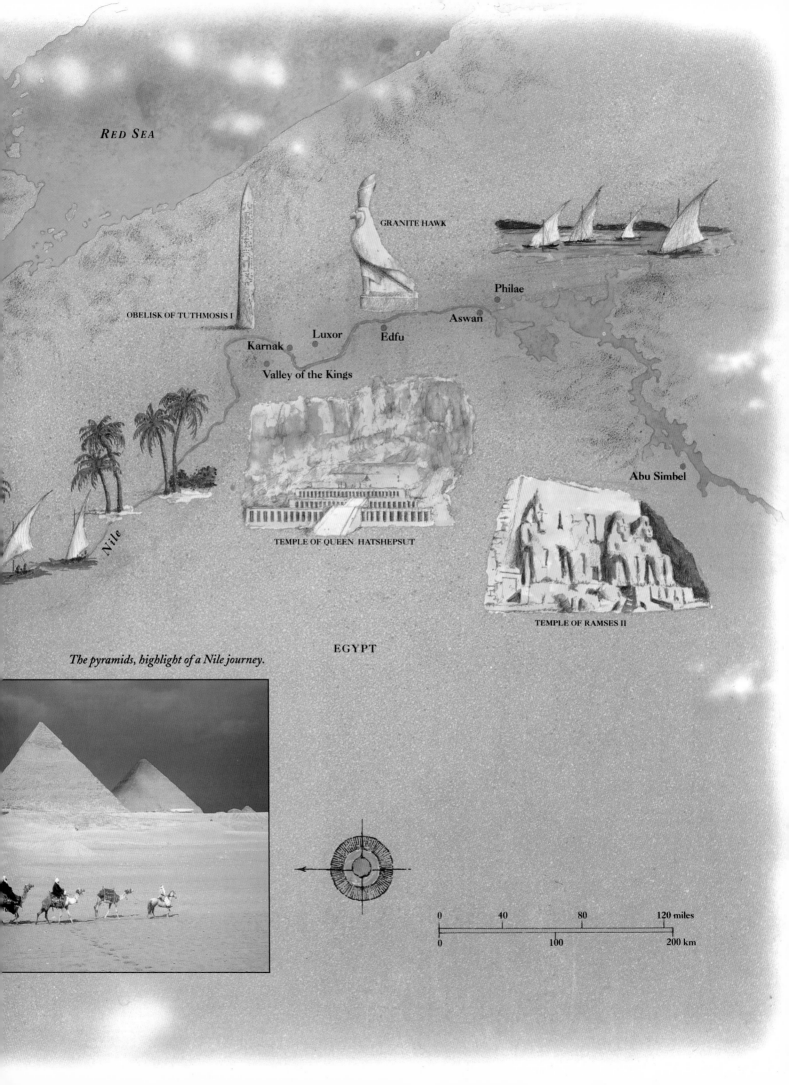

RED SEA

OBELISK OF TUTHMOSIS I

GRANITE HAWK

Philae

Aswan

Luxor

Edfu

Karnak

Valley of the Kings

Nile

TEMPLE OF QUEEN HATSHEPSUT

Abu Simbel

TEMPLE OF RAMSES II

EGYPT

The pyramids, highlight of a Nile journey.

| | 0 | 40 | 80 | 120 miles |
| 0 | 100 | 200 km |

Chichén Itzá
Heart of a lost civilization

On the hot plains of the Yucatán peninsula, a tiered monument of burnished gold rises against a royal-blue sky. This is the Pyramid of Kukulcán, one of the 50 or so major buildings – temples, stepped platforms, a domed observatory – that remain of Chichén Itzá. In the last 50 years, the site has been excavated and much restored, but the motivations of the people who built this city remain a puzzle. For Chichén Itzá was a city of the Maya, one of the "lost" civilizations of the Americas who left few records besides their impressive ruins, a handful of rare books written in obscure glyphs, and legends.

After its founding in around A.D. 450, Chichén thrived for five centuries, during the Classic period of Maya civilization. A number of the surviving buildings at Chichén Itzá, most grouped to the south of the town's later ceremonial heart, date from that era. Many of them have the distinctive corbeled roof of Maya architecture, in which the stone tapers upward to a peak, creating a triangular vault.

In this period the Maya Empire covered not only the Yucatán, but also Guatemala, western Honduras, and northern El Salvador. To the south rose Tikal, Palenque, and Copán, equally impressive ceremonial centers complete with pyramids and palaces, and a rich heritage of sculpture and stone carving. Then, in the middle of the ninth century, for reasons that can only be guessed at – perhaps drought, crop failure, social upheaval, or all three – the Maya Empire evaporated. The cities were abandoned, and reclaimed by the tropical jungle.

Although built in about A.D. 900, the so-called Observatory resembles many such buildings constructed later in the West to house telescopes. Possibly used to track the paths of the stars and planets, it played a key role in the life of Chichén Itzá, where ceremonies were conducted accordingly to a complex but highly accurate calendar.

To the rear is the Pyramid of Kukulcán. The four staircases each have 91 steps, which, with the single step of the summit, add up to 365 – the number of days in a year.

CHICHÉN-ITZÁ

MEXICO

1 Temple of the Bearded Man
2 Tzompantli
3 Ball court
4 Platform of Venus
5 Platform of the Jaguars and Eagles
6 Temple of the Jaguars
7 Temple of the Warriors
8 Pyramid of Kukulcán
9 The Thousand Columns
10 Market
11 High Priest's Grave
12 House of the Corn Grinders
13 Observatory
14 Temple of the Carved Panels
15 Steam bath

Sacred Causeway

Xtoloc Cenote

0   0.5 km
0   ¼ mile

This occurred at Chichén, too, but shortly before the millennium, the city was reoccupied by a Maya-speaking people called the Itzá, giving the city its full name. They were in close alliance with the Toltecs, then the main force in central Mexico. In this so-called Post-Classic period of Maya culture, Chichén Itzá was transformed, with new buildings which clearly broadcast the Toltec connection – notably in the motifs used in the relief carvings, such as marching jaguars and eagles on the platform named after them, and the skulls of sacrificial victims depicted on the Tzompantli platform.

The Thousand Columns (in fact, 360) belong to this period and feature the first use of wooden beams with palm-leaf thatching (as opposed to stone corbels) for roofing. A part of the Thousand Columns probably gave shade to a busy market place, where goods from the Maya's extensive trading links were exchanged. These included exotic items such as gold, gems, iridescent quetzal feathers, chicle chewing gum, and cocoa beans, from which a frothy savory drink – an integral part of the Maya vision of heaven – was made. The city soon had a population of some 200,000 people, housed outside the ceremonial center that is there today. But their dwellings, made of wood and thatch, have not survived.

Chichén Itzá also imported Toltec gods, including the feathered serpent Quetzalcoatl, the sky god. Giant serpent heads carved in stone adorn the Temple of the Warriors, the Platform of the Jaguars and Eagles, and the balustrades of the Pyramid of Kukulcán. Chac Mool, the Toltec rain god, also came to Chichén Itzá during this era.

The Maya were gifted astronomers and mathematicians, and had developed a complex calendar based on accurate observations of the heavenly bodies, and this formed the framework of a ceaseless round of religious ceremonies. These were spectacular affairs, even if they entailed human sacrifice. They included dancing and theatrical performances in extravagant costumes on the platforms, as well as ball games on the huge walled ball court, the largest of seven such courts at Chichén Itzá, covering an area equivalent to 30 modern tennis courts. Spectators wagered their clothes and jewels on the outcome of these games. The steam baths may have played a role in the ritual of this game, although bathing was part of Maya daily life.

Wealthy Mayas of this period lived in lavish style. They adorned themselves with rings, bracelets, belts, jewelry, and headdresses; they covered their bodies with tattoos, put golden rings through their pierced ears, and jeweled plugs into their pierced noses.

Chichén Itzá was in decline as a religious center – although not as a market – when the Spanish conquistadors arrived in the 1520s. They dealt the city, and the late flowering of Maya culture that it had come to embody, its death blows. Chichén Itzá was soon abandoned and lay in ruins, taken over by thorn bushes and scrub. Its rediscovery in the nineteenth century opened the eyes of the world to the tantalizing concept of an entire civilization that had vanished – to the idea that whole cities might be awaiting discovery in the depths of the Central American jungle. Such dreams of discovery may have faded at Chichén Itzá, but not the sense of awe and wonderment that these monumental ruins still inspire.

"They had no fiesta in which they did not get intoxicated, drinking a kind of mead into which a certain root was added by which the wine became strong and stinky."

DIEGO DE LANDA, BISHOP OF YUCATÁN, c.1560

The heritage of the Maya lives on in the people of the Yucatán, many of whom bear a striking resemblance to faces carved in stone on the monuments, or depicted in the rare surviving illustrated manuscripts and in frescoes – including those in many of the temples at Chichén Itzá. Maya nobles – ever fastidious about their appearance – exaggerated the facial features deemed desirable by flattening the skull between boards in infancy, and artificially creating a hooked nose with lumps of clay.

The Sacred Cenote, a well, was the focus of pilgrimage and religious devotion. Valuable offerings, such as jewelry and gold and silver ware, have been recovered from it, as well as female human bones. These seem to confirm the legend that, in times of drought, virgins were thrown into the well at dawn in honor of the rain god. A rope was reputed to be lowered into the well at noon so that survivors could be hauled to safety.

At Chichén Itzá, the rain god Chac Mool reclines before the ranks of stone columns beside the Temple of the Warriors. He may have played a significant role in the ritual of human sacrifice, which so appalled the Spanish conquistadors and their missionary priests. For a city in a region that was prone to drought, it was perhaps only a logical progression to adopt this god from the Toltecs, although in return for life-giving rain he exacted the price of countless human hearts.

OUTPOSTS
of the
BEYOND

THE VERY WORD OUTPOST HAS A DESOLATE SOUND. By their nature, outposts exist at the edge of a known world, with only the unexplored beyond. But outposts also have their own glamour, a call of the wild. It was this, coupled with lucrative trade, that attracted travelers to journey vast distances across inhospitable terrain, to find cities with fabulously exotic names, and to lay down routes that in their turn became famous.

Havana was born of the Spanish need for a port through which to siphon wealth from the Americas; and Samarkand of the necessity for staging posts along the Silk Road. Kathmandu, ringed by a natural fortress of high peaks, was hidden for centuries from all but the most determined travelers, while Kyoto was deliberately isolated by generations of inward-looking rulers. Shanghai, on the fringe of Asia, was the only city in China open to foreigners. And Bangkok, a glittering capital of temples, pagodas, and canals, was indescribably different from Western cities. Perhaps today, when travel is easy, these hard-won routes and exotic destinations retain a special fascination, for in their very names is the glory of the unknown, of what may lie beyond.

To Westerners, the Great Wall of China is the ultimate symbol of otherworldliness – a defensive bastion both repeling invaders and deterring visitors from entering the secretive nation beyond. The wall stretches some 4,000 miles (6,400 km).

Kathmandu

Hidden valley in the heart of Asia

On the night of January 15, 1934, the Nepalese capital Kathmandu was gripped by an earthquake. When the tremors stopped, one of the most beautiful and remote cities in the world was under rubble. The houses of small bricks with their heavily carved wooden windows and doors; the timber pagodas which echoed the shape of the Himalayan pine trees; the innumerable temples with their wind chimes, their statuary, their bells and gongs – all had been squeezed into oblivion by the surrounding fist of mountains.

Today, its medieval heart faithfully rebuilt and restored, Kathmandu can be reached by highway from India or by plane from almost anywhere in the world. Yet somehow the place known to its poets as Devbhumi (Home of the Gods) has preserved an elusive quality in the face of progress.

For millennia, the fertile Kathmandu valley lay cradled by the Mahabharat Lekh and Great Himalaya mountain ranges, inaccessible to all but the most determined travelers. Although, at around 4,300 feet (1,300 m), it was not high – compared to the spectacular peaks that surrounded it – trade developed slowly over difficult passes and dangerous terrain. The Kiratis, probably antecedents of today's Newar people, founded a kingdom in the valley as early as the eighth or seventh century B.C. In the third century A.D., Indo–Aryan Licchavis from India came to the area, bringing with them an elaborate caste system, a new set of deities, and great artistic skills.

Lying peacefully at the confluence of the Bishnumati and Bagmati rivers, in the western reaches of Kathmandu city, the Hindu Indreni Temple faces the Buddhist Bijeswari Temple across the water. This is the city's area of ghats – steps leading down to the river and used by Hindus for cremations and worship – and the riverbank is littered with temples and statues.

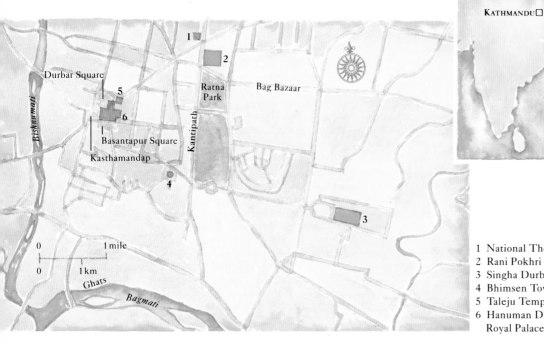

1 National Theater
2 Rani Pokhri
3 Singha Durbar
4 Bhimsen Tower
5 Taleju Temple
6 Hanuman Dhoka (Old Royal Palace)

As befits the capital of a Hindu country which has Buddhist, Tantric, and animist roots, the origins of Kathmandu are swathed in beautiful and complex legends. The Lord Buddha was born in the Nepalese lowlands, and Buddhists believe that the Kathmandu valley was once a turquoise lake. On it floated a lotus flower that gave off an entrancing blue light, a manifestation of Swayambhu, the Primordial Buddha. The devout were drawn to live and worship in caves along the lake's shore. So that he could worship more closely, Manjushri, a Chinese patriarch, sliced through the valley wall with his sword to drain the lake, and built a stupa (a shrine to Buddha) where the lotus had been. This became Swayambhunath – the Monkey Temple – which stands on a hill outside the city to this day.

In Hindu versions of the tale, Krishna hurls a thunderbolt at the lake, or Vishnu breaks the valley wall with his discus. The geological explanation is that the whole valley was once submerged under a lake of glacial ice which eventually melted. Whichever is true, the Bagmati River rushes down from the mountains on its way to feed the Ganges, grazing the sacred steps of the Pasupatinatha Temple and leaving the valley through the narrow slice of the Chobar Gorge. Beyond it, the Taudah Pond is reputed to be the home of Karkot Raja, king of the *naga* serpent gods, whose wriggling subjects are carved on the roofs of palaces and temples in the city.

Work really began on Swayambhunath in 460 B.C., and it set the pattern for a style of shrine that came to be known as the Kathmandu stupa. Under lines of fluttering prayer flags, some 300 steps curve up the hillside, patiently trodden by Tibetan monks and Buddhist pilgrims from across the world. The stupa itself, which protects the Divine Light of Swayambhu, has five important elements. Its base is ringed by 211 copper prayer wheels, spun by the pilgrims as they pass clockwise around the stupa; each spin of the wheel represents the Buddhist mantra *Om mani padme hum* (Hail, o jewel in the lotus). The solid, whitewashed dome represents the womb of the Lord Buddha's mother. On it are painted two eyes (the sun and moon) and a question mark (the flame of his knowledge). Thirteen diminishing rings, the thirteen steps to purity, lead up to the gold crown which signals the attainment of nirvana and the end of all sorrows.

Traditionally, almost all art in Nepal is religious: carved prayer wheels, intricately painted *thangkas* (prayer scrolls), bronze statues of the Hindu pantheon. The artists that came from India with the Licchavis were highly skilled and, in the sixth century, under the first of the Thakuri dynasties, a beautiful temple built from a sacred tree and known as Kasthamandap (the House of Wood) gave the city its name. It stands in Durbar Square, now a refuge for priests and the tutelary divinities of the royal family, and a home for sacrificial animals and flocks of sacred pigeons.

But the truly great flowering of art and architecture in Kathmandu came with the Newars, who built more than 2,500 temples and shrines across the valley. By the Middle Ages, the Malla kings had become the most powerful Newar dynasty; and under their control, the medieval Kathmandu that is there now came into being. The

Sunrise over the white stone steps of the Swayambhunath Temple is a tranquil affair. A matter of hours later, the peace will be shattered by children, tourists, monks, and pilgrims, as well as the hundreds of monkeys which give the edifice its other name, the Monkey Temple. Every surface of the temple is covered in monkeys. The traditional explanation for their presence is that the Chinese patriarch Manjushri cut his hair on this spot, and where it fell the hairs turned into trees and the lice into monkeys.

A Newar woman hangs out a newly washed piece of traditional homespun, or khadi, *to dry in the hot back streets of Kathmandu city. In winter, men and women alike swathe themselves in fine shawls of* pashmina – *the Nepali equivalent of cashmere – to keep out the Himalayan cold.*

squares and streets west of Kantipath – the "way of kings," which divides the old city from the new – bristle with Malla palaces and temples. They were the first to use wood and brick construction, with latticed wooden windows which lean out from the walls, carved doors, and high balconies, today stuffed with drying hay and maize. Two other cities, Patan and Bhakhtapur, rose to prominence in the valley, which was a trading crossroads between India, China, and Tibet.

Although the Newars – some 45 percent of the valley population – are Buddhist, the ruling classes in Nepal tend to be Hindu. The durbar (palace) of the Malla kings includes the sixteenth-century Hindu Taleju Temple, the main gate of which is guarded by the monkey god Hanuman, and the square is dotted with shrines to Ganesh and Shiva. Overlooking all is the vengeful gaze of Black Bhairab, a form of Shiva and the settler of disputes, streaked with red powder and yellow petals from numerous daily *pujas*, or prayer offerings. This statue was found outside Kathmandu in the seventeenth century, blocking one of the city's water sources, and was placed in the square, facing the court of justice. Once a year, on the Black Night of Dasain, the blood of sacrificed animals spurts onto his statue in appeasement.

The Mallas eventually became complacent, and by 1768 their era was at an end. The Shah Gorkhas, ambitious mountain rulers who had long looked enviously on the rich loam of the valley and its jewels of Kathmandu, Patan, and Bhakhtapur, conquered the three Malla kingdoms and founded what became the modern state of Nepal.

But the story does not end there. Prithvi Narayan Shah sealed the country's borders, a state of affairs which lasted for almost 200 years and increased the aura of mystery surrounding the small mountain kingdom. Overtures from the British were repelled, and Nepal garnered a reputation as a zone of peace, a buffer between the increasingly complex politics of India and China. Within the country, a powerful family of hereditary prime ministers, the Ranas, gained control over the royal family and began to build houses and palaces on a massive scale before they were overthrown. The borders were eventually opened and the monarchy restored in the early 1950s, ushering in a wave of Western flower children.

Nepal really entered the twentieth century in the 1970s, with an energetic program of road and airport building. But its capital city always had two identities – the ancient and the modern – and even today extraordinary anachronisms exist. The Milk Yogi – a holy guru who lives at Pasupatinatha – is still fed only on cow's milk throughout his life, and is considered to be an incarnation of Vishnu. And, like other cities in the valley, Kathmandu has its Kumari, or "living goddess," a virgin selected by a mysterious process of divination and sacred "tests" at the age of four or five, whose feet must never touch the floor and who must have the 32 features of beauty required for her role. Once a year, the king must kiss her feet and make a *puja* to guarantee an auspicious year. If she bleeds in any way – from losing a tooth or menstruation – her reign is over, and the search for another Kumari begins. In many ways, the ancient city of Kathmandu is as remote from the rest of the world as it ever was.

Exquisite carved facades abound in Kathmandu. Palaces and temples built by the Malla kings were richly decorated with legends and characters from the Hindu pantheon, and heavy latticed windows allowed women to look out into the streets without being seen.

Women in celebratory red clothes bathe in the waters of the Bagmati River from the steps of the Pasupatinatha Temple, as part of an annual ritual celebrating Tij. This festival takes place on the third day after the new moon of Bhadau, some time during late August or early September.

The painstaking detail of a thangka *– a religious painting on prepared and stiffened canvas – tells the life story of Buddha, progressing clockwise from the top right-hand corner. A genuine* thangka *(rather than one executed for the tourist market) adheres to strict religious principles of design and may take the artist hundreds of hours to complete.*

"Kathmandu is a name to conjure with — it has a restless magic in its very syllables."

PERCEVAL LONDON,
EARLY TWENTIETH CENTURY

Samarkand
Fabled city of the Silk Road

When the Mongol chieftain Tamerlane made the Silk Road town of Samarkand his capital in 1369, he turned a largely rubble-strewn ruin into a legend. From that time on, a mirage of azure domes, steepling minarets, palaces sleekly attired in sea-green and turquoise tiles glimmering within the mountainous depths of central Asia would seep into the imaginations and dreams of the West.

Samarkand became – and remains – a symbol of inaccessible Eastern mystique. European poets and dramatists, including Marlowe, Milton, Goethe, and Keats, dropped the city's magical name into their verse as a way of conjuring up Oriental exotica. James Elroy Flecker, for example, wrote "We travel not for trafficking alone; By hotter winds our fiery hearts are fanned; for lust of knowing what should not be known, We take the Golden Road to Samarkand."

Even today, Tamerlane's faded monuments retain their peacock colors and allure. The Bibi Khanum mosque, named after his favorite wife; the Gur-i-Mir tomb, where his body was laid to rest; and the great Registan Square all evoke the days when camel trains arrived bearing goods from all over Asia. In the shade of arches, merchants haggled over skins and linen from Russia, cinnamon and cloves from India, silks and diamonds from China, or Samarkand's own cornucopia of grapes, melons, pears, and other fruits.

Samarkand's origins go back some 5,000 years, making it one of the oldest cities in the world. According to tradition, it was founded by a semi-mythical king named Afrasayib. The ancient Greeks

Tamerlane's love of azure and turquoise is nowhere more apparent than in the exteriors of Samarkand's mosques, minarets, and madrassas. Terracotta tiles, which were carved and then glazed, and underglazed painted tiles combine with gold, faience, and mosaics to create a magical whole.

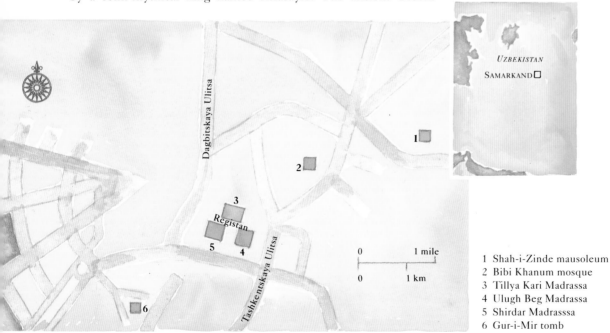

UZBEKISTAN

SAMARKAND ☐

0   1 mile

0   1 km

1 Shah-i-Zinde mausoleum
2 Bibi Khanum mosque
3 Tillya Kari Madrassa
4 Ulugh Beg Madrassa
5 Shirdar Madrasssa
6 Gur-i-Mir tomb

knew the city as Marakanda, and the Macedonian conqueror Alexander the Great entered it in 329 B.C.

In later centuries, the city came within the political orbit of the Chinese Empire. Then, during the early Middle Ages, Samarkand fell to the zealous armies of Islam, whose religious and cultural stamp the city and its people still bear. But disaster came in the early thirteenth century when Genghis Khan and his Mongol armies rampaged across Asia, conquering and destroying all that lay in their way. In the words of a contemporary chronicler, the Mongols "came, uprooted, burned, slew, despoiled, and departed." In 1220, the great Khan reached Samarkand and reduced it to rubble. It remained a ruin for the next 150 years.

Tamerlane was born in 1336 near Samarkand and took pride in claiming that he was descended from Genghis Khan. Like his ancestor, Tamerlane was powerful and ruthless. According to one chronicler, he loved "bold and valiant soldiers, by whose aid he opened the locks of terror, tore men to pieces like lions and over-turned mountains." He was tall and well built, with a ruddy complexion and long beard. He also had a lame right leg – which gave him the name Timur-i-Leng (Timur the Lame), from which Tamerlane is derived.

From every one of the cities that he conquered, Tamerlane culled the best craftsmen, scholars, and artists and sent them back to his capital. From Delhi in India and from Shiraz and Isfahan in Persia came potters, masons, sculptors, and mosaicists. And these men set about creating a city worthy of a great conqueror. They made bricks from desert sand mixed with chopped straw, camel urine, and clay. They shifted stone slabs with the help of Indian elephants. Little by little, the city rose like a phoenix from the rubble of Genghis Khan's depredations.

Perhaps the greatest structure was the Gur-i-Mir, a huge mausoleum built for Tamerlane's favorite grandson and which later housed his own body. The mausoleum was – and is – topped by an immense ribbed dome and sheathed in brilliant azure and turquoise glazed tiles. Below this swelling beacon of ultramarine, a band of white letters in flowing Arabic Kufic script proclaims "God is immortality" around the dome's supporting drum. Inside the mausoleum lie commemorative tombstones – the bodies were actually laid to rest in the crypt below.

The mosque of Bibi Khanum, Tamerlane's favorite wife and a daughter of the Chinese emperor, was started on May 11, 1399, a day deemed auspicious by astrologers. For five frenetic years, 200 master craftsmen, 500 laborers, and 95 elephants toiled away, raising the mosque by the sweat of their brows.

Only the giant ribs and bones of the mosque complex remain; but its dome and 60-foot (18-m) portal are still one of the great sights of the city. One chronicler wrote that the dome "would have been unique had it not been for the heavens, and unique would have been its portal had it not been for the Milky Way."

According to legend, the mosque's architect, a Persian from Meshed, bribed Bibi Khanum for a kiss, whose telltale imprint on

The first madrassa built on the Registan was that of Ulugh Beg, completed in 1420. The second, the Shirdar (lion-bearing) Madrassa, was finished in 1636, ten years before work began on the third, the Tillya Kari – literally "decorated with gold" – Madrassa (right), which opens onto the northern side of the square.

The tchai-khana, or "tea shop," is an essential part of any central Asian market. It has been estimated that, at the height of Samarkand's importance as a market, half the goods traded in Asia passed through the city.

her cheek was reported to Tamerlane. Chased by guards up to the pinnacle of the mosque's loftiest minaret, the architect miraculously sprouted wings and flew off back to Meshed.

Nor was Samarkand embellished simply with bricks and mortar. On the city's outskirts, Tamerlane created a series of garden retreats with alluring names such as the Bagh-i-Dilgusha (garden of the heart's delight) and Bagh-i-Behisht (garden of paradise). Persian and Iraqi craftsmen adorned the walls' exteriors with faience from Kashan. And Syrian architects and craftsmen paved the walls and grounds with such precise intricate designs that they were compared to the ebony and ivory creations of marquetry workers. The gardens enclosed palaces and kiosks whose walls were sometimes covered by silk hangings ornamented with spangles of silver-plate gilt, each spangle set with an emerald, pearl, or other gem.

Tamerlane died in 1405, not in battle but having become ill on his way to invade China. His body was brought back to Samarkand, the city that he had created. Just before he died, he had murmured to his hushed attendants: "Only a stone, and my name on it." But the slab that his grandson Ulugh Beg procured for his body was the world's largest block of dark green jade, which he had carted all the way from Chinese Turkestan. Tamerlane's body was duly laid to rest; and a legend arose that if the body was ever disturbed from its tomb, the world would suffer a disaster greater than any caused by Tamerlane himself. In 1941 a Russian scientist was given permission to exhume and examine the body. On June 22, Tamerlane's skull, after more than 500 years of darkness, greeted a bevy of onlookers. On the same day, Germany invaded Russia.

After Tamerlane's death, a power struggle ensued; it lasted for four years until his youngest son Shah Rukh took control of the empire, making Herat in Persia his capital and installing his son, Ulugh Beg, as governor of Samarkand. In 1447, Ulugh Beg assumed the throne. A scientist with a photographic memory, the new ruler continued to embellish Samarkand. Perhaps his most notable monument was a three-story astronomical observatory set on a hill outside the city. Here, with the help of a massive double sextant mounted on a bronze track, Ulugh Beg plotted the positions of 1,018 stars as well as the movements of the sun, moon, and planets. From this data, he produced the Zij-i-Gurkani, the world's first precise star map.

With the assassination of Ulugh Beg in 1449, Samarkand began to decline. In the early sixteenth century, a Turco-Mongol tribal confederation known as the Uzbeks took control of the city. In the eighteenth century, with new European powers on the world stage which had new trade routes and were interested in different commodities, Samarkand's decline accelerated. From about 1720, it was uninhabited for 50 years.

In the late nineteenth century, the Russians took control of the city, established a railroad there, and made it capital of Uzbekistan. Today travelers from the West take the Golden Road to Samarkand, to witness for themselves what was once an exotic rumor, an imagined realm evoked in lines of poetry, and gaze upon a dream of turquoise that Tamerlane made a reality.

Sharp light brings into play the brilliant tilework of the three madrassas, or religious colleges, that enclose the once bustling inner space of Samarkand's Registan.

Ulugh Beg is reputed to have taught mathematics in the madrassa which bears his name and which attracted students from all over Asia. About 100 were housed in two-story dormitories, some of which are still visible.

On a visit to Samarkand in 1888, Britain's Lord Curzon declared: "I know of nothing in the East approaching it in massive simplicity and grandeur and nothing in Europe."

Impressed by the dome which topped the Umayyad mosque in Damascus, Tamerlane, a keen architect himself, had it copied for his magnificent tomb, the Gur-i-Mir. The style, which was also used by his successors, was highly influential and from Samarkand found its way north into Russia and south into India.

The Silk Road

In the first century B.C., a trade route began to flourish across the remote desert and vast mountain wastelands of Asia. It became increasingly busy and lucrative as both the Han dynasty in China and the Roman Empire reached their apogees some 300 years later. It was named the Silk Road after the most famous product to travel its length.

Silk was the world's most luxurious cloth, prized by the Romans (who could only guess how it was made), but it was not the only product traded along the road. Spices, lacquerware, fine porcelain, precious woods, tortoiseshell, and gemstones moved westward, in return for gold, silver, glass, pearls, coral, woolens, and linen. More important still was the transportation of technologies and ideas. The Chinese invented paper made from pulp, printing, gunpowder, and the magnetic compass, all of which filtered through to the West, where they were further developed.

Buddhism spread along the Silk Road from India to China, and Chinese Buddhists in turn traveled westward along the road as pilgrims. From the fourth to the tenth centuries A.D., Dunhuang was a major Buddhist center, its honeycomb of caves decorated with thousands of votive statues and murals. After the seventh century, Islam spread eastward along the route, so great Islamic centers of learning grew up at important trading cities such as Khiva, Samarkand, and Tashkent.

Although it is commonly referred to as the Silk Road, there was not just one route but many, and their courses changed with

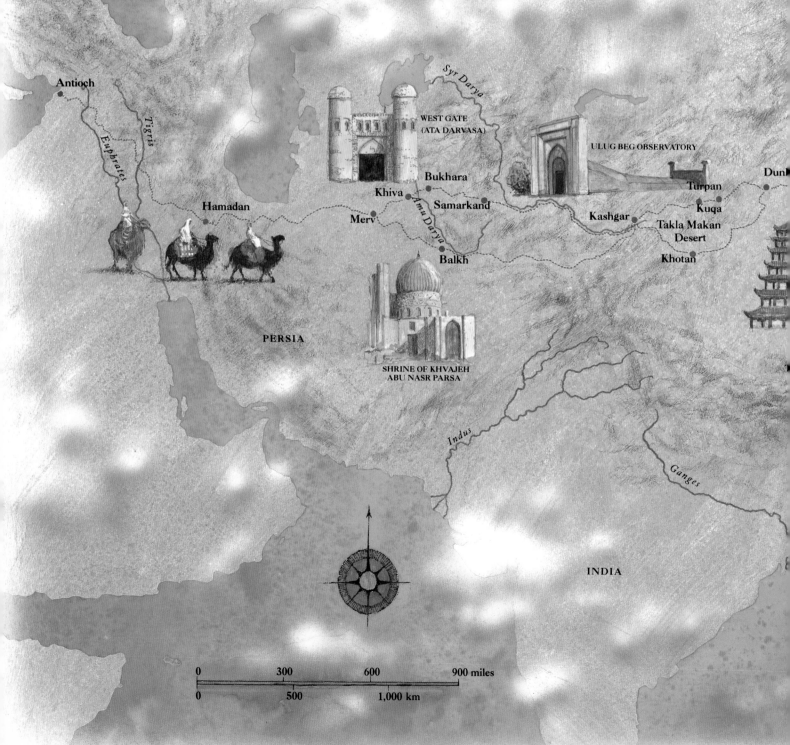

Antioch

Tigris

Euphrates

Syr Darya

WEST GATE
(ATA DARVASA)

ULUG BEG OBSERVATORY

Dun

Bukhara

Turpan

Khiva

Samarkand

Kuqa

Hamadan

Amu Darya

Kashgar

Merv

Takla Makan
Desert

Khotan

Balkh

PERSIA

SHRINE OF KHVAJEH
ABU NASR PARSA

Indus

Ganges

INDIA

0	300	600	900 miles
0	500	1,000 km	

the political and economic climates of the regions they crossed. Few traded along the whole length of the route; instead, goods passed through the hands of a series of intermediaries, along a chain of cities and oasis towns from the Mediterranean coast to the Chinese capital Xi'an. Cities such as Kashgar became cultural melting pots.

Asia attained its greatest stability during the Mongol Empire of the thirteenth century, when almost the entire route was under the authority of a single power. It was during this period that the most famous of the few Europeans to travel the route, Venetian merchant Marco Polo, made his 24-year-long voyage to the East, between 1271 and 1295.

The disintegration the Mongol Empire in the fifteenth century disrupted the flow of goods across Asia, and it was only then that Europeans considered investigating sea routes to the Far East. Portuguese ships – equipped with magnetic compasses and weapons charged with gunpowder – reached China in 1515, paving the way for a rapid growth in sea trade that rendered the Silk Road redundant. The trading centers, oases, caravanserais, Buddhist monasteries, and Chinese imperial gateways were gradually swallowed by the vastness of the inhospitable landscape that surrounded them.

Only in recent years have these places reawakened to a growth of traffic, this time of travelers inspired by the notions conjured by the very name Silk Road. Since 1992 – when the railroad was completed – it has been possible to travel between Samarkand and Xi'an by luxury train, or by one of the buses which ply the mountain passes and desert plains. Once again, the lure of the Silk Road draws travelers from all over the world, exchanging stories and ideas in the ancient tradition of the world's greatest highway.

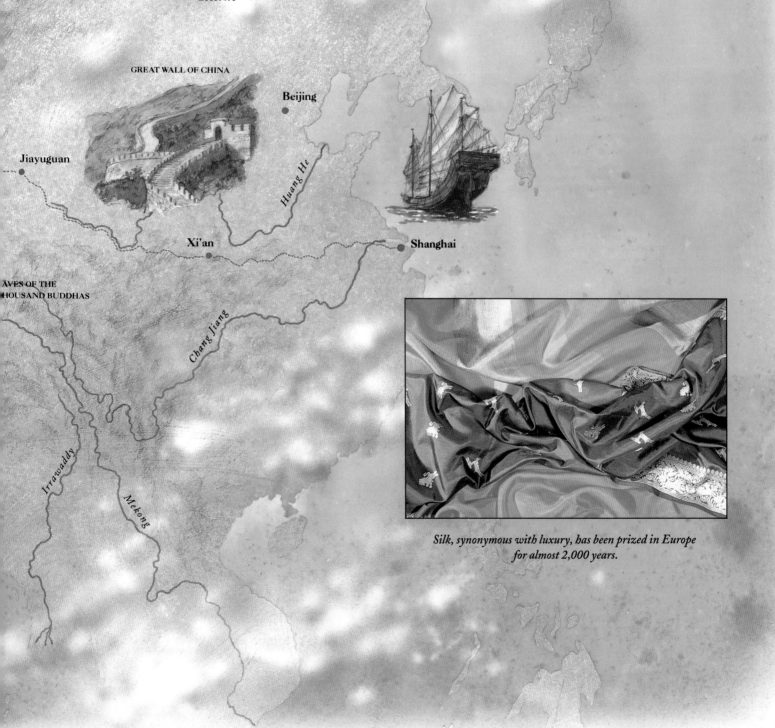

CHINA

GREAT WALL OF CHINA

Jiayuguan

Beijing

Huang He

Xi'an

Shanghai

AVES OF THE
HOUSAND BUDDHAS

Chang Jiang

Irrawaddy

Mekong

Silk, synonymous with luxury, has been prized in Europe for almost 2,000 years.

Bangkok

Waterborne capital of Siam

In the early nineteenth century, visitors to Bangkok had to break their journey in the deep blue waters of the Gulf of Siam. Anchoring by the sandbank which guarded the mouth of the Chao Phraya river, they awaited permission to enter the city. Once it was granted, they transferred to lighters for the 25-mile (40-km) trip upstream, threading their way through the delta among strings of teak barges laden with rice, sand, and charcoal, farmers' boats full of vegetables and livestock, and long-tailed ferries swooping passengers to the city and back. And they waited for their first glimpse of the roofs and pagodas of Bangkok, the glittering capital of Siam (present-day Thailand).

Bangkok was conceived in the 1770s as a great capital by King Rama I, a fitting riposte to the Burmese, who had sacked the old capital Ayutthaya in 1767. The inherent problems of its site on the tidal plain between Ayutthaya and the Gulf were solved by the cutting of *khlongs*, or canals, as a means of transportation and a method of drainage. On the *khlongs* people lived, worked, traded, and traveled. The Chao Phraya (River of Kings) was the mightiest thoroughfare of all, carving its way between the two sides of the city, Thon Buri and Krung Thep, and lined with spectacular houses, palaces, and temples.

The old city was guarded on three sides by the river, and to the east by the swampland known to locals as the Sea of Mud. Along with Wat Po, or the Grand Palace, it was protected by a 4½-mile (7.5-km) wall,

In the floating market at Damnoensaduak, vegetable-laden barges poled by women wearing wide trousers and curved hats are the last remnants of a city life that once revolved around the water. On the khlongs, *away from the busy city streets, families still live in houses of teak and atap thatch, which stand on pontoons made of bamboo stems and areca palms.*

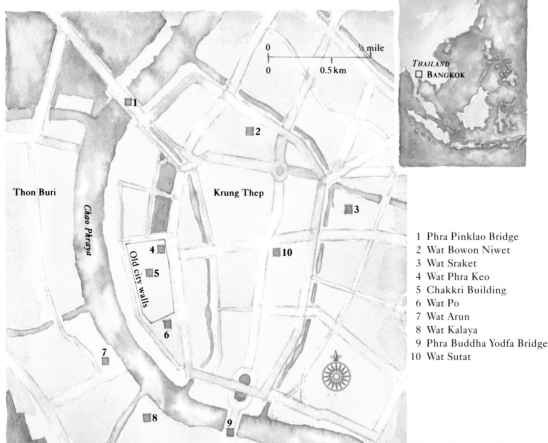

THAILAND
□ BANGKOK

Thon Buri

Krung Thep

Chao Phraya

Old city walls

1 Phra Pinklao Bridge
2 Wat Bowon Niwet
3 Wat Sraket
4 Wat Phra Keo
5 Chakkri Building
6 Wat Po
7 Wat Arun
8 Wat Kalaya
9 Phra Buddha Yodfa Bridge
10 Wat Sutat

which bristled with 63 gates and 15 forts. Secure in their capital, the Siamese succeeded in keeping the Burmese at bay and controlling the delta traffic, so that their country became a rare haven of peace.

Bangkok has suffered more than most cities from the depredations of motor traffic. The Thais had no indigenous wheeled transportation, and the first rickshaws and bicycles were imported. With the advent of the car, hundreds of *khlongs* were filled in and surfaced as roads, changing the character of the city and filling the cramped streets with fumes. Even so, Bangkok is steeped in the past: a spirit house seen through the glitter of traffic; barges poled through floating markets; the elegant colonial facades of the Portuguese and French embassies or the stately Oriental Hotel, where Joseph Conrad, Somerset Maugham, and Noël Coward stayed and marveled at what they saw.

To capture that past, it is necessary to journey back in time some 150 years, to the days when the city awoke to the sonorous beating of gongs from a turret of the Regent's Palace and took to the *khlongs* for the day's business. Houseboats from outside the city floated into Bangkok to sell sugar cane and mangosteens, coconuts, and durians. Officials emerged in the cool of the night to conduct their business around the Grand Palace. The palace itself, home to the Siamese court, was a city within a city, with its own stores and police force and an inner sanctum for 3,000 wives, consorts, dowagers, and children (the last inhabitant died as recently as the early 1960s).

To Westerners, Bangkok was a world of extraordinary beauty and strangeness; of fighting fish and painted kites, of exquisite dancers and gilded temples, of elaborate and idolatrous worship. Stories were told of the sacred white elephants found in the northern jungles and brought to Bangkok to be feted and treated like kings, or the painstaking rituals surrounding the severing of a child's topknot as a mark of adulthood. Small wonder, then, that *The King & I*, Anna Leonowen's story of her time as a governess at the court of King Rama IV, was hugely popular outside Siam.

All the Rama kings were great builders of wats, the Buddhist temple complexes which serve as places of worship, monasteries, and community centers, and there are more than 400 of them dotted across Bangkok. The temple in the palace at Wat Po, for example, is both a center of traditional education and home to the 150-foot (46-m) long Reclining Buddha. Chinese influence can be seen in the brilliant tiles, gilt decoration, and garish mosaics which cover the walls and roofs, and in their distinctive curving gables, decorated with double *naga* snakes and golden finials, known as *chofas*.

As the modern city of Bangkok goes about its daily business, the spiritual is never far away. Offerings of jasmine petals and incense are left every day in the spirit houses, perched on their posts beside the river. Taxi drivers raise their hands, palms together, when they reach a crossroads. Every February, the Royal Field is aswoop with male kites known as *chulas*, trying to snare the smaller, nimbler females, or *pukpaos*. And, during the eleventh lunar month, the river and *khlongs* sparkle with miniature boats shaped like lotus blossoms, each with its own candle and incense offering, celebrating the rice festival of *Loy Krathong*. At heart, Bangkok is still a city of water.

Ornate demon and monkey statues, clad in the jeweled headdresses and elaborate costumes worn to this day by traditional Thai dancers, support a masonry roof at Wat Phra Keo.

The gilded spires of Wat Phra Keo, home to the statue of the Emerald Buddha, tower above distinctive nested gables and curling finials. The wat is alive with chimes and mythical animal statues, overstudded with mirrors and gold, as befits the spiritual center of the nation.

Discovered when lightning struck an ancient stupa in northern Thailand in 1434, the priceless statue was placed in Wat Phra Keo when Bangkok was founded. At the beginning of every season, the king still visits the Buddha – which is actually made of jade – to change its robes.

Some of Bangkok's wats are fabulously endowed with gold leaf, teak, mother-of-pearl, black lacquer, and precious stones, fitting surroundings for the images of Buddha they hold.

In the Wat Po temple complex, the Golden Buddha stares serenely over offerings laid before him. Idols were first modeled in wax, then covered in plaster and clipped in brass. They did not become sacred until the eyes and precious outer layer were added.

"It makes you laugh with delight to think that anything so fantastic could exist on this sombre earth."

WILLIAM SOMERSET MAUGHAM,
ON THE WATS OF BANGKOK

Kyoto
Capital of peace and tranquillity

Its cherry blossom, Zen gardens, and hundreds of glorious temples tempt the belief that Kyoto, for more than 1,000 years the imperial capital of Japan, has had a peaceful history. Instead it has been frequently ravaged by fire, earthquake, and civil war, many of its finest buildings have been destroyed, restored, and destroyed again; and for centuries it was at the heart of political intrigue and upheaval. But, surrounded by temple-clad hills and miraculously unscarred by World War II, it remains Japan's most beautiful city.

Created as the imperial capital on the orders of Emperor Kammu, who moved his court here in 794, Kyoto – then known as Heian-kyo, "the capital of peace and tranquillity" – was conceived on a grid system, following the model of major Chinese cities. In the center of the northern boundary was the great Imperial Palace, a city within a city, covering some 400 acres (160 hectares) and containing, in addition to the imperial residences, government buildings, treasuries, store-houses, and barracks. There was no temple in the palace itself. Indeed, Kammu deliberately had only one temple built in the entire city as a reaction against the rising power of the Buddhist monks in his previous capital, Nara.

The present palace was rebuilt after a fire in 1855, but is a faithful reproduction of the original. In the Hall of Ceremonies stands the emperor's throne, topped by an octagonal canopy which bears a phoenix and the imperial insignia. The empress sat on a smaller throne, to the right of the emperor. Entrance to the palace was

In common with many of Kyoto's temples, the Daigoji is eclipsed by the beauty of its garden, typical of the landscaping which abounds in Kyoto. The pagoda itself is one of the oldest in the city, dating from 951.

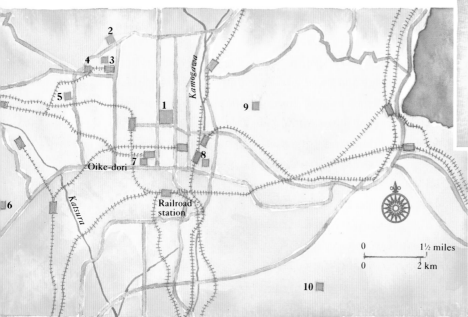

1 Imperial Palace
2 Daitokuji Temple
3 Golden Pavilion
  (Kinkakuji)
4 Ryoanji Temple
5 Ninnaji Temple
6 Moss Temple (Saihoji)
7 Nijo Castle
8 Kiyomizu Temple
9 Silver Pavilion
  (Ginkakuji)
10 Daigoji Temple

subject to strict protocol: one gate was reserved for the exclusive use of the emperor, another for the empress and dowager empress, others for junior wives and lesser members of the royal family and court. Even today, visitors may enter the palace only through the West Gate.

Kammu was the last emperor for centuries genuinely to rule Japan. Although the emperor remained titular head and continued to claim descent from the gods, power fell increasingly into the hands of the nobility, in particular the Fujiwara family, who infiltrated the government, acquired vast estates, accumulated great wealth, and extended their influence by marrying their daughters into the imperial family. The theory was that generations of emperors would feel unswerving loyalty to their Fujiwara fathers-in-law or grandfathers; in practice, the Fujiwaras were regents – and effective rulers – of Japan for more than 300 years.

During the Fujiwara period, Japanese arts and culture flourished. The great work of Japanese literature, *The Tale of Genji* – relating the accomplishments of a courtier in the art of courtly love – dates from the early years of the eleventh century. And poetry, calligraphy, and papermaking all reached great heights under Fujiwara influence. These years also saw the emergence of the warrior class, the shoguns and samurai who played a crucial role in later Japanese history.

Kammu's concern in restricting the number of temples had been to control the power of the monks, but Buddhism was never suppressed. One of Kyoto's greatest temples is a seventeenth-century reconstruction of a building begun in 798. Kiyomizu, built on a steep hill to the east of the city center, is dedicated to the eleven-headed goddess of mercy, Kannon, whose benevolence could ease the pains of childbirth. The temple's main hall is supported by 139 pillars, and the view from its veranda so spectacular that it gave rise to a proverb: having the courage to jump from the veranda of Kiyomizu means being bold enough to undertake a new and risky venture.

Kyoto's Golden Pavilion (Kinkakuji) and Silver Pavilion (Ginka-kuji) were constructed as retirement villas for shoguns who ruled Japan in all but name in the fourteenth and fifteenth centuries. Like many such villas, they were converted into temples after the death of their owners. Ginkakuji was built for Yoshimasa Ashikaga, who devoted so much time to such cultural arts as moongazing and tea drinking that – despite its name – he never carried out his intention of covering the building with silver. His great legacy is the temple's tearoom, believed to be the oldest in Japan: rooms used for the traditional tea ceremony are still based on this design.

The tea ceremony is the incarnation of the concept of *wabi* – meaning "impoverished" or "lonely" – which arose from Zen Buddhist thinking. It brought simplicity and restraint into fashion, emphasizing the importance of grace and thoughtfulness in the most mundane acts. Host and guests are deemed to participate equally in the ceremony, sharing an esthetic experience in a carefully cultivated atmosphere.

Zen exerted a powerful influence on many aspects of Japanese culture, not least in landscape gardening. A garden could incorporate such traditional features as water – as at the Golden Pavilion – trees, shrubs, and bridges, but was created according to strict principles of

"For 1,000 years Kyoto served as the capital, the jewel case of Japan, and the Japanese adorned its precincts with the finest that their minds, hands and souls could conjure."

J.D. BISIGNANI, 1983

Taizoin Temple combines a dry-stone garden and cherry blossom – the twin emblems of beauty and tranquillity that make Kyoto in spring the most romantic city in Japan and one of the most beautiful in the world.

Shimmering with gold leaf, the Golden Pavilion extends out over the lake, so that it is reflected in its peaceful waters – a design feature intended to symbolize the building's position halfway between heaven and earth. The Golden Pavilion was destroyed several times by fire, and the present building, although a faithful replica of the original, dates only from 1955.

harmony and taste to give the impression that it had occurred naturally. The greatest Zen landscape gardener was the monk Muso Soseki (1275–1351), who spent his early years wandering Japan in search of enlightenment. In the course of his travels, he founded many small temples with gardens that made the most of natural features. Kyoto's Moss Temple (Saihoji), where he spent his old age, is his masterpiece, a lush green lakeside park composed almost entirely of moss.

Very different is the Zen dry-stone garden, *kare sansui*, of which the finest example is at the temple of Ryoanji. A layer of white gravel, representing water, is broken up by fifteen rocks, carefully positioned in groups to give a visual balance and to convey to the observer the sense of infinity and detachment which is an integral part of Zen. In Buddhist thinking, fifteen denotes completeness, and it is significant that only with an uninterrupted view of the entire garden are all fifteen rocks visible – there are many angles from which one or more of the stones are hidden. And in the dry-stone garden at Daisen-in, part of the Daitokuji Temple complex, the gravel is replaced by sand which, like water, flows around rocks, creates waterfalls, and passes under a bridge. It is said to represent the course of life passing through the unchanging aspects of Nature.

One of Kyoto's loveliest gardens is the one at Nijo Castle – a combination of water, plants, and eye-catching rocks. Its deciduous trees are a recent addition, however: the seventeenth-century shogun for whom the castle was built, Ieyasu Tokugawa, considered dead leaves an unwelcome reminder of the transitory nature of life. A short walk from the Imperial Palace, Nijo is ostentatious and luxurious, designed to make it clear to emperor and people alike who was really in charge in Kyoto. The stone walls and moat which constitute the castle's defenses are the only modest touches, suggesting that Tokugawa knew his political and military position to be unassailable.

Within the building, concealed rooms allowed the shogun's agents to keep an eye and ear open for potential treachery, and as in several other important buildings in Kyoto, the floors were designed to squeak so that no intruder could approach undetected. The wall paintings in the castle are the work of the Kano School, which dominated the Japanese visual arts for eight generations from the mid-fifteenth century. Under their influence, non-religious subjects were acceptable for the first time. The Kano artists drew their subjects from nature, mainly landscapes and animals. When the work was for palaces and wealthy temples, as was often the case, the painting might be laid over a background of gold leaf.

But even all the opulence of Nijo did not encourage the ruling shoguns to spend much time there, and it quickly fell into disrepair. Only in the nineteenth century, when the shoguns' power was decreasing and they were forced into negotiations with the emperor, did they once more take up residence. It was at Nijo that the last shogun, Keiki Tokugawa, resigned in 1868 and that the imperial decree ending 264 years of shogunate rule was issued.

On the Meiji restoration which followed this decree, the court and seat of government were moved to Tokyo. Politically, Kyoto sank into insignificance, but culturally, it remains the center of Japan.

In the Zen garden, stones are often used to indicate life's ebb and flow. The word "Zen" means meditation in Japanese, and the Zen garden was designed as a work of art for the thoughtful visitor to contemplate.

"Kyoto's beauty is elusive and has to be sought out with patience and forethought ... the best of what Kyoto has to offer is often small in scale and of a delicacy that the encroachment of raucous modernity seems always to underline, and sometimes enhance."

ALAN BOOTH, 1991

Beautiful decorated screens – shoji – serve as room dividers in many of Kyoto's temples and palaces, as they do in traditional Japanese homes. Those in Ryoanji Temple are adorned with natural subjects, motifs introduced by the Kano School.

Ninnaji Temple was built as a palace for Emperor Omuro in the ninth century, but none of the original buildings remain. The current complex is seventeenth century, with the Main Hall, a national treasure, housing the Amida Buddha. The gardens are particularly beautiful at the beginning of April, when the cherry blossom – the symbol of romance in Japanese theater – is at its most abundant.

The Trans-Siberian Railway

Some 5,900 miles (9,500 km) long, the rail journey from Moscow to Vladivostok takes eight days and crosses eight time zones. Conditions aboard are not luxurious – small, four-berthed cabins, basic food, no alcohol – although a steaming samovar at the end of each carriage provides a constant supply of hot water for tea or coffee. The main reason for undertaking the trip is simply that it is there, the world's longest train journey across some of the world's last great wildernesses.

Construction of the railroad began simultaneously from Vladivostok and Moscow in 1891, on the orders of Tsar Alexander III, and the link was completed in 1916. It is a remarkable achievement, built largely on permafrost and in climatic conditions which made work impossible for eight months a year. As a transporter of freight, the railroad is one of the world's busiest, with trains sometimes running as frequently as every three minutes in western Siberia. The passenger train, the *Rossiya*, or "Russia," runs once a day every day of the year, although only two a week go all the way to Vladivostok – the rest stop thirteen hours short, at Krasnoyarsk.

From Moscow, the train takes more than a day to travel the 1,104 miles (1,777 km) to the point in the Urals, marked by an obelisk,

ST. BASIL'S CATHEDRAL

Moscow

Nizhniy Novgorod

TRINITY MONASTERY OF ST. SERGIUS, ZAGORSK

Kazan

Perm

Volga

Yekaterinburg

Ob

Irtysh

Omsk

STEEL BRIDGE OVER THE OB

Novosibirsk

CASPIAN SEA

0   200   400 miles

0   300   600 km

where Europe ends and Asia begins. And beyond lies Siberia. The first Asian city on route is Yekaterinburg, where the Russian royal family was executed in 1918.

Western Siberia is flat, marshy, and almost devoid of vegetation, but soon the railroad climbs on to the Central Siberian Platform and enters the vast forests of the taiga. Most are coniferous, although there are areas to the east where deciduous birch and larch predominate. Small and widely spaced, the trees battle for life against infertile soil and poor drainage.

Four days after leaving Moscow, the railroad reaches Irkutsk, "the pearl of Siberia," close to the shores of the world's deepest freshwater lake. With a maximum depth of 5,712 feet (1,741 m), Lake Baikal contains one-fifth of the world's fresh surface water.

Rivers and river systems also abound in Siberia. The longest river is the Lena, which marks the boundary between the Central Siberian Platform and the Eastern Uplands, and flows for 2,670 miles (4,300 km) north and east from Lake Baikal to the Arctic Ocean. Longer still is the Ob–Irtysh, which

at 3,362 miles (5,410 km) is only a little shorter than the Mississippi–Missouri. After Lake Baikal, the train enters the valley of the Amur River where, protected from the hostile weather by their long, dense coats and layers of fat, the world's last 200 Siberian tigers may survive.

Journey's end is Vladivostok, long forbidden to Westerners because of its strategic significance: the rail link was reopened only in 1991. Here ice-breakers keep the harbor open throughout the winter, battling, like the railroad, against the vicissitudes of Nature.

The railway became an enduring symbol of human power over Nature.

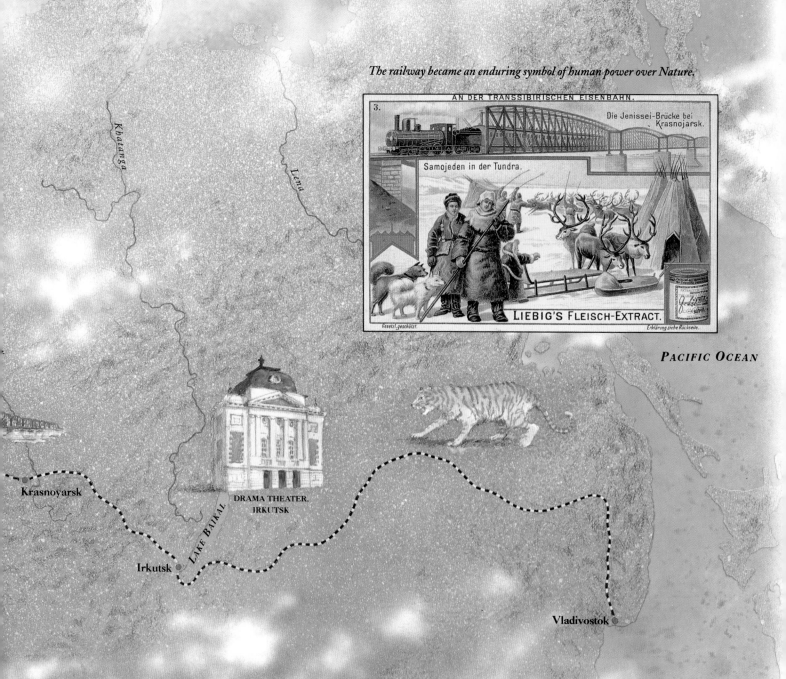

PACIFIC OCEAN

Krasnoyarsk

DRAMA THEATER.
IRKUTSK

LAKE BAIKAL

Irkutsk

Vladivostok

Shanghai

Meeting place of East and West

Early in the morning, as mighty cargo ships hoot from the harbor downriver and the traffic begins to build along the Bund, hundreds of Shanghai residents begin to make the slow, graceful movements of shadow boxing in parks across the city. Shops and stalls produce breakfast for the office workers. Tourists begin their day with a visit to the Peace Hotel and a stroll beside the Huang P'u River. The mood of the city, like the weather, seems mild.

Shanghai's position on the Huang P'u – a tributary of the Chang Jiang – halfway down the east coast of China, makes it a natural port and trading spot. Even by the eighteenth century, it had attracted the interest of Western powers, who had never been allowed a base in China. After the Opium Wars of 1840–42, the victorious British moved into the city and established a concession by force; they were followed five years later by the French. Foreign money poured in, factories were built, laborers arrived in search of work, and the shipping industry boomed. The population expanded from 50,000 in the mid-nineteenth century to just under one million at the start of the twentieth, of whom more than 60,000 were foreigners.

Suddenly it was the most fashionable place in Asia. The Bund was lined with gigantic buildings representing the great business names of the Orient: Jardine & Matheson, Sassoons, and the Chase Manhattan Bank. Junks, steamers, and oceangoing ships poured into

The magnificent floodlit facades of 1920s buildings line the Bund, Shanghai's most famous thoroughfare, which looks out over the Huang P'u River. When Shanghai – literally meaning "going up to the sea" – was the greatest port in China, the Bund – from an Anglo-Indian word for "muddy banks" – was a symbol of Western decadence.

CHINA

SHANGHAI

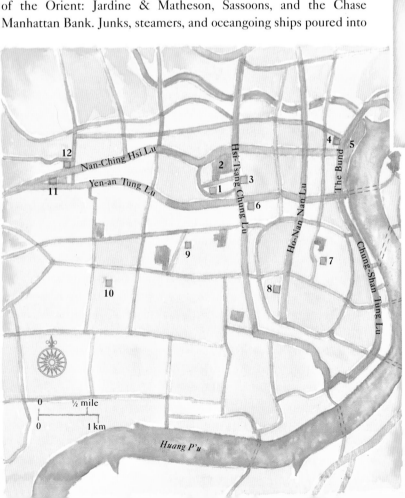

1 Renmin (People's) Square
2 Renmin (People's) Park
3 Workers' Cultural Palace
4 Huang P'u Park
5 Peace Hotel
6 Youth Palace
7 Yu Garden
8 Site of first Communist Party meeting
9 Former Temple of Confucius
10 Culture Square
11 Municipal Children's Palace
12 Ching-an Temple

and out of the harbor, loading goods from thousands of godowns, or warehouses, in the docks. With money came decadence, as Shanghai embraced the capitalist way of life.

In the 1920s and '30s, the dome of the Hongkong & Shanghai Bank building was home to the RAF Club and its legendary excesses. Today's Dongfeng Hotel was once the exclusive Shanghai Club. Western men and women drank and danced the nights away in clubs like Delmonte's Casino, Roxy's, and the Lido. The city had taller buildings, more cinemas, and better cars than anywhere else in Asia. Each concession had its own laws, independent of Chinese regulations, and was patrolled by its own soldiers. This was the Shanghai described by J.G. Ballard in *Empire of the Sun*, as "This electric and lurid city, more exciting than any other in the world."

Behind all the frivolity, however, was a darker side. A visit to the French concession today is like a walk through Shanghai's history. The French licensed prostitution and gambling, and the concession became a natural magnet for black marketeers, protection racketeers, opium dealers, and pimps. Most activities were controlled by Shanghai's legendary gangs, which became increasingly involved in the suppression of early communist uprisings on behalf of the nationalist Kuomintang government.

The first meeting of the Chinese Communist Party was convened in the French concession in 1921, and one of its first speakers – Mao Zedong – walked there from his room nearby. Like many Chinese, he was disgusted by the corruption that had come with Western involvement in national affairs, and with the factories – often using child labor – which generated vast wealth for foreign governments. Shanghai, with its huge new population, harsh conditions, and close proximity to foreign powers, became a hotbed of radical politics.

When the communists came to power in 1949, they made Shanghai a showcase, dispatching people to the country to work the land, and improving workers' rights and housing conditions. But the city also became headquarters of Mao's personality cult and of the dogmatic communism espoused by his wife and her "Gang of Four." It was the engine of the Cultural Revolution of the 1960s, when the youthful Red Guard killed and imprisoned thousands of artists, intellectuals, and liberals in the name of communism and started the "revolutionary committees" that controlled Chinese life.

What little there was of Shanghai's culture was largely destroyed by the Red Guard. Today the city has come full circle and is once again a mighty trading entity with foreign investment at an all-time high, but the landmarks to its past are few and far between: the Bund with its Peace Hotel and Customs House still emblazoned with a red star; the Temple of the Jade Buddha, marooned in the suburbs just as it was spiritually marooned in communist days; the Old City with its narrow cobbled streets and washing hanging on bamboo poles; a few remnants of the buildings which housed brothels and nightclubs; a number of European suburban villas on the way out to the zoo. They are memories treasured more by foreigners than by residents. The citizens of Shanghai are on their way to building another city of dreams, and this time it belongs to China.

A string of red silk lanterns hangs outside a building with perfect Art Deco detailing, for the benefit of today's tourists. Earlier this century, red lanterns – each with a prostitute's name on it – were hung outside the "singsong houses" to attract foreign sailors.

Bound for the open sea, a traditional Chinese junk heads out of Shanghai's colossal harbor. The sight of a junk used to strike terror into the hearts of foreign sailors for, in the days when Shanghai was the wealthy entrepôt of eastern Asia, the ribbed sails and curved prows meant only one thing: piracy.

Still water holds a perfect reflection of the tea house at Yuyuan. Tea houses, with their traditional architecture and pagoda-style tiled roofs, were once the preserve of the rich. Tea ceremonies could take days, using exquisite porcelain utensils much sought after in the West, and the tea consumed was virtually priceless.

Havana

Treasure house of the Americas

With crumbling ocher plasterwork, peeling shutters, storm-dampened cobbled patios, and gap-toothed wrought-iron balconies, the colonial backwaters of Old Havana still excite a nostalgia, tinged with melancholy, for bygone days when time hung more heavily – days of lace and carriages, oil lamps and pomanders, Sunday prayer and whispered conversation behind flickering fans. For several decades, Fidel Castro's government had more pressing concerns than the restoration of the colonial past, and Old Havana gradually faded under the depredations of the relentless tropical climate. But in 1982 it was designated a World Heritage Site by UNESCO; slowly but surely, the historic city center is beginning to re-emerge and claim its place as one of the great treasures of the Americas.

Havana was conceived not simply as a town, but also as a statement – an expression of Spanish might, of Christianity, and of order

The old Hotel Regis is one of many bold buildings constructed on and around the Prado during the heyday of Cuban tourism in the interwar years. It is typical of the traditions of Cuban architecture: a happy-go-lucky mixture of Classical, European, and North African styles, enlivened by a wash of vivid color.

1 Castle of the Three Kings "El Morro"
2 Fortress of San Carlos de la Cabaña
3 Castle of San Salvador de la Punta
4 Old Havana Amphitheater
5 Old Presidential Palace
6 Old National Capitol
7 El Floridita restaurant
8 Cathedral of San Cristóbal
9 Palace of the Captains General
10 Castle of the Royal Forces "La Real Fuerza"
11 Hotel Ambos Mundos
12 House of the Obrapia
13 Bishop's House
14 Convent of St. Francis of Assisi
15 Belén Church and Convent
16 Church and Convent of St. Clare of Assisi

It was laid out to a plan, a grid of intersecting streets and avenues, meeting here and there at open plazas flanked by churches, colonnades, and the facades of stately *palacios*. It became the richest and largest city in the Americas, the central point in an empire that stretched from California to Tierra del Fuego.

The city owes its wealth partly to its position: it is situated at the edge of one of the best natural harbors in the New World. On a voyage of exploration from the Spanish base on neighboring Hispaniola, Sebastian de Ocampo recognized in Havana harbor the perfect place for ships to be cleaned or repaired – as early as 1508. Three years later, Diego Velásquez sailed from Hispaniola with 300 men to claim Cuba for the Spanish crown.

Havana was founded in 1519, the year that Hernán Cortés set out from the island's only other town of significance, Santiago de Cuba, to begin his conquest of Mexico. In 1538 a fortress, the Castle of the Royal Forces (La Real Fuerza), was constructed in Havana. At that time it was surrounded by a cluster of crude *bohíos* – simple huts of coral stone and dung, thatched with palm fronds – but a mere fifteen years later, Havana was sufficiently developed to be acknowledged as a key port in the Spanish Empire and became the capital of Cuba.

Gold, silver, emeralds, precious hardwoods, and the other rich spoils from the Spanish colonies on the mainland were shipped through Havana, and it was here that the treasure fleet assembled for its annual Atlantic voyage to Spain. Although this made the city rich, it also made it attractive to pirates and privateers. French pirates demolished Havana in 1555; Sir Francis Drake lay siege in 1586; and in 1632 the entire fleet of Spanish treasure ships was captured by the Dutch off Cuba.

To combat this harassment, the Spanish built castles on both sides of the mouth of the entrance to the harbor – the Castle of San Salvador de la Punta and the Castle of the Three Kings "El Morro" – both designed to withstand the latest developments in munitions. At night a chain was pulled across the harbor mouth between the castles. And in 1633 construction of a city wall began, although it was not completed until 1767. It was demolished in 1863, but its course still defines the limits of Old Havana – a diamond-shaped enclave on the western side of the harbor.

In the eighteenth century, Havana stood alongside Mexico City and Lima as one of the most prosperous cities of the Spanish Empire, growing rich from its trade and its services to passing ships, which it supplied with fresh water, as well as produce from the fertile hinterland. Tobacco, which Columbus had first seen smoked on Cuba, was also becoming an increasingly valuable commodity.

From 1762 to 1763, the British occupied Havana during the Seven Years' War. Although the city was returned to Spain at the end of the war under the Treaty of Paris, the British occupation opened the port up to all comers. Suddenly this great harbor was on the trading routes of every nation with interests in and around the Caribbean. During the boom years which followed, Old Havana took on much of the shape it has today. The splendid, chandeliered Palace of the Captains General (now the city museum) was built on the Plaza de

Outside the Palace of the Captains General is a statue of Christopher Columbus, the first European to set eyes on Cuba, which he described as "the most beautiful land that human eyes have ever beheld."

The Castle of the Royal Forces, surrounded by a clover-shaped moat, was the first defensive bastion built by the Spanish in Havana. The weather vane on top of the tower, depicting a woman holding a cross, is known as Giraldilla or La Habana and is said to represent Isabela de Bobadilla who from 1539 to 1542 waited in vain here for the return of her husband, the conquistador Hernando de Soto. He had died at the mouth of the Mississippi.

Ernest Hemingway, one of Havana's most celebrated residents during the 1940s and '50s, lived in a house known as La Vigia (the lookout) set in a cliff-side property in the suburb of San Francisco de Paula. To its north lies Cojimar, the once quiet fishing village used by Hemingway as the setting for his masterpiece The Old Man and the Sea *(1952).*

Armas to house the Spanish colonial government. The elegant city mansions of the plantation owners were built around the Plaza Vieja and along streets such as Obispo; the flamboyant Baroque cathedral was completed in 1778; the harbor was strengthened with the massive Fortress of San Carlos de la Cabaña; the Prado, the broad avenue sweeping down the western side of the walls, was laid out, helping to give the city an air of European grandeur; and Havana's first theater and coffee house were opened.

Following the revolt of slaves in Haiti in 1791, many French plantation owners relocated to Cuba, and the island soon became the Caribbean's prime sugar producer. Around this time, too, cigar-smoking was approaching the height of its popularity in Europe. Revenue from these crops, along with its continued importance as a trading center, underpinned Havana's building boom in the mid-nineteenth century. The city's rich built comfortable mansions behind huge wooden carriage doors leading to shaded patios. Inside were cool, tall rooms, simply decorated with whitewash and perhaps polychromatic tiles or a dado of Tuscan-style painted decoration, handsomely offsetting family portraits and dark wooden furniture. In the middle of the living room stood a smoldering coal on a dish – for lighting one of Havana's most famous exports.

After some 30 years of increasingly bitter struggle, Cuba gained her independence from Spain in 1899. But it was independence in name only: the Americans (heavy investors in the island's businesses) reserved the right to intervene in internal affairs. None the less, as the price of sugar rose, Cuba continued to prosper. In the 1920s, '30s, and '50s, Havana was one of the world's most desirable holiday destinations, famous for its casinos; for the dancing girls in its night-clubs, including the junglelike Tropicana; and for its bars and restaurants, notably El Floridita, one of Ernest Hemingway's haunts.

Wealthy expatriates were also drawn back to the city, building the suburb of Vedado, with its hotels and private homes in racy Art Deco style. Havana became the playground of millionaires and film stars, as well as of writers and artists attracted by the warm climate, the liberal atmosphere and heady pulse of the music and dance. The city also acquired touches of pseudo-grandeur, such as the Capitol, built in 1930 in imitation of Washington's Capitol.

This glamorous veneer was, however, concealing a world of corrupt politics and racketeering. Mafia-led gangsters controlled the gambling, the smuggling syndicates, and the numerous brothels, while the majority of ordinary Cubans lived in pitiful poverty; a quarter of the population was suffering from malnutrition. On January 1, 1959, a group of revolutionaries, led by the young lawyer Fidel Castro, succeeded in ousting the dictatorial government of General Fulgencio Batista. After the United States enforced an economic boycott in 1961, Castro turned to the Soviet Union for help.

In a world changed by the collapse of communism, a new era is dawning in Cuba. Perhaps it can find comfort in the deep historical roots of Old Havana. The city was born out of a dream of a new age and built on the cusp of two worlds – the Old and the New. History may be in the balance, but Havana is no stranger to that sensation.

Havana's clubs were renowned for their pulsating music and energetic dancing. In this heady, pleasure-seeking atmosphere were practiced the conga and cha-cha, and the mamba and rhumba, described by a commentator in the 1950s as "dances of an extraordinary erotic ferocity."

Laid out at the end of the eighteenth century, the Prado runs between the Castle of San Salvador de la Punta and the Capitol to the west of the line of the old city walls. It has been renamed Paseo de Martí after José Martí, a revolutionary hero who died in 1895 during one of the uprisings against Spanish colonial rule.

The lively holiday atmosphere of Havana drew thousands of visitors to pre-revolutionary Cuba, attracted by the warm climate, the casinos, and the clubs. For Americans in particular, life only 90 miles (150 km) from the mainland provided an agreeable contrast to the more austere conditions back home. Behind the easy-going atmosphere, however, lay a darker world of mafia-led racketeering and corruption.

Gazetteer

NORTH AMERICA

Cities of Romance and Creation

Acapulco, Mexico
As the best port on the whole of Mexico's Pacific coastline, Acapulco was "discovered" by the Spanish in 1530 and rapidly became a major trading town. Here, galleons arrived laden with goods from the other side of the Pacific, in particular the Philippines and China. But Mexican independence – achieved in 1821 – and a steady decline in trade spelled the end of Acapulco's first period of prosperity.

It was in the 1950s, when a road link to the capital was completed, that Acapulco's fortunes were revived. Suddenly the area's beautiful coastline, deep semicircular bay, and sheltered beaches were within easy reach of vacationers from Mexico City and farther afield. Today Acapulco – and in particular La Quebrada inlet, where divers plunge 150 feet (45 m) from the cliffs to the crystal clear waters below – is a mecca for sun worshippers.

Atlanta, Georgia
In the mid-19th century, Atlanta was one of the wealthiest and most sophisticated cities in the U.S.A. Thanks largely to its situation in the foothills of the Blue Ridge Mountains, the city was at the hub of the ever-expanding railroad network and was chosen as the terminus of the Western and Atlantic Railroad. Its importance may have proved its undoing: invaluable as a supply depot to the Confederate forces during the Civil War, it was an obvious target for the Federal army; and on September 1, 1864, it was captured by General Sherman. Before he left some two months later, nearly 90 percent of the town had been destroyed.

But Atlanta did not wholly succumb, and after the war, it came to epitomize the character of the "New South," rebuilding itself and reconciling with its former enemies in the North to restore business. Its population doubled in the first year of peace, and the city is today the commercial and financial capital of the Southeast. Appropriately, Atlanta's seal, chosen in 1887, shows a phoenix rising from the ashes accompanied by the motto "Resurgence."

Georgetown, Washington, D.C.
Some 2½ miles (4 km) northwest of the national capital, Georgetown lies at the confluence of the Potomac River and Rock Creek. The area was described by the architectural historian Elbert Peats as "a beautiful old dogwood, always in flower." He was referring to the elegant row houses that flank Georgetown's cobbled streets – reminders of its postcolonial heyday when it was a thriving commercial center, independent of Washington.

Georgetown's wealth was based on the imported tobacco that flooded through its quays on the Potomac River. The coming of the railroad reduced traffic on the waterways, and the town's commercial importance dwindled. But, although it was annexed to Washington in 1878, Georgetown managed to retain its small-town elegance and in 1950 was declared a national historic district.

Further testimony to its past lies in Georgetown University, the nation's oldest Catholic college, founded in 1789.

Philadelphia, Pennsylvania
A harmonious blend of old and new, the city of brotherly love is a thriving and energetic place that retains elements of its colonial past. Its apparently modern gridiron street plan was, in fact, the first of its kind in the U.S. and was devised by William Penn. Trees, parks, open spaces, and colonial-style buildings echo the city's origins as a Quaker settlement in the 17th century.

At the center lies Penn Square, site of City Hall, surrounded by four shady, fountained squares. To the east lie the oldest sections of Philadelphia, with Independence National Historical Park, home of Independence Hall and of the cracked Liberty Bell, tolled on the occasion of the first reading of the Declaration of Independence on July 8, 1776. Close by is Elfreth's Alley, some 33 houses that comprise the oldest continuously inhabited street in the U.S. Typically, these older parts of the city reflect the colonial style – two- or three-story houses that face directly onto leafy sidewalks.

San Francisco, California
The city of San Francisco overlooks the peaceful waters of San Francisco Bay, which is some 13 miles (21 km) across at its widest point. In spite of this superb natural harbor, the region around the modern city was not explored by sea, and the first permanent settlement was established here only in 1835. But the discovery of gold and later silver in the 1840s caused a massive influx of people from all over the world eager to make their fortunes. Within a couple of years, San Francisco was transformed from a small frontier town into a thriving metropolis.

Virtually destroyed by earthquake and then fire in April 1906, the city was rebuilt in only four years. Today it is an elegant, cosmopolitan seaport, crisscrossed by steep, hillside streets, and is home to a rich variety of ethnic groups from around the world, including Chinese, Italian, and Spanish.

Entangled in History

Boston, Massachusetts
During the War of Independence, this genteel city on the eastern seaboard was one of the focal points of unrest. Despite initial good relations with Britain, the road to revolution was sealed by such events as the Passage of the Stamp Act in 1765, the Boston Massacre of 1770, and – most notoriously – the Boston Tea Party of 1773. In this act of defiance, a small band of colonists dumped three shiploads of tea into Boston harbor as a protest against Britain's monopoly of the tea trade. Among the group was the silversmith Paul Revere, who some two years later was able to warn Bostonians of the approaching British army. This allowed the Americans to form a militia to intercept the "Redcoats" at Lexington, thereby beginning the War of Independence.

The city was initially occupied by the British, but was relieved by Washington in March 1776. Since the war, Boston has retained its distinctive colonial feel, and many 18th-century buildings remain, including the Old State House and Faneuil Hall.

Monticello, Virginia
Thomas Jefferson, third president of the U.S. and principal author of the Declaration of Independence, is intrinsically linked with Monticello. He inherited some 5,000 acres (2,000 hectares) of land overlooking the sweeping plains of Virginia's Piedmont farmlands at the age of 14. He started building Monticello in 1770 and took nearly 40 years to complete the house and its idyllic setting of woodland, plantation, and landscaped gardens.

The design for Monticello was inspired by Jefferson's time in Europe as the American ambassador and reflects the Neoclassical style prevalent at the end of the 18th century. Dominated by a centrally domed space, the house mimics an ancient temple, and inside it is scattered with Jefferson memorabilia. A seven-day clock that he designed sits in the entrance hall; the weights of the pendulum hanging through a hole in the floor tell the day of the week. Other intriguing inventions include a double door, both sides of which open when only one of them is pushed. The entrance hall itself served as a private museum for some of Jefferson's personal collection of Native American artefacts and fossils.

Plymouth, Massachusetts
The Pilgrim Fathers arrived in the Plymouth area on December 21, 1620, an event commemorated to this day in the U.S. as Forefathers' Day. Five days later, the 102 pilgrims crowded onto the *Mayflower* landed at Plymouth Rock. Conditions for the settlers were far from comfortable, and in the first winter alone, nearly half of them died; the others were saved through the intervention of the native tribes nearby, who gave them food and showed them how to plant and raise corn. In return, the Indians were invited to a three-day festival the following autumn, held in thanksgiving for their year's labor. Since then, Thanksgiving Day has become a national holiday throughout the U.S.

Savannah, Georgia
The state of Georgia owes its origins to the vision of James Edward Oglethorpe, who was granted a royal charter in 1732 and set out to establish a colony, providing land on which the British working poor could cultivate semitropical silks, grapes, and spices. The first area he settled, in 1733, was at the mouth of the Savannah River. Named after the river, Savannah was designed following a system of squares, many of which accommodated small parks planted with semitropical flora.

In order to stem the massive expansion and moral degradation that characterized other American colonies, the buying of land for large plantations was strictly limited in Georgia, and alcohol and slavery were banned. The pace of growth was sedate, and Savannah developed as a graceful seat of colonial power, with none of the hustle or cramped atmosphere of some of its colonial neighbors.

The War of Independence did little to affect the city and, almost 100 years later during the Civil War, Savannah avoided the fate of its neighbor Atlanta in Sherman's "march to the sea"; instead it was offered to President Lincoln as a Christmas present in the winter of 1864. As a result, Savannah retains the charm of previous centuries, still typified by open spaces hemmed with Georgian colonial and Greek revival style houses.

Paradise Found

Banff and Jasper National Parks, Canada

The towering peaks and glistening glacial lakes of the Banff and the Jasper national parks cover some 6,760 sq. miles (17,500 km²) of the Canadian Rockies, part of the immense chain of mountains that stretches from Alaska in the north to the Mexican border.

Bright green lakes nestle beneath imposing crags, from which spill the series of glaciers that form the Columbia ice field, a vast sheet of ice some 2,500 feet (750 m) thick. Meltwater from the ice field charges the Athabasca, Saskatchewan, and Columbia rivers that flow into three different oceans: the Atlantic, the Arctic, and the Pacific.

This is not just an area of ice and snow, however. The lofty peaks that dominate the parks are fringed with evergreen forests of spruce, larch, pine, aspen, and fir, which in turn play host to a variety of wildlife including mountain lions, elks, and grizzly bears.

Blue Holes, Bahamas

Off the coast of Andros, the largest island in the Bahamas, sit several pools of inky blue water. These mysterious "holes," which stand out from the bright turquoise water that surrounds them, were until recently shrouded in mystery. At high tide, inflowing currents swirl around the holes creating powerful whirlpools that suck objects into the vortex. Then as the tide recedes, water is spewed in great mushrooms above the sea.

Local legend attributes these strange occurrences to the monster Lusca, half-shark, half-octopus, which uses its arms to drag boats into the murky blueness of the holes, and then throws out what it does not wish to eat. It was not until the 1960s that the first explorations of these mysterious portals were undertaken. Instead of being the home of a mythical beast, the blue holes proved to be doorways to an immense system of caverns and cathedral-like vaults, dug out by the ocean in the limestone beneath the sea bed.

Despite the powerful forces that sweep water in and out of these impressive caves, life has still been able to find a perch. Nurse sharks rest along the floor while crayfish feed on debris dragged into the holes. Most unusual of all is the lucifuga, a blind cavefish that feels its way around the inky depths.

Everglades, Florida

Tropical forests filled with luscious ferns, orchids, bromeliads, and epiphytes characterize the Everglades and provide an ideal home for waterbirds, such as the flamingo, and a huge variety of fauna including the endangered Florida panther and the manatee. The waters of the third largest freshwater lake in the U.S., Lake Okechobee, empty into the Everglades, a region covering some 4,000 sq. miles (10,500 km²) of southern Florida.

Much of the open scenery is covered with sawgrass, a type of sedge that grows up to 16 feet (5 m) in height and whose edges are covered with minute sharp teeth. But, scattered among the sea of grass and water, small islands – or hammocks – offer opportunist tropical plants a foothold.

Grand Canyon, Arizona

The Grand Canyon is vast: the awesome power of the Colorado River carves a ribbon through the

Arizona countryside. The canyon is 277 miles (446 km) long, between one-tenth of a mile and 18 miles (0.2 and 29 km) wide, and over 1 mile (1.6 km) deep. But its size alone does not make it one of the world's supreme natural wonders. It is also a multicolored chronology of the earth's history. The river's action has exposed layers of rock, ranging in hue from gray-green and pink to brown slate and violet. Rocks on the valley's floor are some of the oldest on earth, dated at around six billion years old. Those higher up, in the southeast, are less than 1,000 years old.

Kauai, Hawaii

The smallest and most westerly of Hawaii's major islands, Kauai is breathtakingly beautiful. The Pacific crashes against its 90 miles (145 km) of beaches, above which tower cliffs and steep pallisades. Rich volcanic soil and high rainfall combine to earn Kauai the nickname the "garden isle," and mean that its jagged inland mountains are draped year-round in lush tropical jungle.

Mount Waialeale, which at 5,148 feet (1,569 m) is the highest point on the island, is all that remains of what was once the massive volcano that gave birth to Kauai. The sides of the peak are threaded

NORTH AMERICA

1 Ellesmere Island, Canada 2 Anchorage, Alaska 3 Queen Charlotte Islands, Canada 4 Banff and Jasper National Parks, Canada 5 Redwood National Park, California 6 San Francisco, California 7 Grand Canyon, Arizona 8 Rainbow Bridge, Utah 9 Monument Valley, Arizona/Utah 10 Mesa Verde, Colorado 11 Cahokia, Illinois 12 Niagara Falls, New York/Canada 13 Plymouth, Massachusetts 14 Boston, Massachusetts 15 Philadelphia, Pennsylvania 16 Georgetown, Washington, D.C. 17 Shenandoah Valley, Virginia 18 Monticello, Virginia 19 Atlanta, Georgia 20 Charleston, South Carolina, pp.66–71 21 Savannah, Georgia 22 Bermuda 23 Vieux Carré, New Orleans, pp.34–39 24 Everglades, Florida 25 Key West, Florida 26 Blue Holes, Bahamas 27 Havana, Cuba, pp.194–99 28 Teotihuacán, Mexico 29 Acapulco, Mexico 30 La Venta, Mexico 31 Palenque, Mexico 32 Chichén Itzá, Mexico, pp.158–61 33 Kauai, Hawaii

with crystal waterfalls, the most spectacular of which are the Wailu Falls, which plunge some 80 feet (25 m). It was here that Hawaiian chiefs traditionally proved their courage by diving into the plunge pool at the foot of the falls.

Monument Valley, Arizona/Utah

The massive rock sculptures that stand proud of the countryside on the Arizona and Utah border are possibly the most recognizable features of the American landscape, chosen to represent the archetypal Old West in the movies of John Ford and others.

Although named after the geological term for the remnants of erosion, these "monuments" towering above the red desert sand are in fact reminiscent of ruined and crumbling castles and temples. Flat-topped massifs – gigantic blocks of sandstone with a tough, resilient cap – soar some 1,000 feet (300 m) above the ground. And pinnacles, or free-standing fingers of rock, are scattered over the valley. Among the best known are Castle Rock, The Mittens (two separate formations, each with a narrow column of rock, the thumb, next to a broader block), and Hen-in-a-Nest, resembling a squatting chicken.

Niagara Falls, New York/Canada

At more than 3,500 feet (1,070 m) along its curved edge, and some 160 feet (50 m) high, Niagara Falls is not the world's largest waterfall; but it is one of the most beautiful. Its sediment-free waters roar over the falls in a crystal-clear cascade into the veils of a permanent mist at their foot. Into this mist, according to legend, members of the local tribe threw their fairest maiden in an attempt to appease the thunder god. Behind this veil, indeed behind the falls themselves, lies the Cave of the Winds, a cavern carved naturally by the tumbling water.

To guarantee the continued beauty of the falls, national parks have been established in both the U.S. and Canada, and extensive engineering works on the Niagara River are designed to prevent further erosion. Left unchecked, this erosion would push the falls back at a rate of about 3 feet (1 m) each year.

Rainbow Bridge, Utah

The largest natural bridge in the world was unknown to all but the Paiute Indians until 1909. Although it is named after its shape, Rainbow is an apt epithet: its sandstone takes on different colors as light levels alter in the course of the day. The pink of early morning becomes dark lavender under the noon desert sun, shading to deep reds and browns toward evening.

Towering some 290 feet (90 m) above a small creek that flows on to the Colorado River, the bridge owes its outline to the action of extremes of temperature that occur between day and night. These fractured and weakened the rock, which succumbed to the irresistible force of the stream's flash floods which washed the debris away. Over the years this powerful combination of the forces of wind, rain, and floods have gouged out the bridge.

Redwood National Park, California

Before the last Ice Age, a vast redwood forest covered much of North America. All that remains today is a comparatively tiny pocket of land in northwestern California, hugging the Pacific coastline from Big Sur to the Oregon border. More than 160 sq. miles (415 km²) in size, the Redwood National Park contains some of the tallest trees in the world, the redwoods *Sequoia sempervirens*, which regularly reach more than 325 feet (100 m) in height. The park's tallest tree stands at 367 feet (112 m). Redwoods are also tough trees, with a massive 12-inch (30-cm) thick acidic bark to protect them from both insect and fire damage.

Although the redwoods are the undeniable stars of the park, the region also boasts some ruggedly beautiful coastline scenery. Cliffs edge onto both rocky and sandy beaches, with rocks and stacks jutting into the Pacific. This is home to an exotic abundance of wildlife, including the California seal and brown pelicans.

Shenandoah Valley, Virginia

The Shenandoah Valley lies cradled between the Allegheny Mountains to the northwest and the Blue Ridge Mountains to the southeast. The valley and the river that flows along its floor take their name from the Native language for "daughter of the stars." This especially verdant stretch of land was the sole domain of the Shawnee and Iroquois tribes until the arrival of the first settlers – chiefly German Lutherans and Scottish and Irish Presbyterians in the 1720s. They compared the area to the biblical promised land, and the soil did indeed prove fertile; a strong farming community was established.

The valley marks the triumph of Nature over man's worst depredations. In 1824, the order given by General Philip Sheridan of the Union forces to destroy anything that could possibly be of use to the Confederates led to the wholesale burning of farmhouses, crops, livestock, and barns. But Nature repaired the scars, and today the valley is once again a luscious pasture of woodlands, meadows, and orchards.

From the Mists of the Past

Cahokia, Illinois

To the east of St. Louis are the remains of what was once the greatest American city north of the Rio Grande, abandoned in the 15th century. At its peak Cahokia, which means "wild geese," covered 6 sq. miles (16 km²) and was populated by more than 20,000 souls. It was the capital of the Mississippians, the last major culture in North America, which first came to preeminence in about 800 A.D. and lasted until the arrival of Europeans on the continent. The vast Mississippian kingdom covered the present states of Mississippi, Alabama, Georgia, Arkansas, Missouri, Kentucky, Illinois, Indiana, and Ohio.

Cahokia is scattered with about 120 earth mounds of varying shapes and sizes, some retaining the remains of wooden buildings on their flattened tops, others containing the buried bodies of some of the city's former inhabitants. The largest of these mounds, the Monk's Mound, is an awesome feat of engineering: it is a four-terraced mound that is 100 feet (30 m) high, covers 14 acres (6 hectares), involved the displacement of 22 million cu. feet (623,000 m³) of earth, and took some 300 years to complete. Archaeologists believe it formed a platform for the home of the city's ruler-priest. The building of the monument coincided with the peak of the Mississippian culture around the years 1050 to 1250 A.D.

La Venta, Mexico

Parts of the settlement of La Venta have been dated to 1500 B.C. This was the second major settlement – after San Lorenzo in Vera Cruz – of the Olmecs, one of the oldest civilizations in Central America. La Venta was a center for sculpture, typified by the enormous carved stone heads – measuring up to 6½ feet (2 m) in height and weighing 25 tons – that abound both here and in San Lorenzo. Archaeologists still do not know how these massive blocks of stone were moved from quarries up to 60 miles (100 km) away, without the use of the wheel. Sculptures of manatees, monkeys, and jaguars adorn other monuments in the city.

The Olmec culture was highly sophisticated. La Venta is dominated by a 100-foot (30-m) earth mound which may well have been the burial site of a ruler. This is but one such site in the city, where the dead were frequently interred with ornate jewelry, such as concave iron-ore mirrors.

Mesa Verde, Colorado

Built by the Pueblo tribe around 1000 A.D. as a defense against the Navajo and Apache, the settlement at Mesa Verde is set in a sandstone cliff and is accessible only by easily defended stairways carved out of the overhanging rock. Now a ruin, it was once a vast single-building complex with some 220 rooms housing between 250 and 350 people.

The building itself was constructed from hewn stone blocks and mortar, with each floor set back from the one below, like a series of massive steps up to the roof. Entry was through a hole in the ground floor, and higher stories were reached by ladders through holes in the ceiling. This thriving community was abandoned toward the end of the 13th century, probably as a result of drought. (Tree rings point to a severe drought between 1272 and 1299.) It seems likely that the city's inhabitants moved in search of water holes farther south.

Palenque, Mexico

Lush rainforest in southern Mexico surrounds what was once the thriving capital of the Maya Empire. Brightly colored toucans and parrots now flit between the ruins of a city that covered 8 sq. miles (20 km²). The majority of Palenque still remains hidden in the forest that reclaimed the land once the settlement had been abandoned, but archaeologists have excavated 30 buildings, and estimates suggest that a further 5,000 may be hidden in the thick undergrowth.

The largest edifices restored so far are six pyramids, including the Temple of Inscriptions, named after the 620 hieroglyphs that adorn the structure. Inside were found the remains of a ruler identified in the hieroglyphs as Pakal, meaning "hand shield." He was buried with an impressive collection of ornaments, including a death mask made from 200 pieces of jade. The hieroglyphs also relate that the city of Palenque reached its peak under the leadership of Pakal, who came to the throne at the age of 12.

Queen Charlotte Islands, Canada

Some 175 miles (280 km) off the coast of western Canada lies a group of around 150 islands that together make up the Queen Charlotte archipelago. These form the Haida Gwaii, or "the home of the

Haida," a tribe of Native Americans who first settled the islands during the early years of human colonization in the Americas.

On these islands, which cover some 3,700 sq. miles (9,600 km²), life has changed little for centuries, with the Haida – essentially a race of hunter-gatherers – still living off Nature's bounty. The verdant land, covered in brooding temperate rainforests of cedar, spruce, and hemlock which harbor black bears and deer mice, provides plenty of food; and waters warmed by the Pacific Current provide an equable climate.

Far from the nomadic lifestyle of similar societies in other continents, the Haida have established a semi-settled way of life. They live in permanent wooden buildings at different sites throughout the islands, moving between them as the seasons change. Without a constant battle for survival, the Haida have developed highly complex crafts, in particular sculpture. Totem poles adorn their villages, generally one for each family, sometimes up to 65 feet (20 m) tall and decorated with events from the family's history.

Teotihuacán, Mexico
Known to the Aztecs as "the place of the gods," Teotihuacán was the site of their grandest monuments. At its peak, this massive complex of stone pyramids, temples, and houses covered an area greater than imperial Rome. Its layout was designed along a rigid geometric grid, with the result that a nearby river had to be diverted in order to provide conformity to the strict pattern.

Running through the city's center is the Avenue of the Dead, linking the marketplace at one end with the two massive pyramids dedicated to the sun and moon. These pyramids rival those at Giza in size. The largest and most dominant structure in the whole city is the Pyramid of the Sun. It rises 230 feet (70 m) in a series of massive steps, with sides 738 feet (225 m) long. Its partner, the Pyramid of the Moon, is some 150 feet (45 m) high. Other monuments include the 21,000 sq. foot (1,953 m²) Temple of Quetzalcoatl, the feathered serpent and one of the more powerful Aztec gods.

At its peak, in about 500 A.D., the city sheltered more than 200,000 people and was the largest settlement in the Americas. But it was gutted by fire and abandoned in around 750 A.D.

Outposts of the Beyond

Anchorage, Alaska
Surrounded on three sides by mountains, Anchorage lies at the head of the Cook Inlet, a finger of icy water some 220 miles (350 km) long and up to 80 miles (130 km) across at its widest part, stretching from the northwest Pacific. The city was founded in 1915 as the headquarters of the Alaskan railroad that traveled from Fairbanks in the center of the state. It owes its name to the fact that it was used as an anchorage, or stopping point, for ships navigating the Cook Inlet.

The city's growth has been rapid, and it is now the largest city in Alaska, housing half of the state's population. It also acts as a gateway to the vast and largely unspoiled wilderness beyond. Evidence of this is apparent in the brooding form of Mount McKinley, at 20,320 feet (6,194 m) the highest peak in North America, looming over Anchorage's skyline.

Bermuda
This archipelago of 7 main and more than 150 smaller islands and groups of rocks appears as a mere speck within the immensity of the Atlantic Ocean. The nearest point on the U.S. mainland, Cape Hatteras, is 570 miles (920 km) to the west. Bermuda's beauty is undeniable. The islands are covered in lush subtropical plants and fringed by coral reefs in a climate kept warm by air currents that waft from the Gulf of Mexico.

The first settlers arrived in 1612, and the islands were rapidly established as a major port of call on the trade routes between Britain and the American colonies. Today's population – the descendants of African slaves, British colonists, and Portuguese laborers who arrived from the Azores and Madeira in the mid-19th century – bears witness to this past.

Ellesmere Island, Canada
Cape Columbia, Ellesmere Island's northernmost point, is a mere 500 miles (800 km) from the North Pole. The few hundred people who inhabit this icy wilderness – where winter temperatures average –22°F (–30°C) – are spread over an area the size of Britain. They are the latest in a line of humans that has lived here since the 12th century. Other life forms are adapted to the conditions: the largest trees are diminutive hardy dwarf willow shrubs, and animals include white-haired Arctic wolves and shaggy musk oxen.

The countryside is typical tundra, dotted with peaks that rise up to 8,500 feet (2,600 m). Pack ice surrounds the northern and western coasts of the island, and permanent ice caps sit among the inland mountains. Despite its frozen climate, the land is classified as desert, since only 2½ inches (65 mm) of snow falls throughout the year.

Key West, Florida
Lying more than 100 miles (160 km) south of the Florida mainland, Key West is the most southern settlement within the continental limits of the U.S. It forms the last of the Keys, a chain of coral and limestone islands that stretch in an arc from the southern tip of Florida. They derive their name from the Spanish *cayo*, meaning "small island."

Initially settled as a salvage center for the ships that came to grief on the reefs of the Caribbean, it later became home to British colonists escaping the War of Independence. It has also offered sanctuary from metropolitan life to the likes of Hemingway, who worked here on *For Whom the Bell Tolls* and *A Farewell to Arms* between 1931 and 1940.

Today the islands are less remote than they once were, and the Keys are linked by a chain of some 42 bridges that make up the Overseas Highway. But Key West has clung to its "outpost" atmosphere, typified by its "Conch" houses – highly ornamented 1½- and 2½-story houses, built to last, which have withstood the hurricanes that often lash the area.

CENTRAL & SOUTH AMERICA

Cities of Romance and Creation

Panama City, Panama
Located near the Pacific entrance to the Panama Canal, Panama City is the gateway between the Western and Eastern worlds.

Old Panama was founded in 1519 on the site of an Indian fishing settlement – the name *panamá* means "many fish" in the native tongue. The settlement sprang to prominence as a storage site for gold and silver from the Andean countries in the south before it was shipped back to Spain. As such, it became a prime target for pirates and privateers.

In 1671 Henry Morgan successfully destroyed the town, and New Panama sprang up at a site some 5 miles (8 km) farther west. But the city did not prosper, and in 1751 the region was absorbed into Colombia. It gained independence in 1903, and its resurgence was guaranteed in 1914 with the opening of the Panama Canal. Now more than 40 ships every day travel the 36 miles (58 km) of the canal that link the Caribbean and the Pacific, bringing enormous wealth to the town.

Rio de Janeiro, Brazil
For four days every year, the city of Rio de Janeiro springs into life as countless brilliantly costumed dancers parade through the streets to samba rhythms in the world-famous pre-Lenten Carnival. Although lively throughout the year, Rio surpasses itself in this expression of joy and celebration.

The landscape around echoes the vivacity of the city: a mixture of golden beaches (such as those found at Copacabana), hills, ridges, and peaks. The most prominent of these peaks, including the cone of Sugar Loaf Mountain, are those at the entrance to Guanara Bay, around which the city nestles. To the west, built upon the summit of Mount Corcovado, is the monument to Christ the Redeemer, a giant statue of Christ with arms outstretched.

Rio de Janeiro owes its name to a geographical mistake. When the site was first spotted by Portuguese navigators on New Year's Day in 1502, they believed that the bay must be the mouth of a giant river and named it accordingly: "rio" meaning river and "janeiro" January. The town's status grew when the Portuguese royal family settled there in 1808 and, seven years later, declared the region a kingdom. Since then, expansion of the coffee, cotton, sugar, and rubber trades has brought a steady stream of wealth into the city.

Paradise Found

Amazonia National Park, Brazil
The mighty Amazon River drains an area the size of Australia. In 1974 the Brazilian government established the Amazonia National Park, covering some 4,000 sq. miles (10,360 km²) of the Amazonian jungle and straddling the Tapajós tributary. The park guarantees that the Amazon basin's incredible diversity of life is preserved.

Creatures previously uncharted are found here, and the area supports species found nowhere else. The park's plant life is characterized by ferns, vines, bromeliads, and lianas, in addition to mangroves, rubber trees, and palms. This rich flora supports a dazzling array of fauna, including manatees and river dolphins in the water and deer, capybaras, armadillos, tapirs, and monkeys on land. The tree canopy, in turn, is aflutter with birds, including toucans, parrots, and hummingbirds.

Antarctic Peninsula, Antarctica
Perhaps the world's last great wilderness, Antarctica is a continent of massive icy peaks and steep-sided

valleys. The most prominent feature in this land of breathtaking natural beauty is an 800-mile (1,300-km) peninsula, a finger of rock and ice jutting out into the sea to reach within 600 miles (1,000 km) of South America. Thanks to warm ocean currents, this is one of the milder areas of the Southern Ocean, with balmy midsummer temperatures of around 59°F (15°C).

This is one of the few places where life can maintain a foothold on the continent. The only two types of flowering plants throughout Antarctica are found here, as well as varieties of moss, liverworts, and algae. Animals have yet to achieve any significant permanent presence, but during the summer months, the waters teem with microscopic life that attracts a huge number of animals to these shores. These visitors include seals, whales, petrels, gulls, and penguins.

Dominica

This emerald jewel of the Caribbean has, to a large extent, remained unspoiled. Dominica cannot boast the sandy beaches that lure tourists to the other islands, and so it has not succumbed to the developers' bulldozers. Instead, it has the largest area of tropical forest in the whole of the Caribbean, covering some 40 percent of the island's land area.

Each year up to 236 inches (6,000 mm) of rain fall on the mountains at the center of the island, feeding an untouched paradise of verdant trees, giant ferns, brilliant birds, and – evidence of the island's volcanic past – steaming lakes. As water percolates through the soil, it reaches a region of rock heated by molten rock below. The heated water rises through small holes, or fumaroles, to the surface, where it results in a steaming lake. Boiling Lake on Dominica is the largest such lake, known as a flooded fumarole, in the world. Gases from the volcanic rocks below have also escaped to the surface, staining the rocks with rich reds, yellows, and browns.

Galápagos Islands, Ecuador

Straddling the equator, the group of 19 islands with islets and rocks that make up the Galápagos are populated by a collection of wildlife that enthralled the English naturalist Charles Darwin when he visited them in 1835. Here he discovered animals whose specialization and development confirmed his belief in the theory of evolution.

The fascinating array of wildlife, including Galápagos finches and land tortoises, owes much to the islands' isolation: they are scattered over 23,000 sq. miles (59,500 km²) of the Pacific and lie more than 600 miles (1,000 km) from the coast of Ecuador. Any life that has reached the islands has been able to flourish without the threat of competition. This remote Eden was declared a wildlife sanctuary in 1959.

Pampas, Argentina

Vast plains of tall pampas grass dominate the heart of Argentina, stretching from Gran Chaco in the north to Patagonia in the south and from the Atlantic coast to the foothills of the Andes. The pampas gets its name from the Quechua Indian term for "flat surface," and as on the prairies of North America, the sea of waving grass extends to the horizon.

This is the home of Argentina's meat industry and of the legendary gauchos, a disappearing breed of South American cowboys famed for their skill in the saddle and their lawlessness. The pampas itself is split into two parts. The western area is typically dry with sandy deserts in parts and brackish streams. In the east, however, the climate is more humid as the region is subject to powerful storms. Consequently this eastern region, reaching down to the River Plate, has become the most densely populated area of the country.

Tepuis, Venezuela

Thrusting several thousand feet above the Venezuelan jungle floor are vast blocks of rock, consisting of flat summits atop near-vertical sides. (The highest, Mount Roraima, stands a dizzying 9,220 feet/2,810 m high.) Known by the Penom Indian name of "tepuis," these towering isolated blocks have become the source of legend and fired many a creative imagination. Sir Arthur Conan Doyle wrote of an isolated land populated by prehistoric monsters in *The Lost World*. In many respects, truth has mimicked fiction, for the flat summits of the tepuis support wildlife that exists nowhere else on earth. Cut off from the world below, these plants and animals have evolved into unique forms.

The tepuis, which are scattered across much of southeastern Venezuela, are the remains of a large sandstone bed which over the eons has been shattered by the movements of the continents and then eroded by wind, rain, and rivers. Evidence of this is nowhere more apparent than at Angel Falls, which plummet 3,212 feet (979 m) – more than nine times the height of Africa's Victoria Falls – over the side of Auyan tepuis into a fine veil of misty spray.

From the Mists of the Past

Copán, Honduras

The ruins at Copán remained hidden in the tropical jungle of Central America until the mid-19th century, when archaeologist John Lloyd Stephens and artist Frederick Catherwood made the first detailed study of the remains of this great city of the Maya, the civilization that flourished some 1,500 years ago.

The city was built around four main plazas on the banks of the Copán River. In each plaza sits a stepped pyramid, which served either as a temple or as a palace. The most impressive of these is decorated with a stairway covered in more than 1,250 pictures relating the history of the settlement's rulers, from the first warrior kings to the stairway's builder. Consisting of some 72 steps, the 52-foot (16-m) wide hieroglyphic stairway was built by a ruler known as Smoke Shell who ascended the throne in 749 A.D.

Today only 30 of the steps are in place; the others are being painstakingly restored. Among the other attractions on the site are ball courts and stellae, or statues, some 10 feet (3.4 m) high. They were erected by the rulers of Copán as monuments to themselves and symbols of their own power.

Nazca Lines, Peru

More than 100 designs litter some 200 sq. miles (520 km²) of Peru's desert floor, forming the largest display of art in the world. The carvings fall into two categories: depictions of animals; or astonishingly straight lines, some stretching for more than 5 miles (8 km), many crisscrossing in an apparently random collection of squares and triangles. The representational drawings, too, are formed by a single, uninterrupted line and include a monkey, hummingbird, spider, and orca, many of which are more than 330 feet (100 m) long.

Both lines and pictograms were formed by scraping away the red gravel on the desert floor to expose the yellow sand beneath, and there is no evidence that anything other than human hands was used. Inscriptions from relics scattered over the area suggest the lines were the work of the Nazca Indians and were created between 500 B.C. and 500 A.D. Little is known of the people who carved these images in the soil, or of why they did so. Theories include that the lines were ancient highways, a giant astronomical calendar, or even a landing strip for spaceships.

Outposts of the Beyond

Altiplano, Bolivia

Flanked by the Western and Eastern Cordilleras of the massive Andes chain, the Altiplano could not be more different from the lofty mountains and volcanoes that surround it. Some 500 miles (800 km) long and 80 miles (130 km) wide, this gap in the mountain chain is filled with an immense level plain, about 12,000 feet (3,650 m) above sea level. Rain seldom falls here, and any that does quickly evaporates, leaving vast salt flats, or *salars*, which give the region a brilliant white floor that casts a powerful glare in the sunlight.

Little life has penetrated this remote spot. Hardy plants, including cacti and the giant puya – a distant relative of the pineapple which produces a flowering spike that can reach up to 30 feet (9 m) in height – are able to survive in the rarefied air. In the more fertile regions, toward Lake Titicaca in the north, members of the Aymara tribe live, herding llamas and alpacas, and harvesting potatoes and quinoa grain from the fragile soil and thin air.

Easter Island, Chile

Situated more than 1,200 miles (2,000 km) from its nearest neighbor and over 2,000 miles (3,200 km) from the South American mainland, tiny Easter Island lies surrounded by the wide blue waters of the Pacific Ocean. In this unlikely setting are scattered more than 600 stone statues, ranging from 10 to 40 feet (3 to 12 m) in height. All are similar: known as Moai, they consist of the upper body of a man, with a stylized head, inlaid eyes, and elongated ear lobes. Later statues also have a huge red topknot.

The earliest of these sculptures – which are the legacy of an extremely wealthy culture, able to expend time and energy on carving sculptures from the island's volcanic rock – dates from 380 A.D. The culture that carved them flourished for more than 600 years, harvesting yams, sweet potatoes, and bananas, and exploiting the abundant forests that once covered the island for their houses and boats.

Mysteriously, however, they all but died out in a short space of time. A party of Spanish explorers noted a population of about 3,000 in 1770. Contact was extremely limited with this remote spot, and four years later, when Captain James Cook arrived, he found around 600 men and only 30 women. Blame for this has been laid on a civil war brought about by food and wood shortages. Today only the enigmatic statues remain, offering little insight into the life of the Easter Islanders.

and shelters the world's most southerly city, Ushuaia. Although poetically named "the land of fire" by the Portuguese navigator Ferdinand Magellan, who first saw the coast lit by the fires of the local tribe as he sailed past in 1520, the area is better known for its gusting winds, which blow up to 115 mph (185 km/h), and its 16 feet (5 m) of rain each year. The area's isolation and inhospitability to humans have made it an ideal haven for animal life, and the waters around the archipelago teem with krill which support fish, birds, sea lions, dolphins, and whales.

AFRICA & THE MIDDLE EAST

Cities of Romance and Creation

Jerusalem, Israel

The city of Jerusalem is the meeting place of three continents and three religions. It was traditionally seen as the hub of the Old World, the center around which Asia, Africa, and Europe revolved, and is revered by Islam, Christianity, and Judaism.

The Dome of the Rock is the most identifiable feature of the Jerusalem skyline, a glittering cupola originally made from solid gold sheets, but today replaced by aluminum and gold alloy. Originally constructed by the Muslim leader, Caliph Omar, between 687 and 691 A.D., the dome is said to house the rock from which the prophet Muhammad rose to heaven with the Archangel Gabriel. The Church of the Holy Sepulcher contains the sites where Christians believe Christ was crucified and where his body was subsequently laid to rest by Joseph of Arimathea. The present building was rebuilt in 1927 after its ancestor was destroyed by an earthquake. The Western, or Wailing, Wall is the most sacred site to the Jews. It is said to be the last remains of the Temple of Jerusalem built by Herod the Great in 19 B.C. and destroyed by the Romans some 90 years later.

Marrakesh, Morocco

In the center of the fertile, irrigated Haouz plain, between Morocco's Atlantic coast, the Oued Tensift River and the Atlas Mountains, lies the ancient city of Marrakesh. It was founded in 1062 by Yusuf ibn Tāshufin, ruler of the Almoravid dynasty, and is one of Morocco's four imperial cities, acting as its capital at various points in the country's history.

Also known as the "red city" because its buildings are made from beaten clay, Marrakesh boasts a superb collection of Moorish architecture. The oldest part of the town, the medina, is surrounded by a vast palm grove. At the medina's center lies the colorful and vibrant marketplace, the Place Jema al-Fna. Around this, a collection of buildings document the life of the city since its birth.

Patagonian Desert, Argentina

The Patagonian Desert, in the south of Argentina, is the largest desert in the Americas, covering nearly 260,000 sq. miles (673,000 km²). This vast steppelike plain rises in huge terraces from the coastal cliffs of the Atlantic coast to the foothills of the Andes in the west.

Little more than 8 inches (200 mm) of rain falls here each year, since humid westerly winds from the Pacific lose their moisture in the Andes. The watercourses that cross the land are, at best, intermittent, but usually no more than dried-up river beds, with a few salt pools in the deep depressions. This environment does, however, support a diverse number of species, including herons, shielded eagles, armadillos, guanacos, and pumas.

Tierra del Fuego, Argentina/Chile

Covering 28,450 sq. miles (73,700 km²), Tierra del Fuego forms the southern extreme of the Americas

The 12th-century Koutoubia mosque to the east has a 220-foot (67-m) high minaret built by enslaved Spanish captives. Also dating from this period is the highly ornamented Rabat Gate, which forms one of the entrances to the old city. Later buildings include the Sa'di Mausoleum, constructed in the 16th century, the Dar el Bëida Palace and the Bahia Royal residence. Marrakesh is also renowned for its parks, in particular the Menera olive grove and the walled 1,000-acre (405-hectare) Agdal gardens.

Mecca, Saudi Arabia

As the world's most sacred Islamic site, Mecca is the destination every Muslim dreams of visiting at least once in a lifetime. This journey, or *hajj*, centers upon the Ka'aba, a cube-shaped stone building that, according to tradition, was built by Abraham and Ishmael as the house of God. The Ka'aba is now housed by the enormous al-Haram mosque, which can hold 300,000 worshippers at one time. Other important sites are the Zamzam Well, the two hills of al-Safwa and al-Marwa, and the neighboring towns of Mina and Arafat, all of which the pilgrim must visit during the *hajj*.

Mecca is situated on an oasis and was a stopping place on old caravan routes. In 570 A.D., the prophet Muhammad was born here, and it was in the hills around the town that he saw many visions and received the verses of the Qur'an. Forced to flee from the city in 622, he returned eight years later to cleanse the Ka'aba of idols and dedicate it to Allah, the One God. Today, during the Muslim month of *Dhu-al-Hijjah*, the month of pilgrimage, more than two million worshippers flock to Mecca from all over the world.

Entangled in History

Congo River

One of the last areas of the African continent to be explored, the Congo basin remained a blank spot on maps of the world until the end of the last century. The Portuguese explorer Diego Cão was the first European to set eyes upon the river mouth in 1482 and erected markers here claiming Portuguese sovereignty. Cão believed it to be the opening to an inlet that would lead to the heart of the legendary realm of Prester John, a priest-king said to preside over an empire of enormous wealth. But treasures on offer in the Americas interrupted the exploration of this area of Africa for more than 400 years.

David Livingstone, journeying with Henry Morton Stanley, established that the Lualaba was part of the Congo River system, not the Nile as many had believed. Livingstone, however, was perhaps the last great "scientific" explorer of Africa. After his death, the territorial ambitions of the European powers and of the Africans themselves prompted further exploration. The economic arguments for exploration hinged around the valuable trade in ivory. If Europeans were to reap the vast potential profits from this trade, a route from Lake Tanganyika west to the coast had to be found.

In November 1876 Stanley set out from Nyangwe on the Lualaba. In January the following year, he charted the seven major falls and rapids on the Congo that bear his name. Seven months later, he reached the coast, having successfully navigated the whole length of the Congo. The stage was set for European powers to become increasingly embroiled in the partitioning of West Africa.

Gold Coast, Ghana

This stretch of the West African coastline has, since the 15th century, been an area associated with amazing wealth. Although originally established as a refueling stop on the trade routes to the East Indies, this strip of coast – where immense riches could be traded for simple raw materials such as iron and copper – soon achieved an importance of its own.

The first Europeans to reach this area, the Portuguese, were keen to maintain a monopoly on access to the large stocks of gold that appeared to flow unceasingly from the interior (they even called the area *la mina*, "the mine"). For a while they were successful in keeping other European powers away. In turn, however, the local tribes, including the Akan and the Ashanti, proved extremely adept at keeping the Portuguese at arm's length, and they were never allowed any claim to sovereignty over the land. When trading with the Portuguese proved unprofitable, the local tribes simply started to deal with the Dutch and then the British.

Timbuktu, Mali

Situated roughly halfway between the North African states and the Gold Coast on the Gulf of Guinea, Timbuktu was ideally placed on the trade routes that ran across the Sahara. The settlement was founded on the southern edge of the Sahara some time in the 12th century as a seasonal camp for the Tuareg nomads, but its importance to trade was quickly recognized, and it was soon incorporated into the Mali Empire that stretched from the Atlantic deep into the center of northern Africa. By the time African traveler Ibn Battutah arrived at Timbuktu in 1353, the town had become an important focal

AFRICA & THE MIDDLE EAST
1 Marrakesh, Morocco 2 Kerkuane, Tunisia
3 Leptis Magna, Libya 4 Timbuktu, Mali
5 Gold Coast, Ghana 6 St. Helena 7 Congo River,
Congo (Zaire) 8 Okavango Delta, Botswana
9 Victoria Falls, Zambia/Zimbabwe, pp.102–5
10 Madagascar 11 Seychelles 12 Mount
Kilimanjaro, Tanzania 13 Ngorogoro Crater,
Tanzania 14 Serengeti National Park, Tanzania
15 Ruwenzori Mountains, Zaire/Uganda
16 Meroë, Sudan 17 Mecca, Saudi Arabia
18 Luxor, Egypt, pp.152–55 19 Jerusalem,
Israel 20 Dead Sea, Israel/Jordan 21 Petra,
Jordan, pp.128–33 22 Damascus, Syria, pp.26–33
23 Cape Verde Islands

point for trade in gold and salt. Merchants arrived from Wadan, Tuwat, and Morocco to buy slaves and gold in return for Saharan salt, cloth, and horses. The city reached its peak during the Askia period between 1493 and 1591.

A decline in trade and increasing raids by the Tuareg, Fulani, and Bambara tribes saw a downturn in its fortunes. It was captured and restored a little by the French toward the end of the 19th century, but could not recapture its former glory. Today small salt caravans still arrive at Timbuktu from the south, but there is no gold to trade, and the trans-Saharan routes are no longer used.

Paradise Found

Dead Sea, Israel/Jordan
The unique climate of this area of Israel and Jordan has led to the creation of an exotic wilderness. The surface of the Dead Sea is 1,312 feet (400 m) below sea level – the lowest point on any of the continents. It is thus a natural area for inflowing water – chiefly the River Jordan – but also one from which water rarely drains. Instead, due to the high temperatures, water evaporates, perhaps by as much as 1 inch (2.5 cm) a week. As it does so, it leaves behind large amounts of minerals, raising the saltiness of the Dead Sea's water to about 10 times that of ocean water. Dazzling crystalline towers of salt and minerals line the water's edge. But the salinity has one more noticeable effect for human visitors, and it is this that has attracted tourists. It is impossible to sink in the buoyant waters of the Dead Sea. In fact, it is possible to sit in them.

Mount Kilimanjaro, Tanzania
Some 200 miles (320 km) south of the equator sits "the mountain that glistens." The translation of the Swahili name by which the peak is known is apt: its white, snow-capped summit flashes in the brilliant equatorial sunshine. First reports to reach Europe of a mountain covered with snow in the heart of the African continent were scoffed at. Yet at 17,564 feet (5,354 m), the peak is well above the snowline, and while its base bakes in the heat, its summit experiences arctic conditions year-round.

Kilimanjaro is massive – some 60 miles (100 km) long and 47 miles (76 km) wide – and is made the more impressive by standing alone, looming over the grasslands of the Masai Mara. Its slopes are a world within a world: above the savanna lies a strip of cultivated land where bananas, millet, and coffee are grown. Above this sits dense tropical forest, home to leopards and blue monkeys. Higher still are regions of moorlands and high-altitude desert.

Madagascar
The wildlife paradise that is Madagascar is rivaled perhaps only by the Galápagos. Its fauna is unique, due to the island's isolation from the rest of the world over millions of years. For instance, it is home to all the world's species of lemur. On the African continent, the evolution of the higher monkeys caused the lemur to die out there, but on Madagascar lemurs were able to survive without competition. Half of the world's chameleon varieties are also found on the island, and the coelacanth – a fish long thought to be extinct and rediscovered only earlier this century – swims off its shores.

But the island's isolation is only half the story. For Madagascar was covered by lush tropical rainforest sheltering an estimated 9,000 species of plants, and despite the destruction of tracts of forest, the island remains an Eden for flora and fauna.

Ngorogoro Crater, Tanzania
This natural bowl-shaped depression in northern Tanzania is an island sanctuary from the fluctuating conditions of the savanna that surrounds it. Inside the crater verdant plains, saline lakes, and marshes offer food and shelter to up to 30,000 herbivores, including wildebeest, zebra, gazelles, and the rare black rhino. In contrast to those outside the crater which must endure the vagaries of the rainy season and migrate accordingly, those within Ngorogoro enjoy year-round comfort and grazing, thanks to a natural irrigation system that keeps the crater fertile.

The crater itself is all that remains of a once-vast volcano that is a part of the Great Rift Valley, the longest continuous crack in the earth's crust. The top of the mountain, which has long been extinct, has collapsed in on itself, leaving a huge, nearly circular bowl some 12 miles (20 km) in diameter. The crater's rim sits some 2,000 feet (600 m) above the valley floor, up steep and gullied slopes.

Okavango Delta, Botswana
The vast spread of the Okavango Delta stands out of the African countryside as a gem of emerald green in stark contrast to the barren wilderness of the neighboring Kalahari Desert. The delta is a region rich in both plant and animal life, thanks to the waters of the Okavango River that flow from the highlands of central Angola nearly 700 miles (1,100 km) to the northwest. As the river enters the plain, it fans out into numerous tributaries, feeding the shallow backwaters, lagoons, and swamps that make up the largest inland delta in the world, covering more than 6,000 sq. miles (15,500 km²).

It is a landscape subject to constant change as watercourses change direction or even dry up completely, to be replaced by new ones. Every year, heavy rains in Angola mean a flood of water that replenishes and cleanses the delta. Having lost most of its impetus by the time it reaches the region, the floodwater gently stirs the soil, releasing and distributing oxygen and nutrients, taking nearly five months to get from one end of the delta to the other.

Inhabiting this rich environment are a whole host of mammals, including hippopotamus, zebra, buffalos, elephants, and sitatungas, antelope that have developed splayed hooves to allow them to walk on the floating reeds.

Ruwenzori Mountains, Zaire/Uganda
In the second century A.D., the Greek mathematician and geographer Ptolemy mentioned a group of peaks, lying 2,000 miles (3,200 km) south of the Mediterranean, in which lay the source of the Nile. He called them "the mountains of the moon." The peaks do indeed have a certain unearthly quality, which is emphasized by the "otherworldly" aspects of the wildlife they support. This includes giant lobelias with 6½-foot (2-m) flowering spikes, triple-horned chameleons, and tree hyraxes, diminutive relatives of the elephants that inhabit the land surrounding the Ruwenzori.

In contrast to the lush greenery that swathes the lower slopes of the mountains, the summits glisten with brilliant snow all year round. Nine of the peaks stand at more than 16,000 feet (4,880 m), the highest being Mount Margherita at 16,763 feet (5,109 m). Little was known about these fabled peaks until the 19th century, when the Anglo-American explorer Henry Morton Stanley became the first Westerner to set eyes on them, some 150 miles (240 km) west of Lake Victoria, in 1888.

Serengeti National Park, Tanzania
The Serengeti game reserve is famed for its vast herds of grassland animals that both graze in the park and move in enormous annual migrations. During the wet season between December and May, the animals become concentrated on the plains southeast of the park. Then, with the arrival of the dry season, they move west and north to the grasslands of the Mara that border the park and stretch into neighboring Kenya. As many as 1.5 million wildebeest and more than 200,000 zebra move through the reserve during this migration. Other animals include gazelles, giraffes, elephants, hippopotamus, lions, and leopards, and the reserve is also an important refuge for the endangered black rhino.

The reserve covers more than 5,700 sq. miles (14,800 km²) of grassland and thorn tree woodland savanna, and is situated about 100 miles (160 km) east and southeast of Lake Victoria. It is fringed by several impressive and permanently snow-capped peaks, including Oldeani at 10,459 feet (3,188 m).

Seychelles
A paradise of silver-sanded beaches, the Seychelles are lapped by the brilliant turquoise waters of the Indian Ocean and fringed by lush, tropical jungle. Over the centuries, the islands have remained untouched by human hands. The first recorded landing was in 1609, but no serious attempt at colonization was made until the latter half of the 18th century.

There are about 115 islands in total, scattered over around 150,000 sq. miles (400,000 km²) of ocean. They divide into two distinct types. The first, the Mahé group of some 40 islands, are typically mountainous, draped in tropical rainforest at their center and surrounded by a narrow coastal strip. The outer, surrounding islands are small coral atolls rising only a few feet above sea level. The islands' remoteness – they lie 680 miles (1,100 km) northeast of Madagascar and 1,000 miles (1,600 km) from the mainland of Africa – contributes to the sense of paradise. Wildlife, though limited, includes giant tortoises and sea turtles.

From the Mists of the Past

Kerkuane, Tunisia
Buried in the sands for hundreds of years, the ruins at Kerkuane have been well preserved against the ravages of time. These are the remains of a Punic settlement (the word Punic derives from the Roman name for the Carthaginians), part of the Carthaginian Empire which stretched across northern Africa and the western Mediterranean.

Kerkuane was founded c.570 B.C., and the town itself was well designed around broad streets. The houses, which were covered in colored clay, were similar in shape and design, but their size and orientation gave a clue to their inhabitants' social standing. Most remarkable are the beautiful mosaics – still almost intact – which line the decorated pools of the town's baths. Figurines in one temple imply that it was dedicated to a god of hunting or fishing. Kerkuane remained a lively and thriving settlement until the town was sacked by the Romans in 256 B.C. during the First Punic War.

Meroë, Sudan

The site at Meroë, some 175 miles (280 km) north of Khartoum on the east bank of the Nile, is the remains of the one-time capital of the ancient Cush civilization. From the eighth century B.C., the Cush controlled most of what is now Egypt and Sudan. Around 650 B.C., however, they were defeated by the Egyptian pharaohs and lost their northern territory, and their rulers, the 25th, or "Ethiopian," dynasty of ancient Egypt, were forced to move their capital from Napata to Meroë in the south. The city flourished as the focus of an Egypto–Cushite culture that thrived quite separately from its Egyptian ancestry until the arrival of the Romans. Weakened by Roman conquest, the town was open to attacks from indigenous tribes and finally fell around 320 A.D. to the Christian Askumite armies.

Excavations have revealed that Meroë was a great and populous city, housing a culture famed for its skill in iron smelting. Buildings within the town include several palaces and a riverside quay, in addition to the great temple of Amon and a copy of a Roman public bath. Evidence of the similarities between the Cush and Egyptian cultures is evident from the groups of pyramids near the site.

Leptis Magna, Libya

The remains at Leptis Magna are the most spectacular in the Roman Empire. Preserved under layers of sand over the centuries, the town has yielded an amazing collection of buildings, including a forum, amphitheater, basilica, an ornate triumphal arch, a variety of temples and baths, and a 1,500-foot (460-m) long circus. The town's center was marked by a street 1,350 feet (410 m) long, flanked on either side by elaborately arcaded porticoes. Outside the town, the remains of a 12-mile (19-km) long aqueduct have also been found.

Leptis Magna was established in the seventh century B.C. by the Phoenicians. Its position on a natural harbor offered easy access to the trans-Saharan trade routes to the south. It continued to flourish under the Romans and reached its zenith – with a population of about 80,000 – in the third century A.D., when Septimius Severus, a native of Leptis Magna, was crowned Roman Emperor. And it was during his reign that most of the buildings now standing were erected. After the decline of the Roman Empire, the city was overrun and occupied in turn by Vandals and Byzantine Christians.

Outposts of the Beyond

Cape Verde Islands

Uninhabited before the arrival of the first Portuguese settlers in 1462, the Cape Verde Islands – situated some 385 miles (620 km) off the west coast of Africa – proved an invaluable provisioning station on the route between Europe and the Portuguese territories in South Africa and South America, notably Brazil. Their name is taken from the westernmost cape of Africa.

The islands possess the classical attributes associated with a tropical paradise. They enjoy a rich tropical climate and are surrounded by white shimmering beaches and fringed by tropical flora, with tall impressive volcanic peaks looming in the background. The 15 islands and islets that form the chain are split into two groups: the Barlavento, or windward islands, and the Sotavento, on the leeward side. The islands' mountainous interiors are high enough to generate rain. But beyond the rain belt, there is no moisture. Grasses and pines coat the upper slopes where there is rain; those beyond experience near desert conditions. This is further exacerbated by the fact that the islands are subject to frequent and severe droughts.

St. Helena

The tiny island of St. Helena is surrounded by the expanse of the Atlantic Ocean, some 1,150 miles (1,850 km) off the western coast of Africa. A mere speck, St. Helena is only 10½ miles (17 km) long and 6½ miles (10.5 km) wide, covering an area of only 47 sq. miles (122 km²). Steep cliffs between 450 and 2,000 feet (140 and 600 m) high line the eastern, northern, and western coasts. These lead up to a mountainous interior, largely consisting of a semicircular chain of peaks, including Mount Actaeon at 2,683 feet (818 m). From these heights, deep valleys carve through the volcanic rock south to James' Bay, the only port on this remote island.

Discovered by the Portuguese in 1502 on the saint's day after which it is named, the island served as a refreshment base for the trading routes between Europe and the East Indies. It was here that Napoleon was banished after the Battle of Waterloo in 1815. Unlike Elba in the Mediterranean, which had proved too close to Europe and unable to hold the defeated emperor, St. Helena was the ideal spot, and Napoleon spent his last years at the country house Longwood, dying there in 1821.

SOUTHEAST ASIA, AUSTRALASIA, & THE PACIFIC

Cities of Romance and Creation

Jakarta, Indonesia

The population of Jakarta has doubled since 1940, and the city today is booming, experiencing a rate of economic growth that is almost unrivaled in Southeast Asia. Its importance as a center for commerce, however, dates from its period as a Dutch colonial settlement, and some of the buildings constructed at that time remain. They include a Portuguese church dating from 1695, the old city hall built in 1710, and the present ministry of finance, which is housed in a building originally constructed for the region's governor.

Jakarta's layout, however, owes more to British influences than to the Dutch, who governed the colony until 1949. Its pattern is broken up by large squares, including Medan Merdeka, or "freedom field," and Lapangan Banteng, meaning "place of the large wild ox." Since it sits on a vast, flat alluvial plain, the city has been allowed to sprawl and has now spread to cover an area of some 230 sq. miles

(600 km²). The site upon which the city stands has been used since the fifth century A.D.

Manila, Philippines

That Manila is a city of myriad cultural contrasts is reflected in its architecture, which includes elements of American, Spanish, Chinese, and Malay styles. Situated on Luzon, the largest island in the Philippines, Manila lies on the eastern shore of Manila Bay, a large inlet that leads via a 12-mile (19-km) wide channel into the South China Sea. The city – which now sprawls over some 15 sq. miles (40 km²) – has developed around its excellent sheltered port. The Spanish came here in the 16th century and built the fortress city of Intramuros, meaning "within walls," in place of the original Muslim settlement that occupied the site. Present-day Manila has developed from this fortress city and now encompasses, in addition, some 13 villages that once surrounded Intramuros.

The city is bisected by the Pasig River, and its streets are dotted with tropical trees, including palms, banyans, and acacias. Open spaces include the Rizal Park, named after the Philippine author and nationalist José Rizal, which contains Japanese and Chinese gardens as well as an open-air theater and a grandstand.

Sydney, Australia

Not only the oldest and largest city in Australia, Sydney is also the most vibrant and energetic, largely due to the cosmopolitan make-up of its population. Peoples from Britain, Ireland, Greece, Italy, China, and other parts of Asia make an ethnic contribution to this melting pot.

The city's sights include the world-famous Opera House, opened in 1973; the Sydney Harbour Bridge, completed in 1932, which spans the bay linking north and south Sydney; and – a few miles from the city center – Bondi Beach.

In 1788, the fleet carrying the first settlers arrived from Britain and discovered the entrance to Port Jackson, which led to the bay upon which Sydney is situated. The captain of the fleet, Arthur Phillip, described it as "the finest harbor in the world." Since the establishment of the colony, Sydney has spread from the Pacific coast along the harbor, with its innumerable bays and inlets, inland toward the Blue Mountains, and it now covers a massive 4,790 sq. miles (12,400 km²).

Entangled in History

Botany Bay, Australia

This inlet in the Tasman Sea is said to be the spot where Captain James Cook first set foot upon the Australian mainland in 1770. Having originally called it Stingray Harbour, Cook changed the bay's title because of the huge variety of new plants found there by the expedition's naturalist, Joseph Banks.

It was thought to be an ideal site for establishing Australia's first colony. However, when the first fleet arrived some 18 years later, under the leadership of Captain Arthur Phillip, they found that Botany Bay had insufficient water and soil that was too poor in quality to support a settlement. They were forced to look farther north. Up the coast they discovered and explored the opening to Port Jackson, which Cook had ignored on his previous visit. They landed and established a settlement at what is now the heart of modern Sydney. Botany Bay itself, fed by the Georges and Cooks rivers, is roughly circular in shápe, with a 1-mile (1.6-km) wide opening to the sea which broadens to almost 5 miles (8 km) inside the harbor.

Pitcairn Island Dependency
This isolated group of islands in the Pacific, midway between New Zealand and South America and some 1,350 miles (2,170 km) southeast of Tahiti, owes its fame to the mutineers aboard HMS *Bounty* who, under the ship's first mate, Fletcher Christian, cast Captain William Bligh adrift. The mutineers reached Tahiti, where some remained. But nine, with a group of Tahitian men and women, set sail again, eventually reaching Pitcairn, where they burned the ship, in 1790. The mutineers survived in obscurity with their Tahitian partners until American whalers found them in 1808. An attempt at resettlement to Tahiti in 1831 failed when many islanders returned to their home. Today there is one settlement – Adamstown on the northeastern coast.

Although it covers an area of only 2 sq. miles (5 km²), Pitcairn is the largest and only inhabited island of the group. The land is rugged and mountainous, and most of its coastline is lined with cliffs. It enjoys a subtropical climate, and its soil is fertile enough to support today's islanders, who are all descendants of the original mutineers.

Paradise Found

Bali, Indonesia
The Balinese countryside reflects that of the neighboring island of Java: palm-fringed beaches leading down to deep blue waters and jungle-draped mountains, the largest of which is the still-active volcano Mount Agung, 10,303 feet (3,140 m) high and known locally as "the navel of the world."

Bali's color is enhanced by its vibrant religion, a cocktail of Hindu, Buddhism, Malay ancestor cult, animism, and magical beliefs. These are exemplified by the island's funerals, in which huge, decorated coffins – some animal shaped – are paraded through the streets prior to cremation to liberate the soul from the body. The body is surrounded by musicians and dancers, who scare away evil spirits.

The arts are all highly important. As in the funeral, dancing takes on a magico-religious purpose, warding off spirits or recounting stories. Musical accompaniment is provided by the gamelan orchestra, which consists of various percussion instruments, a two-string violin, and a flute.

Bora-Bora
This 4-mile (6-km) long island is situated in the south-central Pacific some 140 miles (225 km) northwest of Tahiti. A jewel set within the brilliant turquoise of its immense ocean surroundings, Bora-Bora belongs to the Society Islands, themselves part of French Polynesia. The shoreline of the island is indented with picturesque bays whose silver-white sands are overhung by coconut palms.

Beyond the gleaming beaches, the island is surrounded by coral reefs, which encapsulate a lagoon on the west side. The reef is capped by small sandy islets, known as motus, on which the island's runway has been built. Inland, jagged crests and peaks mark all that remains of a once-massive, now extinct, volcanic peak. The summits

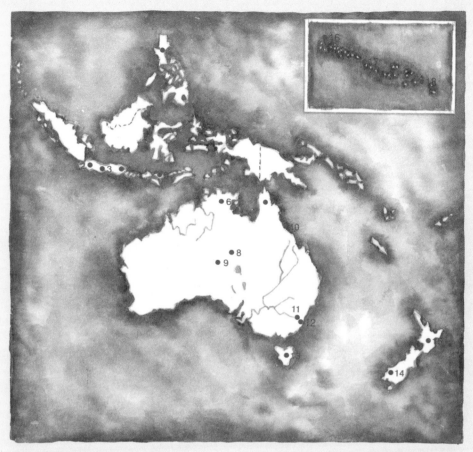

of Mount Pahia and Mount Otemanu soar to more than 2,000 feet (600 m), their slopes swathed in lush greenery. The island was first described by Captain James Cook on his voyage in 1769.

Great Barrier Reef, Australia
Stretching for more than 1,250 miles (2,000 km) off Australia's northeastern coast lies one of the wonders of the natural world. In terms of diversity, the fauna of the Great Barrier Reef is matched only by the jungles of the Amazon. Here are found an amazing array of creatures, including scorpion fish, sharks, groupers, giant sea turtles, and dolphins.

The reef has been built over the past 500,000 years by tiny animals known as polyps. More than 350 different species of these polyps create a multitude of different forms, from staghorn corals, with their antler-shaped constructions, to brain coral, whose foldings and indentations look like a 6-foot (1.8-m) human brain.

The reef is composed of some 3,000 individual interlocking coral rafts and islets separated by narrow channels. At places such as Cape Melville, the reef is just a narrow ribbon of coral; farther south at Cape Manifold, huge coral rafts are almost 200 miles (320 km) across. Constant temperatures of between 70° and 100°F (21° and 38°C), and rich provisions of oxygen and nutrients, maintain the coral polyps, and a variety of wildlife that live off them. In 1979 the region was declared a marine park, covering 134,600 sq. miles (348,600 km²).

Komodo, Indonesia
The island of Komodo – part of the Lesser Sunda Islands of Indonesia, covering some 200 sq. miles

SOUTHEAST ASIA, AUSTRALASIA, & THE PACIFIC
1 Manila, Philippines 2 Jakarta, Indonesia 3 Borobodur, Indonesia, pp.146–51 4 Bali, Indonesia 5 Komodo, Indonesia 6 Arnhemland, Australia 7 Cape York Peninsula, Australia 8 Alice Springs, Australia 9 Uluru, Australia 10 Great Barrier Reef, Australia 11 Sydney, Australia 12 Botany Bay, Australia 13 Tasmania, Australia 14 Milford Sound, New Zealand 15 Rotorua, New Zealand 16 Bora-Bora 17 Tahiti 18 Pitcairn Island

---

(520 km²) – is famed for one particular species of animal that lives within its shores. This is the Komodo dragon, a species of monitor lizard that, at 10 feet (3 m) in length, is the largest living species of lizard in the world. This bulky animal may well be the source of many of the Eastern dragon legends.

Despite its weight of nearly 300 pounds (135 kg), the Komodo dragon moves surprisingly quickly. It feeds mainly on carrion, but has been known to kill small deer and even humans with its sharp curved teeth. Like other large reptiles, such as giant land tortoises, the Komodo dragon can live to a very great age, in many cases exceeding 100 years old. But the lizard is currently under threat because of a drop in prey numbers and shrinkage of its habitat due to human influence on the island, so its numbers are now being carefully monitored.

Milford Sound, New Zealand
Rudyard Kipling referred to Milford Sound as "the eighth wonder of the world." He was overawed by the cliffs that hang suspended over the glittering

deep blue waters below. Towering to a breathtaking 5,280 feet (1,600 m), they are the tallest sea cliffs in the world. Above them is the most striking feature of Milford Sound, the 5,550-foot (1,692-m) Mitre Peak.

The Sound is a 12-mile (19-km) fjord that carves its way from the Tasman Sea into the countryside of New Zealand's South Island. Ice sheets that covered this region until 10,000 years ago gouged out a deep channel that was filled by rising water as the glacier retreated. The water itself is composed of three distinct layers. The high levels of run-off from streams and waterfalls maintain a layer of fresh water that sits on the surface down to a depth of about 10 feet (3 m). Below this is a brackish layer where the fresh water mingles with the sea water that lies underneath.

The waters are particularly rich in life, with coral colonies growing on the sides of the fjord and an abundance of fish, such as the red-striped perch. The landscape around Milford Sound is shrouded by dense forest, home to the kakapo, a ground-dwelling parrot.

Rotorua, New Zealand
A region famed for its remarkable array of hot springs, boiling mud pools, and spouting geysers, Rotorua is situated in the middle of North Island's thermal region some 150 miles (240 km) southeast of Auckland, on the southwestern corner of Lake Rotorua, from which it takes its name. To the south of the area, where the air is filled with the pungent aroma that emanates from the sulfur springs, lies Whakarewarewa, site of New Zealand's largest geyser. Each eruption of Pohotu, which in Maori means "splashing," produces a fountain of boiling water which spurts 100 feet (30 m) into the air.

To the east is Tikitiere, an area of boiling pools and hot flats where heated mud bubbles to the surface. At Orakei-Korako, there are huge silica terraces as well as a fern-framed cave in which a bright blue pool is set.

Tahiti
From Mount Orohena, which soars to 7,339 feet (2,237 m), swoop deep, lushly vegetated valleys, down which flow swift streams, such as Papenoo to the north of the island. The mountains of Tahiti – which, in addition to Orohena, include the two eroded volcanic cones, Tahiti Nui and the Taiarapu peninsula, connected by the Isthmus of Taravao – are largely devoid of human settlement. Cultivation is limited to the thin, fertile strip that fringes the island, most of which is draped in tropical flora, including coconut palms, pandanus, lantana, and hibiscus. Beyond this lie blue-green lagoons surrounded by coral reefs.

Some 33 miles (53 km) long and covering 402 sq. miles (1,041 km²), Tahiti is the largest of the windward Society Islands, part of French Polynesia in the Pacific Ocean. The island was first visited by Europeans in 1767, when Captain Samuel Wallis landed there. Subsequent visitors included Captains Cook and Bligh. Tahiti's most celebrated inhabitant, however, was the artist Paul Gauguin, who spent his final years on the island, immortalizing its beauty until his death in 1901.

Tasmania, Australia
This heart-shaped island covers 26,383 sq. miles (68,332 km²), just one percent of Australia's total land area, yet it holds some of the country's most verdant and lush areas. The island is swathed in some of the world's last temperate rainforest, with trees such as the King Billy, the huon pine, the leatherwood, the sassafras, and the blackwood covering the mountainous slopes that peak at Mount Ossa, which soars to 5,305 feet (1,617 m) in the center of the island.

Tasmania also includes tracts of eucalyptus forest and savanna woodland, home to a host of unique and bizarre creatures, including the Tasmanian devil, the duck-billed platypus, and the extremely rare and possibly extinct thylacine, or Tasmanian tiger.

Outposts of the Beyond

Alice Springs, Australia
In Australia's Northern Territory, Alice Springs is an oasis in the middle of thousands of miles of scrubland at the very heart of the continent. Surrounded by large areas of red desert and rocky ridges, such as the Macdonnell Ranges, the town is the only major center of human population for hundreds of miles. It lies on the Stuart Highway, a massive road that bisects Australia, with Darwin 954 miles (1,535 km) to the north and Adelaide 1,028 miles (1,654 km) to the south.

Alice Springs was established in 1871 as a station on the Overland Telegraph line. Since these inauspicious beginnings, the opening up of the country's vast interior has led to a rapid expansion in the town's fortunes, and today it serves as a focal point for the tourist industry in central Australia. Alice Springs is also the headquarters for Australia's Flying Doctor Service and for the School of the Air, an educational service that broadcasts to children living in the more remote parts of the countryside.

The Todd River flows – intermittently – through the town, but for most of the year its route is marked by a dry riverbed. The local population exploits this by holding its own "boat race," a regatta in which boats are carried by teams of runners along the parched watercourse.

Arnhemland, Australia
Covering roughly 37,000 sq. miles (95,800 km²) of the northeastern limit of Australia's Northern Territory, Arnhemland stretches between the gulfs of Carpentaria and Van Dieman. Unknown to Europeans until a Dutch ship visited in 1623 (hence the name), this area has been occupied by Aborigines since the Pleistocene age and is still the largest Aboriginal settlement in Australia. Evidence of this long occupation is provided by rock carvings and extensive galleries of cave paintings, such as those at Obiri Rock, which chronicle humanity's earliest colonization of the Australian continent.

The region is also supremely beautiful, consisting largely of a tropical plateau between the Roper and Victoria rivers, where lush vegetation surrounds wetlands that support an incredible host of wildlife. One-third of Australia's bird species and one-quarter of its species of fish live here. The region is also home to both estuarine and freshwater crocodiles, as well as large water buffalo. To the west of Arnhemland lies the Kakadu National Park, another area of outstanding beauty, which covers 5,000 sq. miles (12,950 km²) of the countryside.

Cape York Peninsula, Australia
Only one road leads up this finger of land that forms the most northerly tip of the Australian continent. For six months of the year, during the rainy season, the road is impassable, as heavy rains and flooding swamp the area. This inaccessibility has been Cape York's savior, and despite the richness of its mineral deposits, it has remained largely unspoiled.

The region, covering some 80,000 sq. miles (207,000 km²), is split in two by the Great Dividing Range, which begins its great journey south across the continent. To the west of the mountains lies tussocky savanna, land used by only a few cattle herders. East of the Dividing Range sits a region that is humid and thick with vegetation. Essentially an extension of the great Indo-Malaysian rainforest to the north, the forest consists largely of eucalypts and harbors an enormous variety of fauna. This includes the 6-foot (1.8-m) flightless cassowary, a distant relative of the ostrich; brightly colored birds of paradise; and the sugar glider, a flying possum. The Quinkan Galleries, a region of sandstone escarpment near the town of Laura, hold Aboriginal cave paintings, some 13,000 years old, documenting the first successful colonization of the land.

Uluru, Australia
To the north of the Great Victoria desert, at the heart of the Australian continent, sits one of the largest monolithic rock formations in the world. Uluru, or Ayers Rock, rises 1,142 feet (348 m) above the surrounding countryside, which lies in a flat plain, the horizon broken only by the Olgas to the west. Under the noonday sun, the monolith's sandstone shines a brilliant red. Once the sun begins to descend, however, Uluru undergoes a dramatic transformation. The color of its surface shifts from brilliant red, becoming more golden, then pink, before turning bright crimson and then finally purple as the sun dips below the horizon.

This amazing effect of the light has caused awe in visitors to Uluru for centuries. The site is sacred to the Aboriginal peoples who first populated the continent, holding a special place in their legend of the Dreamtime when the earth was formed. Today tourists flock in droves to witness its color transformation and to scale its peak.

Uluru itself is but the tip of a huge lump of rock that geologists have measured as extending 3¾ miles (6 km) under the surface. Even today, Nature is continuing to sculpt the rock. Extremes of heat and cold shatter it, and blocks of rubble sit at its foot. One such flake is the formation known as Kangaroo's Tail, where a giant sliver of rock sits against Uluru's northern face like a flying buttress on a medieval cathedral.

ASIA

Cities of Romance and Creation

Bombay, India
As one of the largest and most densely populated cities in the world, Bombay is, understandably, a hive of energetic activity. It boasts a population in excess of eight million people who are involved in a kaleidoscope of activities from cotton textile manufacture to finance. Situated three-quarters of

the way up India's west coast, the city has, over the centuries, grown as an important trading station with the civilizations that have emerged to the west.

Bombay's present face reflects its most recent period of history. Its architecture is a mixture of Gothic designs – typical of the 18th and 19th centuries – modern skyscrapers and multistory concrete buildings. Despite this hodgepodge of styles, the site of the city itself is one of immense natural beauty. The sea entrance reveals an extensive panorama of the Western Ghats, a chain of mountains that extends along India's west coast. The wide harbor is studded with islands, the largest of which, Elephanta, is famous for its eighth- and ninth-century cave temples. The built-up area occupies a peninsula composed of seven individual islets that have, over the years, been joined by a series of breakwaters and causeways.

Hong Kong

With more than 5½ million people crammed into 412 sq. miles (1,067 km²), Hong Kong is one of the most densely populated places in the world – bringing the city not only vibrancy and energy, but also incredible wealth and sophistication. Yet despite its modern appearance as a forest of high-rise office and apartment buildings, Hong Kong has been constructed to surprisingly traditional plans.

The principles of *feng shui*, translated as "wind and water," hold that a balance between the natural and the manmade must be maintained to guarantee good luck and prosperity. Any construction work carried out in the city must follow the advice of a *feng shui* consultant, even down to the date and time of the building's completion. Mountains to the rear and water in front of the city provide protection from evil spirits.

The deep waters of Hong Kong's natural harbor proved ideal for trade, especially after the Opium Wars with China in the middle of the 19th century. Since then, the city's growth has been spectacular, and the harbor is ringed with massive skyscrapers that loom over the junks of the Tanka boat people in the water below.

Kuala Lumpur, Malaysia

The name of Malaysia's capital translates as "muddy confluence," a term referring to the settlement's beginnings as a center for tin mining. Founded as a mining camp in 1857, the tin ore was dredged from the bottom of the confluence between the Kelang and Gomback rivers, churning the waters into a muddy soup. This tin ore was, however, the source of the city's wealth.

Kuala Lumpur's growth has been rapid, and its buildings are now a mixture of modern and Moorish architecture, with traditional Chinese shop-houses and Malay stilt villages, or *kampongs*. Old temples sit alongside mosques and oriental shopping streets. An indication of the city's transformation into a major international center is in the construction of the Petronas Towers. These twin skyscrapers, linked by a bridge on the 25th floor, will, when completed, stretch 1,476 feet (450 m) into the sky, making them the tallest building in the world, some 22 feet (7m) taller than Chicago's Sears Tower.

Singapore

Often referred to as "the lion city" or "the garden city" because of its parks and tree-lined streets, the city of Singapore dominates the tiny Republic of Singapore. It sits around the massive port area, which at 36 sq. miles (93 km²) is one of the largest harbors in the world. The surrounding skyline is etched with myriad modern skyscrapers and offices put up alongside buildings of Asian and British colonial design. The juxtaposition of the old and the new reflects Singapore's history, primarily as a trading port and more recently as a financial center.

Although originally a part of the Sumatran trading empire of the 13th century, modern Singapore was shaped by more recent events, beginning with the arrival of Sir Stamford Raffles in 1819. He established trade routes with Britain, and despite competition from other colonies in the area, such as Hong Kong, Singapore flourished. Since achieving independence in 1965, it has become one of the most important financial centers in Southeast Asia. Today its population, although predominantly Chinese, offers a microcosm of the whole Asian continent, and the influx of Indians and Malays lends the city a distinctive cosmopolitan feel.

Varanasi, India

The city of Varanasi in northeastern India was founded about 3,000 years ago by descendants of the Aryan people who invaded northern India *c*.1500 B.C. It is one of the most sacred sites for Hindus, the target every year of thousands of pilgrims, whose prime goal is the Ganges River which flows through the town. To die within the boundaries of Varanasi is, to a Hindu believer, to achieve liberation of the soul from the endless cycle of birth, death, and rebirth known as *samsara*.

The river bank through Varanasi, some 3 miles (5 km) long, is lined with a spectacular array of spires, pavilions, temples, and towers. From these a series of broad steps, known as *ghats*, lead down into the waters of the Ganges. In an amazing display of energy and color, people flock to these *ghats* every day and plunge into the river in order to wash in and drink the sacred Ganges water. Festivals are common throughout the year, particularly Divali, the festival of lights held during October and November. At this time, the houses and streets are decked with lamps, and the river springs to life with flickering points of light as candles are sent floating in its current.

Entangled in History

Beijing, China

At the center of China's capital lie the golden roofs of the imperial palaces that make up the Forbidden City. Now a museum, the buildings were the home of the Chinese emperors from the 15th to the early 20th centuries. Within its 35-foot (11-m) high walls, white terraces rise from immense courtyards to support a labyrinth of buildings, including the Hall of Supreme Harmony (the center of the Chinese world) and the Palace of Heavenly Purity, residence of the emperor himself.

The majority of the Forbidden City was constructed during the Ming dynasty, between 1368 and 1644. However, the site of present-day Beijing has been one of military and trading importance for far longer. The first major settlement dates back to *c*.500 B.C., and since then the town has been destroyed and rebuilt many times. Most notably, in 1272 the Mongol ruler Kublai Khan constructed the city of Ta-tu (great capital) on the site, establishing it as the political center of China.

But Beijing is not simply the city of China's imperial past. It is also a city of the communist present, chosen as the capital of the People's Republic in 1949, and the site of a thwarted attempt at a democratic future when, in 1989, it became a focus of protests, centered upon Tiananmen Square.

Bodh Gaya, India

This village in northeastern India was the site of a spiritual event that altered the religious current of the world some 2,500 years ago. Beneath the shade of a pipal tree, Siddhartha Gautama, an Indian prince who had been filled with a desire to find out the cause of and solution to human suffering, entered a deep meditation. During the night, he reached a state of spiritual enlightenment known as nirvana. He achieved the status of the Buddha, the Awakened One, and for the remainder of his life proceeded to teach what he had learned throughout northern India.

Nearly 300 years later, with the religion of Buddhism established, the emperor Ashoka officially recognized the site of the pipal tree as sacred to Buddhists. Since that time the site has grown to include a number of monuments, shrines, and temples. Among these is the Mahabodhi Temple, a 180-foot (55-m) high honey-colored tower whose tapering sides are covered with ornate engravings. According to the writings of a seventh-century Chinese pilgrim, the original temple was covered with gold, silver, pearls, and other gems. Near the temple stands a pipal tree, said to be a descendant of the very one the Buddha sat beneath. Pilgrims tie scarves to its branches and light incense and lay candles at its foot.

Golden Temple, India

Shimmering in the middle of an artificial lake in the city of Amritsar in northwestern India is the serene form of the Golden Temple. This most sacred of Sikh temples dates, in its present form, from the late 18th and early 19th centuries. Having been destroyed by the Afghan king Ahmad Shah Durrani in 1757, it was rebuilt and later refurbished by the Sikh ruler Maharaja Ranjit Singh, who ruled from 1801 to 1839. This benevolent king donated half a million rupees to decorate the temple in marble and gold leaf.

When completed, it had two stories, and each of its four walls faced one of the main compass points. The lower floor is fashioned from marble and has been inlaid with a host of gemstones, including mother-of-pearl, onyx, lapis lazuli, and cornelian. The upper floor has been covered in sheet copper, which, in turn, is covered with gold. Inscriptions from Sikh holy scriptures carved into its glistening surface decorate the temple, the roof of which is clustered with small gilded kiosks capped with fluted golden domes and spires. Inside by day, beneath a jeweled canopy, rests the Sikh holy book, *Adi Granth* or *Guru Granth Sahib*. It is carried to the Golden Temple early every morning across the water by means of a causeway from the Akal Takht, a domed building that sits opposite.

Ise, Japan

The oldest Shinto shrine in Japan – the Grand Shrine of Ise – dates back some 1,500 years, yet it still retains an air of mystery. The compounds in which the temples, or shrines, are built are closed to all but priests and members of the imperial household: "ordinary" visitors must peer through a silk curtain to get a glimpse of the temples, and then only once they have removed hats and overcoats. What they witness is a collection of buildings constructed with the utmost simplicity and beauty, set within tall groves of cryptomeria trees.

Far from the ornate cathedrals and mosques of the Christian and Islamic worlds, the Shinto temples at Ise are built from pale Japanese cypress wood which is left unpainted and unvarnished. Raised on stilts, the buildings have steep roofs made of a deep, highly manicured brown reed thatch. Every 20 years, the temples are systematically dismantled and replaced with identical buildings made from fresh wood – a system of rebirth that offers a sense of renewal within a continuous tradition.

Isfahan, Iran

During the first half of 17th century, Shah Abbas I the Great, of the Persian Safavid dynasty, built one of the most beautiful and picturesque monuments of the Islamic world. The Royal and Lutfullah mosques at Isfahan epitomize the exuberance of Safavid art. The dome of the Royal Mosque is a brilliant peacock blue, across the surface of which have been draped intricate tendrils formed from thousands of golden-brown mosaic tiles. Inside are yet more delicate mosaics in brilliant blues, yellows, and greens. Outside the two mosques, beyond a 90-foot (25-m) high portal, lies a great square known as the Maidan.

All these buildings were constructed at a time when the Safavid court had become internationally famous. Foreign travelers and dignitaries from England, Portugal, Spain, France, and Russia were frequent visitors to this city of wide boulevards fringed with plane trees and canals, with countless scented parks and pavilions lining the way. With the death of Shah Abbas II, son of the city's builder, however, the great era of the Safavid dynasty came to an end, and the prosperity of Isfahan declined.

ASIA

1 Taymyr Peninsula, Russia 2 Wrangel Island, Russia 3 Kamchatka Peninsula, Russia 4 Lake Baikal, Russia 5 Mount Fuji, Japan 6 Kyoto, Japan, pp.182–87 7 Ise, Japan 8 Beijing, China 9 Shanghai, China, pp.190–93 10 Shi Huangdi Tomb Complex, China 11 Caves of the Thousand Buddhas, China 12 Isfahan, Iran 13 Persepolis, Iran 14 Samarkand, Uzbekistan, pp.170–75 15 Pamirs, Tadzhikistan 16 Mount Kailas, Tibet, pp.108–11 17 Lhasa, Tibet 18 Harappa, Pakistan 19 Vale of Kashmir, India 20 Golden Temple, India 21 Taj Mahal, India 22 Kathmandu, Nepal, pp.164–69 23 Varanasi, India 24 Bodh Gaya, India 25 Pagan, Myanmar 26 Guilin, China 27 Hong Kong 28 Shwe Dagon Pagoda, Myanmar 29 Bangkok, Thailand, pp.178–81 30 Angkor Wat, Cambodia 31 Phuket, Thailand 32 Kuala Lumpur, Malaysia 33 Singapore 34 Bombay, India 35 Goa, India 36 Anuradhapura, Sri Lanka 37 Sigiriya, Sri Lanka

Taj Mahal, India

One of the most romantic sites in the world is on the southern bank of the River Yamuna, in the town of Agra in northern India. Unequaled as a monument to eternal love, the Taj Mahal was built to house the body of Mumtaz Mahal, wife of the Mogul emperor Shah Jahan who ruled from 1628 to 1658. So intense was the emperor's grief for his wife after her death in 1631 that he vowed to create for her the most beautiful tomb in the world. He employed some 20,000 workmen and 1,000 elephants to haul marble from quarries 200 miles (320 km) away. He also had malachite brought from Russia, carnelian from Baghdad, and turquoise from Persia.

The mausoleum was completed in 1643 and formed part of a larger complex, guarded by two huge ornate silver doors, since stolen by a local Hindu tribe, which gave entry to a marble-paved garden. A narrow watercourse runs through the middle of this garden, flanked by cypress trees. Reflected in the still waters, the mausoleum soars upward on top of a huge horizontal plinth, with four minarets, one at each corner. The effect is one of breathtaking visual harmony, made all the more so by the play of sunlight upon the white surface.

Paradise Found

Goa, India

Situated on India's west coast is a small, relatively untouched piece of paradise. Lapped by the seas of the Indian Ocean, the beaches of Goa, a province of India, are among the most beautiful and idyllic in the world. Along Goa's 60 miles (100 km) of coastline, shimmering golden sands are overhung by rich tropical flora. The region's two major rivers, the Mandavi and the Zuari, empty into a vast bay in which there is an island, also called Goa.

The province and island cover a total of some 1,430 sq. miles (3,700 km²) of the Indian countryside. Beyond its beautiful coast, the land is rich and fertile, with crops such as rice, cashew nuts, coconuts, and mangoes. Farther inland, the scenery is dominated by the Sahyadri Hills, themselves a part of the Western Ghats, which run along the entire length of western India. These rise to 3,392 feet (1,034 m) at Sonsagar.

Goa's proximity to Bombay – it is only about 250 miles (400 km) south of the city – and its strategic position on the coast have contributed to its wealth. It has always played an important role

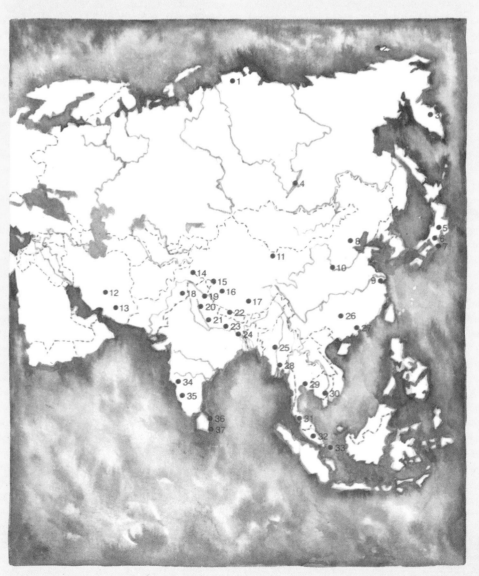

as a trading area with the West, reaching its zenith at the end of the 16th century, when it was made the capital of Portuguese India.

Guilin, China

The town of Guilin is situated in the northeast of the Kwangsi Chuang autonomous region of China. Beyond the city limits, the countryside – which has been celebrated by generations of Chinese painters and poets – is speckled with a host of needle-shaped pinnacles which loom on either side of the banks of the Li River for about 30 miles (50 km).

These dramatic formations are created when rainwater falling on the limestone hills eats away at the stone to leave a forest of pinnacles through which the Li calmly winds its way. On its waters the locals sail, using specially trained cormorants to catch fish. Around them steep-sided slopes are covered with trees that have managed to take root on the near vertical mountain sides, reflecting the meaning of the word Guilin – "forest of sweet osmanthus." The region is also famous for the many underground caves that exist, particularly Lu Ti Yen, "the reed flute cave."

Lake Baikal, Russia

Known as the Pearl of Siberia, Lake Baikal is the oldest and largest body of fresh water in the world. It holds as much water as the five Great Lakes combined and is estimated to be some 25 million years old. The lake shelters an incredible diversity of flora and fauna – perhaps 2,500 separate species – more than half of which have evolved in its waters and are unknown anywhere else in the world. They include huge columnar sponges and abundant algae and shrimps, which in turn support more than 50 species of fish, among them sturgeon and the almost transparent gomulyanka. Baikal is also home to some 70,000 Baikal seals, the only species of freshwater seal in the world.

Its great age is only one of the reasons for this natural wealth: the other is its purity. Nearly 300 rivers empty into the lake, but only one, the Angara, drains it. Not surprisingly, once in the lake, water remains there for a considerable length of time. It has been suggested that incoming water may circulate through the lake for 400 years. Throughout this time, any sediment carried by the water filters out, leaving behind water of incredible purity. And, although the surface of the lake freezes in winter, a few feet below the surface – and down to its depths of 5,370 feet (1,637 m) – oxygen and other nutrients continue to circulate.

Baikal is framed by amazing mountain scenery and swathes of coniferous forest, which are home to sable, among other species.

Mount Fuji, Japan

The slopes of Mount Fuji soar above the Japanese countryside in a portrait of symmetrical beauty. Rising at 45 degrees from the horizon, they meet at the snow-capped summit 12,388 feet (3,776 m) above the ground. For at least 12 centuries, Fuji's breathtaking serenity has inspired Japanese poets and artists. The latter include Katsushika Hokusai who, in the mid-19th century, recorded many views of the mountain in his paintings.

Fuji has been held in high esteem on the islands of Japan throughout human history there. Its name dates back to the first people to arrive in Japan,

the Ainu, who called the peak Fuchi, after their fire goddess. This link with the spiritual was continued, and in both Shinto and Buddhist faith, the mountain is sacred. Buddhists believe that a path encircling the mountain at 8,200 feet (2,500 m) is a gateway to another world. A Shinto shrine near the summit dates back nearly 2,000 years and was built in an attempt to appease the gods when the peak, now dormant, was an active volcano.

. Even today pilgrims climb the mountain to gaze at the countryside below, which in spring is a blaze of colored blossom, and in the fall smolders with reds and browns as the trees shed their leaves.

Phuket, Thailand

Thailand's largest island, Phuket, covers some 310 sq. miles (800 km²) and lies off the west coast of the Thai peninsula in the Andaman Sea, among a group of 37 islands. It was first settled as early as the first century B.C., and today the coast is still lined with traditional fishing villages, whose houses are poised above the water on stilts. Its interior is generally flat, but several hills dot the countryside, some reaching 1,700 feet (520 m) in height.

In recent years the island has become an important vacation center. Visitors are attracted not only to its traditional houses and its beaches, but also to the many surreal rock formations that dot the islands around Phuket. In some places huge pillars of rock rise from the turquoise sea, completely isolated from the other landforms around.

Vale of Kashmir, India

Nestled between the snow-capped peaks of the Himalayas to the north and the summits of the Pir Panjal range to the south is one of the most beautiful, fertile, and temperate parts of the Indian subcontinent. This former lake bed enjoys a climate far milder than its neighboring regions: its altitude means that its average temperature is lower in the summer, and the ranges of mountains protect it from the monsoons common in this part of the world.

Over the years, various rulers of India have chosen to retire to this lush region, which, particularly during the hot summer months, was an oasis of comfort. The Mogul emperor Akbar referred to the vale as his "private garden," while British families flocked to the region during the days of the Raj. Unable to build homes, they chose instead to construct boat-houses where they spent their time. Some of these may still be found floating on the lily-covered waters of Lake Dal. Isolated by huge mountain ranges, the Vale of Kashmir still remains an area removed from the troubles of the outside world.

From the Mists of the Past

Angkor Wat, Cambodia

Hidden among the dense undergrowth of the Cambodian jungle some 150 miles (240 km) north of Phnom Penh lie the remains of what was once the largest city in the world. At its zenith, it covered 75 sq. miles (190 km²), the size of present-day Manhattan. When it was discovered in 1850 by the French missionary Charles-Emile Bouillevaux, little remained to tell of its history, save the relief carvings and engravings in Khmer and Sanskrit that cover the buildings. From these, archaeologists learned that the 100 or so *wats*, or temples, that litter the city

were built between the 9th and 13th centuries A.D. and dedicated to both Hindu and Buddhist religions.

The largest temple is Angkor Wat, built in the 11th century by the Khmer ruler Suryavarman II. Dedicated to the Hindu god Vishnu, it covers an area larger than the Vatican in Rome and was isolated, in true Khmer tradition, from the hustle and bustle of the city by a 650-foot (200-m) wide moat. The temple itself consists of a cluster of central towers that rise like lotus buds above the tangled jungle. Beneath is a labyrinth of corridors, lined with elaborate carvings and sculptures, including one portraying the Hindu creation myth that stretches for 160 feet (50 m).

Anuradhapura, Sri Lanka

The best-known sights of the ancient city of Anuradhapura are the huge bell-shaped *dagobas* on the banks of the Aruvi Aru River in north-central Sri Lanka, 127 miles (204 km) north of Colombo. Built from small sun-dried bricks, these *dagobas*, or Buddhist commemorative shrines, formed part of a city that also included many temples, sculptures, and palaces, as well as drinking-water reservoirs. Leading up to many of these buildings are ornately carved staircases, such as the Ratnapasada, which were decorated with moonstones, stellae, and commemorative pillars.

Adding to the sacredness of the site is an ancient pipal tree said to have to been a branch from the Bo tree at Bodh Gaya under which the Buddha achieved enlightenment. The tree branch was planted in Anuradhapura in 245 B.C., and it may well be the oldest tree for which there is any historical record. Anuradhapura means "city of happy people," and its roots date back to the fifth century B.C. It remained the Sinhalese capital until the 11th century A.D., when invasions from southern India forced its evacuation.

Caves of the Thousand Buddhas, China

Carved out of a cliff southeast of Dunhuang in northwestern China are a series of caves that house the world's greatest collection of Buddhist art. They contain 2,000 statues and 45,000 colored murals, hidden in recesses that range from small grottoes to spacious caverns. These caves were built between the 4th and 10th centuries by Chinese Buddhists who traveled along the ancient Silk Road upon which Dunhuang was situated. On the westbound journey, they prayed here for a successful trip; on the eastbound they offered thanks for their safe return. As thanks offerings for safe passage, the travelers constructed statues or created highly ornate and brightly colored murals.

The caves' most astonishing hoard was only revealed at the beginning of the 20th century. In 1907, explorer Sir Aurel Stein, on an expedition from India, came across an enormous collection of ancient manuscripts that had been carefully preserved within one of the chambers. This extensive library of documents had been collected from all over Asia and included papers in Chinese, Tibetan, Sanskrit, and Sogidan, as well as a printed version of the *Diamond Sutra*, which dates from 868 A.D., making it the earliest known printed book.

Harappa, Pakistan

Excavations carried out on the left bank of what is now a dry watercourse of the Ravi River in eastern

Pakistan have revealed one of the major settlements of the Indus Valley culture. This culture flourished between 2500 and 1700 B.C. and was contemporary with those in Mesopotamia and ancient Egypt. At its peak, the Indus Valley civilization spread from the shores of the Arabian Sea to the Simla Hills, 1,000 miles (1,600 km) to the northeast, and down to within 30 miles (48 km) of present-day Delhi.

Harappa is second in size only to the ruins found at Mohenjo-Daro some 400 miles (650 km) to the west. Both dominated their culture, and both were rigidly designed following a strict grid plan. Along the crisscrossing streets were residential blocks and huge granaries; the focal point of the complex was a massive citadel resting on a raised podium. This was fortified by a tall mud-brick rampart dotted at frequent intervals with impressive bastions.

The buildings and artefacts unearthed from sites such as Harappa have provided the only evidence that exists of this extensive and complex society. Attempts to translate their language have met with only tentative success, and details of their history remain lost in the mists of the past.

Pagan, Myanmar

Rising up in the middle of a hot, dusty plain in the center of Myanmar, formerly known as Burma, is a collection of more than 2,000 Buddhist pagodas, nestling so close together that they form a forest of spires, pinnacles, and conical domes reaching into the sky. The temples stretch for 8 miles (13 km) along the banks of Myanmar's major river, the Irrawaddy, and 2 miles (3 km) inland.

The city of Pagan was founded by the Burmese ruler King Pyinbia in 849 A.D., but the major period of temple building occurred between the 11th and the 13th centuries, following the defeat of the Mons people from the south and their forced exile to Pagan. These extremely skilled artisans were able to construct many of the profusion of temples and pagodas in the city. Most impressive of these is the Dammayangyi Ananda, in which six terraces rise from a square-shaped base in a blaze of brilliant white stucco. However, Pagan's glory came to a swift end when in 1283, the Mongol leader Kublai Khan invaded northern India and the city was evacuated.

Persepolis, Iran

Although the inaccessibility of its site high in the mountains of Iran made Persepolis habitable for only short periods of the year, the capital of the Persian Empire remains a superb architectural achievement.

The great palace, built by Darius I and his successors Xerxes and Artaxerxes, sat upon a vast terrace some 1,600 feet by 1,000 feet (500 m by 300 m), upon which the rooms were constructed from a highly polished dark gray stone. These included the Apadana, which served as Darius's main audience chamber, and a main hall of pillars, each of which was 17 feet (5 m) in diameter and supported the 65-foot (20-m) high ceiling. Beyond the confines of the palace lay a sprawling town provisioned by the fertile plain in which it stood.

Some 4 miles (6 km) to the north, several royal tombs hewn out of a cliff face have been uncovered. The city's prosperity came to an end when Alexander the Great sacked the town and overthrew the emperor in 330 B.C.

Shi Huangdi Tomb Complex, China

The rows upon rows of terracotta soldiers discovered near the city of Xi'an in 1974 are one of China's most mysterious finds. There are more than 6,000 of these statues, each unique, intricately detailed, and larger than life, guarding the tomb of China's first emperor, Shi Huangdi. The emperor was obsessed by his death as early as 247 B.C., when he came to the throne at the age of 13, and ordered the construction of an enormous tomb. Over half a million people were employed in the construction of the site, of which the terracotta soldiers form only a small part. The figures, which include archers, swordsmen, and chariots complete with horses, lie in satellite burial mounds around the central tomb which is as yet unexcavated but is believed to house the emperor's body.

The Hang historian Sima Qian – who lived between 145 and 90 B.C. – gives a tantalizing view of the tomb's contents. He describes the ceiling of the mausoleum as a depiction of the heavens, below which was a three-dimensional model of the kingdom, complete with flowing rivers and seas of mercury. To deter potential grave robbers, crossbows were primed to fire their bolts at the first sign of an intrusion. Finally, the tomb was covered and planted with trees to resemble a small innocuous hill, as it does today.

Sigiriya, Sri Lanka

On top of a huge rock pillar in the center of northern Sri Lanka is what appears to be an almost impenetrable fortress. Kasyapa I, a usurper to the throne who believed he was both god and king, built this ancient stronghold in 477 A.D. to protect himself from his enemies.

Known as Lion Mountain, this palace fortress is nearly 600 feet (180 m) above the surrounding plain and is accessible only by means of a walkway that clings to the side of the overhanging rock. On the way up are paintings that remain to decorate the journey. They portray asparases, or nymphs, that emerge from clouds to scatter flower petals for the traveler. The final ascent is made through the jaws and throat (*giriya*) of an enormous lion (*sinha*), hence the name Sigiriya. Beyond this, the palace is arranged in a series of levels, containing residences, courts, and rock gardens, with the king's audience hall occupying the summit. Beyond the citadel lies a garden complex with ponds and plantations.

Shwe Dagon Pagoda, Myanmar

Buried within a hill to the north of the nation's capital, Rangoon, are said to be relics of the four Buddhas. Above this rises an enormous golden pagoda, in the shape of a giant hand bell, towering over a forest of smaller spires and a collection of mythical animals including leographs (half-lion, half-griffin), sphinxes, and dragons.

This site has been considered sacred for more than 2,500 years, but the present temple complex was constructed only in the 15th century. At that time, Queen Shisawba decided to gild the massive dome with gold leaf. Since then, the rigors of the tropical climate have meant that the gold has to be completely replaced every 20 years, at considerable expense. The effect, however, is breathtaking as the brilliant sunshine glistens on the golden dome creating an aura all of its own. Surmounting the stupa is the *hui* – an elegant umbrella-shaped cap

that is studded with more than 1,100 diamonds, including one on the tip that weighs 76 carats. The complex also houses the Maha Ganda bell, which is 14 feet (4 m) high and weighs 23 tons.

Outposts of the Beyond

Kamchatka Peninsula, Russia

In the western imagination, the word Siberia conjures an image of a vast, impenetrable wasteland far away. Kamchatka is still more remote – the most easterly tip of the continent of Asia, stretching some 750 miles (1,200 km) from the eastern tip of Siberia. The peninsula separates the two icy seas of Okhotsk to the west and Bering to the east. This finger of land, 350 miles (560 km) at its widest part, points south into the Pacific, toward the islands of Japan. Its 147,000 sq. miles (380,000 km²) are sparsely populated, and its countryside remains largely wild and untouched.

Kamchatka is also a land of extreme contrasts. Its two major mountain ranges – the Sredinny, or central, and Vostochny, or eastern – are testimony to its violent volcanic life as part of the Pacific "ring of fire." Twenty-two of these summits still harbor active volcanoes, and one, Klyuchevskaya Sopka, has erupted more than 70 times since 1679.

But alongside the volcanoes, geysers, and hot springs, the peninsula holds more than 400 glaciers. Its lush, mineral-rich soil also supports dense birch and larch forests, and – in spite of its cold climate – a surprisingly diverse range of wildlife. Salmon regularly spawn in its rivers, brown bears roam its forests, and the magnificent Stellar's sea eagle soars in the skies above it.

Lhasa, Tibet

The capital of the Tibetan region lies a breathtaking 12,000 feet (3,700 m) above sea level in the center of a fertile plain lined with poplars and scattered with fields of peas and barley. Beyond this soar the massive peaks of the Tibetan Himalayas.

Translated as "the ground of the gods," Lhasa is isolated physically and spiritually. It was the seat of the Tibetan ruler, the Dalai Lama, from 1391 until Chinese occupation in 1951. During this period, 13 Dalai Lamas governed the state, each believed to be a reincarnation of his predecessor. With the death of each one, a search is made for a suitable boy to continue the line, born at the exact moment of his predecessor's expiration.

The Dalai Lama's winter residence was the imposing Potala Palace, a vast building towering 330 feet (100 m) above the ground. Its height was augmented by its inward-sloping walls, which stretch some 1,000 feet (300 m) from end to end and dominate the bazaars and winding streets below. During the summer months, the Dalai Lama resided in the Jewel Palace.

Pamirs, Tadzhikistan

A remote region at the heart of central Asia is the meeting place of some of the largest mountain chains in the world: the Himalayas, Karakorams, the Kunlun, Tien Shan, Gissaro-Alai, and the Hindu Kush come together at the Pamir Mountains. These peaks occupy a rough rectangle some 155 miles (250 km) across in the eastern half of Tadzhikistan and form a collection of awesome jagged crests and ridges which soar into the sky, while below them sit broad, shallow lakes. The permanently snow-capped peaks reach 24,590 feet (7,495 m) at Communism Peak, their highest point. Massive glaciers sweep into the valleys below, scouring the rock as they move. The largest is the Fedchenko glacier, which stretches for 48 miles (77 km).

The wildlife of the region is sparse but supremely adapted to life at high altitude. Among the creatures that make this area their home are the Tibetan snowcock, the long-tailed marmot, and the shaggy-coated and elusive snow leopard.

Taymyr Peninsula, Russia

Straddling the 75th parallel, the Taymyr peninsula protrudes into the ice-strewn waters of the Arctic Ocean and is the most northerly region of the entire Eurasian mainland.

Essentially flat, the countryside is one of enormous vistas of open tundra streaked with winding rivers and dotted with pools and lakes thawed by the summer sun. Throughout the height of summer the sun hovers above the horizon. During this time, herds of reindeer migrate to the region in order to feed on the mosses and lichens that flourish in the milder climate.

In winter, the delicate glimmer of the northern lights plays upon the dark snow and frozen waterways that cover the surface. The sun disappears for four whole months and the temperature drops to −58°F (−50°C), freezing the ground beneath the surface solid down to a depth of 1,000 feet (300 m). When temperatures rise again, a thin layer of the surface melts, watering the soil. Under this melted surface the ground remains locked within the ever frozen world of permafrost.

Wrangel Island, Russia

This remote outpost of rock lies in the Arctic Ocean, close to the limit of permanent ice that surrounds the North Pole. Even during the warmer summer months the seas around Wrangel are strewn with shifting pack ice, and in winter, the water freezes solid, isolating the island from the rest of the world.

Its remoteness in human terms has made Wrangel Island a wildlife haven, particularly in the summer. Then, the countryside is filled with the cries of migrating birds, well over half a million of which nest here. These include brent geese, common eiders, knots, and gray plovers.

With the retreat of the permanent ice beyond the island's north shore, the coastline becomes host to a variety of sea mammals, drawn to the burgeoning life in the ocean. Bearded and ringed seals compete for beach space with enormous walruses. This concentration of animal life has attracted one other mammal. Polar bears cross to the island on drifting pack ice in order to reach denning areas and raise pups here. Each year nearly 300 are lured by the enormous range of prey they find on the beaches.

Beyond the stunning cliffs that line the shore, the land has been worn flat by successive sheets of ice. Within this environment archaeologists have discovered that Wrangel Island was the final home of the woolly mammoth, which survived here until as recently as 2000 B.C.

EUROPE

Cities of Romance and Creation

Budapest, Hungary

Once known as "the Queen of the Danube," Budapest still holds onto the energy that made it a favorite venue of such composers as Liszt, Brahms, Bartók, and Kodály. Straddling the Danube, the city of more than 200 sq. miles (520 km²) is far from unified. On the west bank of the river at the foot of Castle Hill – itself characterized by a mixture of Romanesque, Gothic, and Baroque buildings, including Budai var (Buda castle) and the Fisherman's Bastion – lies the town of Buda. On the east bank is the later settlement of Pest, which is typified by semicircles of concentric tree-lined boulevards, crisscrossed by avenues. Pest also boasts the Vigado concert hall, venue for the visits of some of the great romantic composers.

Formerly two settlements, the two halves were officially united in 1872 under the name Buda-Pest, although the hyphen was soon dropped and the present name fell into common use. Spanning the Danube to link the two halves of the city are numerous bridges, the oldest of which, the Chain Bridge, was built by the British engineers William and Adam Clarke between 1839 and 1849.

Florence, Italy

The city of Florence sits astride the River Arno in central Italy, a monument to the glories of the medieval and Renaissance worlds. Now extended beyond the confines of the old city fortifications to cover some 40 sq. miles (100 km²), the city is still recognizable as the one that stood on the site 400 years ago. Today the skyline is dominated by the tower of the Palazzo Vecchio, Florence's tallest structure, which was built in the 13th century, and the 15th-century dome of the Duomo.

Florence was once one of the world's major powers and home to some of the greatest creative geniuses of all time – Michelangelo, Dante, and Leonardo da Vinci. Their work and that of others still graces the city, which houses probably the finest collection of Renaissance art and architecture in the world. Painstakingly preserved, these buildings dot the whole of the city. They include the city's original defenses, designed by Michelangelo, the Uffizi, and the Ponte Vecchio, which traverses the river and is today covered by some of Florence's more exclusive shops. On the southern side of the river are the Boboli Gardens, a picturesque collection of grottoes, orchards, pools, and fountains.

Istanbul, Turkey

The city of Istanbul lies at the crossroads between the continents of Asia and Europe and between the Black Sea and the Mediterranean. In the course of its history, the city has been swept along on the tides of religious, political, and cultural change; has been known as Byzantium and Constantinople; and has served as the capital of the Byzantine and Ottoman empires.

The oldest part of the capital occupies a peninsula of land that sticks out into the Bosporus, the channel of water linking the Black Sea and the Mediterranean, and is still graced by a collection of 25 churches that date from the city's Byzantine period. These include Haghia Sophia, which means "divine wisdom." Dating from the fourth century A.D., it is often considered the world's finest sacred building. Capped by a 105-foot (30-m) dome, the church was transformed into a mosque following the capture of the city by the Ottomans in 1453. Minarets were added to create the site as it stands today.

Monaco

Clinging to the hills overlooking the Mediterranean, the principality of Monaco has long been associated with fabulous wealth. The roots of this wealth lie in the state's refusal to charge its citizens income tax, which attracts the world's super-rich as residents. Symbolic of this affluence is the renowned casino which first opened its doors in 1861. State-owned, this playground of the wealthy contributes some 5 percent of the state's budget. But Monaco is also beautiful. Lying in the heart of the Cote d'Azur, just 9 miles (14 km) along the Grand Corniche from the French resort of Nice and 5 miles (8 km) from the Italian border, it enjoys a mild Mediterranean climate.

The palace of the Grimaldi royal family dominates the bay, where luxurious yachts lie at anchor. In 1878, a theater – now home to the Opéra de Monte Carlo – was built by Charles Garnier, designer of the Opéra Garnier in Paris. The Cousteau Museum is one of the finest tributes to the glories of life under the sea in the world. And every year Monaco plays host to one of sport's most prestigious events, the Monaco Grand Prix, when the central streets are transformed into a formula-one racetrack. Monaco can also boast that it is one of the most densely populated regions in the world. Its 30,000 people are housed in ¾ sq. mile (1.94 km²).

Rome, Italy

The streets of Rome testify to the city's history. Over the millennia, it has served as the capital of empires, kingdoms, and republics, and has been the spiritual focus for millions of people. Essentially, Rome is a city of contrasts. Ancient remains, such as the Colosseum, sit tranquilly within the teeming energetic realm of the modern world, where people relax in the cafés that line the plane-tree-shaded streets.

The relaxed attitude of today's Roman citizen contrasts with the ceremonial order represented by the Vatican City, situated within Rome's confines. This tiny state-within-a-city houses some of Rome's most beautiful architecture. The huge keyhole-shaped piazza designed by Bernini leads up to the impressive Basilica of St. Peter. To one side is the Sistine Chapel, where the aging Michelangelo adorned the ceiling with ornate sacred frescoes telling the Old Testament story from Genesis to the Flood, as well as portraying the Last Judgment.

Vienna, Austria

Lying on the Danube between the foothills of the Alps and the Carpathian Mountains is the former imperial city of Vienna, one of the best preserved of Europe's great ancient capitals. Vienna's architecture reflects the period when it served as the major city of an empire that stretched from Germany to the Balkans. The buildings from this golden imperial age are within the Ringstrasse, a massive circular road that encloses the city center. They include the Hofburg – a former imperial palace that houses the treasury of the Holy Roman and Austrian empires – in addition to the town hall, the Vienna State Opera, the Schönbrunn Palace, and the Belvedere, a summer residence for the Habsburg rulers.

As one of Europe's major political centers, Vienna attracted some of the continent's artistic elite. Composers including Haydn, Schubert, Beethoven, and Mozart spent time here, attracted by the patronage of the royal court. Even today, the city's streets are lined with the coffee houses for which it was renowned and which over the years have served as a focal point for local life.

Entangled in History

Alhambra, Spain
An inscription within the palace at Granada reads "nothing in life is more cruel than to be blind in Granada." The truth behind this saying is nowhere more apparent than at the Alhambra, one of the best examples of Moorish architecture ever constructed and the finest in Europe. Built originally as a minor fort, the Alhambra was converted into a royal palace when Christian attacks throughout Spain in the 12th and 14th centuries forced the Moors to move their capital to Granada. Over the reigns of Yussuf I (1333–53) and Mohammed V (1353–91), the Alhambra was extended into the architectural wonder it is today.

Although fairly unassuming from the outside, the Alhambra is best known for its fantastically ornate interiors. The Moorish fondness for water has been incorporated throughout the building's layout, as marble-lined fountains and pools reflect the ornate splendors of the surrounding architecture. In the Court of Myrtles, a tranquil pool of silvery water is flanked by two myrtle bushes, while water cascades from a central fountain over 12 marble lions that support it in the Court of Lions. Most impressive, however, is the stalactite ornamentation that hangs from domes, niches, and arches. The effect creates a honeycomb of thousands of cells across which light and shade dance throughout the day.

Chartres Cathedral, France
The site on which Chartres Cathedral was built has been held sacred by local inhabitants for millennia. Prehistoric people erected a dolmen here in the belief that those who walked beneath its arch were refreshed by tapping into the earth's energy. And Chartres was the site of a druid college. These early structures were replaced by a succession of churches, of which the present Gothic masterpiece is the sixth. Work began in 1194, and since the cathedral was far in advance of its time in terms of construction methods, it is believed that Knights Templar returning from the East brought with them the necessary knowledge to allow its completion.

Chartres is one of the most beautifully ornate monuments in the Christian world. Its porches and portals are covered in more than 2,000 sculpted figures, and the use of flying buttresses allowed for the construction of a high arched roof. In addition to making the cathedral appear larger than it really is, they offer increased space for stained glass, at which the craftsmen of the period were expert. One fine example is the Notre-Dame-la-Belle-Verrière window (Our Lady of the Beautiful Glass) situated in the choir stall.

Elsinore, Denmark
Two legendary characters are associated with the castle of Kronborg, formerly known as Elsinore, which lies north of the Danish capital Copenhagen. The first is a prince, known as Amleth, whose uncle murdered the prince's father and then went on to marry the widowed queen. This intrigue of the Danish court was the inspiration for William Shakespeare's play *Hamlet*. The second is the hero Holger the Dane. Formerly one of Charlemagne's paladins, or knight's-companions, he is said to be sleeping beneath the castle, waiting to return when his country's need is greatest.

Legends aside, the castle has served as a royal residence, a garrison, and a museum throughout its history. The first fortification here was built *c.*1420 by Eric of Pomerania for defense and to collect taxes from ships that passed through the waters between Denmark and Sweden. The present Dutch Renaissance-style castle, however, was built by King Frederick II in 1574. A century later, a whimsical garden was added to the grounds, where visitors could wander through the Kingdom of Heaven, visit a Hermit's Hut, and witness what was said to be the grave of Prince Hamlet.

Iona, Scotland
The tiny island of Iona, off the western coast of Scotland, is the site of the earliest attempts to bring Christianity to the British mainland. In 563 A.D., the Irish prince Columba, later canonized, brought 12 companions here, their purpose – according to the later Ionan monk, Adamnan – "to seek out a foreign country for the sake of Christ." Legend has it that Columba chose Iona because it was out of sight of the coast of his homeland. By the time he died in 597 A.D., a thriving monastery had been founded on the island, and several successful expeditions to the north of Britain had been carried out.

However, the appearance of Viking raiders meant a downturn in the monastery's fortunes throughout the 9th and 10th centuries. A resurgence occurred with the construction of a Benedictine abbey in 1203, but with the Reformation in the 16th century, the buildings once again fell into disrepair. Today the 13th-century abbey has been substantially restored to its former glory and lies in the beautiful isolation that first attracted Columba to the island.

Mont St. Michel, France
Today the conical mound of Mont St. Michel rises above the sandflats of the bay in which it lies, covered with monastic buildings, gardens, terraces, fortifications, and an abbey church. The Mount's only link to the mainland is by a single causeway. Building work began in 708 A.D. when Aubert, bishop of Avranches, was commanded in a dream to construct an oratory on the mount. Prior to this, it had been a tree-covered, isolated land populated only by a few monks. By the end of the 10th century, a Benedictine abbey and some 50 monks inhabited the island.

Work began on the impressive Romanesque abbey church in 1020 A.D. and continued for more than 100 years, as the steep slopes made construction extremely difficult. Later additions included a 15th-century choir to the abbey and a monastery, known as *le merveille*, "the marvel," which was built between 1211 and 1228 by King Phillip II of France. Since then, it has survived the Hundred Years' War with England in the 15th

century, as well as Huguenot onslaughts in 1591. Religious life came to end here during the French Revolution, when the monastery was dissolved and the island was turned into a prison, which it remained until 1863. Today Mont St. Michel is once again a retreat from the outside world, and visitors from all over the world flock here to find tranquillity.

Oberammergau, Germany
This apparently ordinary town nestling in a peaceful valley high in the Bavarian Alps stands as testament to the persistence of human nature, and to the sanctity of a pledge made by previous generations. According to legend, at the height of the plague which ravaged Europe in the 17th century, Oberammergau's surviving residents gathered in the local church and promised to perform the passion play if God lifted the plague. Miraculously, there were no further deaths; and true to their word, the population of the town have staged the play every 10 years for the past three and a half centuries. Neither the Franco–Prussian war of the late 19th century nor two world wars in the 20th have prevented performances.

The passion play, which begins at the start of Holy Week with the triumphal entry into Jerusalem and concludes with Christ's ascension into heaven, lasts for more than eight hours, from 9 a.m. to 5.30 p.m. It involves months of planning by the local residents, many of whom grow their hair and beards in order to perform.

Sagrada Familia, Barcelona, Spain
Conceived to the glory of God, the Church of the Holy Family, which dominates the Barcelona skyline, was designed by Spanish architect Antoni Gaudi, and, although still unfinished, is a testament to his vision and perseverance. Gaudi was commissioned to begin work on Sagrada Familia in 1883, although the early construction was directed by his contemporary, Francesco P. Villar. Within nine years, Gaudi had taken over sole supervision of the project and soon became so obsessed with it that he lived on site and worked on nothing else.

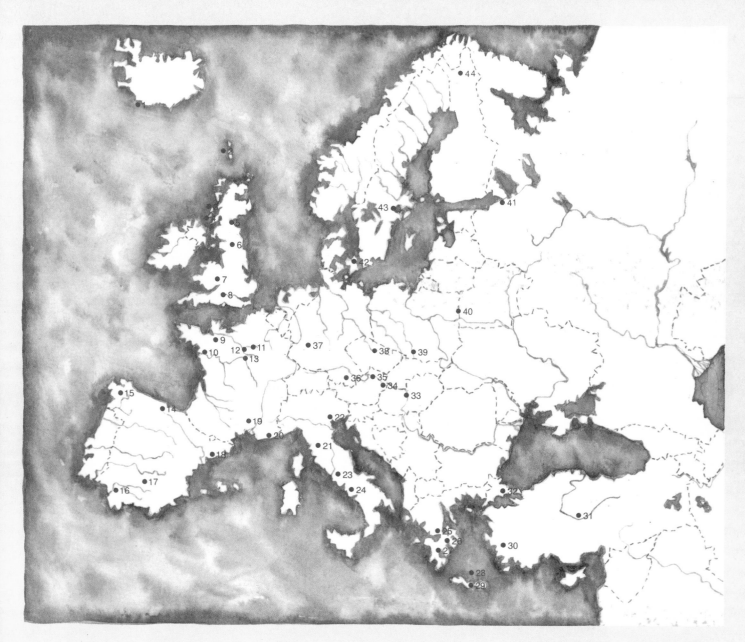

While making his way to vespers in 1926, Gaudi was hit by a trolley car and subsequently died of his wounds. But he left behind comprehensive plans for the cathedral's completion, which at the time consisted of only one transept and one of its four towers. Today three of the towers have been completed, and work on the central tower is underway.

The cathedral is typical of much of Gaudi's work: it is unique. Gaudi wanted his buildings to appear effortless, with none of the buttressing that had characterized every previous great Christian cathedral. His example was Nature – the Casa Mila apartments, for example, are constructed to resemble a series of lily pads. But his style also blends a freedom of form with rich colors and texture. At Sagrada Familia, where the vagaries of construction history have indeed resulted in an organic form, his vision reached its apogee. The effect is almost plantlike in its complexity, creating a forest of piers, vaults, and roofs.

Santiago de Compostela, Spain

For more than 10 centuries, Christian pilgrims have been drawn to the Cathedral of St. James at Santiago de Compostela in northwestern Spain. Legend has it that the site contains the remains of the martyr after which it is named, James (Iago in Spanish) – apostle and cousin of Christ – who was beheaded in Jerusalem. The story goes that James's followers placed his body on a ship, which carried it to the Atlantic coast of Spain. From there it was carried inland to the present site and buried. It remained obscure for several centuries until the arrival in 950 A.D. of the first recorded foreign pilgrim, Bishop Godescala from Le Puy in the Auvergne region of France. Under his influence and thanks to the patronage of the wealthy monastery at Cluny – which built hospitals and priories along the route – Santiago de Compostela flourished as a center for pilgrimage.

The present cathedral was begun in 1078 and is renowned for the Portico de la Gloria, carved at the end of the 12th century, which lies behind the highly ornate 18th-century Baroque facade. The bones of St. James are said to be buried under the silver, alabaster, and jasper high altar, on which stands the bejeweled statue of the saint, cloaked in a silver cape. Pilgrims must hug the statue from behind, after which they are entitled to wear a scalloped shell to symbolize their successful pilgrimage.

Tintern Abbey, Wales

The Cistercian house of Tintern Abbey is the most potent demonstration of the ravages wrought in Britain by the dissolution of the monasteries in 1536–40. Situated on the banks of the River Wye, against the backdrop of the rolling wooded hills of the Welsh countryside, Tintern Abbey was once the wealthiest monastery in Britain. It was founded in 1131, but was substantially rebuilt and enlarged 100 years later. Records show that by that time the abbey and its lands were valued at the phenomenal sum of £150. But on the dissolution of the monasteries, the church and its lands passed into the hands of the Lord of Chepstow. The buildings rapidly fell into disrepair, and today all that remains is the pale sandstone cruciform church, without a roof and with a damaged nave, along with a cluster of monastic buildings that are situated, unconventionally, to the north of the church.

The abbey and its picturesque setting have nonetheless inspired painters and poets, including Turner and Wordsworth, who composed "Lines written a few miles above Tintern Abbey" in 1798.

Paradise Found

Bialowieza Forest, Poland/Belorus

This area of woodland, which straddles the border between Poland and the Republic of Belorus, is the last surviving region of primeval mixed-tree forest in Europe. Conditions within its limits are similar to those found in the forests that covered much of the continent some 2,000 years ago. Today, the establishment of a national park covering about 460 sq. miles (1,200 km²) between the Narew and Lesna rivers insures the preservation of this unique ecological treasure.

There are some 26 species of trees in the forest, including pines, hornbeams, and oaks, and the forest is deliberately left untouched: dead trees lie where they fall. This tradition of protection stretches back to the 15th century, when the forest was preserved as part of the royal hunting grounds of the kings of Poland and the Russian tsars. The wildlife they stalked still roams the forest floor and includes wolves, lynxes, elks, wild boars, and forest bison. In 1921, the forest bison was extinct in the forest, but thanks to the generosity of zoos and animal parks throughout the world, 60 specimens were reintroduced. Today the Polish herd alone numbers more than 250.

Cévennes, France

The Massif Central, a huge upland area in central France, covers over one-sixth of the country. One part of this, known as the Cévennes, is a region of limestone plateaus and granite mountains. It includes Mount Lozère, the highest peak in the Cévennes at 5,574 feet (1,699 m). The region's upper slopes are swathed in forests of pine, fir, oak, and beech, while the lower slopes are carpeted in meadow and heath that blaze with color as wild flowers open in the spring. By contrast, the peaks and plateaus are isolated and bleak places.

The Causses in the west of the region are windswept tablelands with sparse vegetation and no surface water; they are bleak in the winter months and bake under the summer sun. Under this land of extremes is a network of underground caves and rivers whose floors and ceilings are strewn with stalactites and stalagmites that have been built up over the centuries by percolating rainwater. Above ground, the region plays host to red and roe deer, European beavers, Griffon vultures, and the recently reintroduced lammergeier, also known as the bearded vulture because of the bristles on each side of its beak.

Rhine Gorge, Germany

As it flows between the towns of Bingen and Koblenz, the River Rhine enters into a 90-mile (145-km) long gorge. The sheer sides and looming peaks create some of the most picturesque scenery along its watercourse from the Swiss Alps to the North Sea. Terraced vineyards line the route, and at regular intervals medieval castles perch precariously on rocky outcrops overlooking the river. Above the village of St. Goarhausen are the ruins of the Katz Burg, which offers breathtaking views down the rocky cliffs into the gorge below.

The region is steeped in history, myth, and legend. As the river approaches St. Goar, it narrows to flow around a precipitous 433-foot (132-m) high rock, known as the Lorelei. This stretch of water is noted for the echoes generated by the rock and may well be the source of the myth of the sirens. The songs of these maidens lured unwary sailors to their deaths in the treacherous currents around the rock's base. Farther downstream lie the Siebengebirge, or "seven mountains," said to have been formed when giants deposited the earth dug out when making the river. One of these, Drachenfels, or "dragon rock," is reputedly the spot where the Wagnerian hero, Siegfried, killed a dragon.

From the Mists of the Past

Altamira, Spain

In 1868, quite by chance, the caves at Altamira, some 20 miles (30 km) west of Santander, were discovered when a hunter stumbled upon them. Their importance was not immediately recognized, but subsequent explorations revealed evidence of prehistoric human occupation and one of the finest art galleries in the world. The discoveries were dismissed as an elaborate hoax, but by the beginning of the 20th century, this art collection was accepted as dating from the Ice Age.

The caves stretch back 890 feet (270 m) into the hillside, and their floors were scattered with various artistic and practical implements. These include ceremonial staves in addition to engraved animal shoulder blades. But the greatest treasures remain the collections of art, particularly those covering the ceiling of the great lateral chamber, a part of the caves which is 59 feet (18 m) long and 25 feet (7.5 m) high. Across the roof are a host of images of animals – including bison, wild boars, and horses – as well as human figures, hand prints, and outlines. Drawn in charcoal and earth colors, the figures stand out in an array of reds, blacks, and browns, which archaeologists have dated to 13,500 B.C.

Cappadocia, Turkey

High in the uplands of Turkey's Anatolian heartland is a haunting landscape dominated by rock cones. These strange features have been sculpted over the years by wind and rain out of the soft pale rock known as tufa. The countryside here is extremely fertile and has supported generations of people. The region is best known for the dwellings that these people have chosen to make their own: close inspection of the rock cones reveals that many contain houses, and the region is dotted with entire underground towns.

Hewn out of the soft rock, the oldest of these dwellings date from the first century A.D., when early Christians started to carve out churches and hermitages. Soon these had extended into warrenlike excavations containing storerooms, living quarters, wells, air shafts, and pits to catch intruders. Even larger elements of furniture, such as beds, have been sculpted out of the rock. These extensive constructions could house thousands of inhabitants, known as troglodytes, in virtually impenetrable security.

Carnac, France

In the countryside around the village of Carnac in northwestern France is one of the most puzzling man-made constructions in the world. More than 3,000 stones have been arranged into parallel lines and curves in three distinct groups. Row upon row of these tall, free-standing stones, or menhirs, stretch for up to 5 miles (8 km). The largest group, referred to as Le Ménec, is made up of 1,099 stones organized into 11 rows. The stones vary greatly in size, from 3 feet to 23 feet (0.9 m to 7 m) in height. The more massive stones weigh in excess of 350 tons, and scientists have been mystified as to how the people were able to create such a construction as early as 3500 B.C., before the introduction of the wheel to Europe.

Theories for the possible uses of such a collection of stones are wide-ranging. These include the possibility that they make up a huge astronomical clock, or that they were monuments to the dead, a hypothesis borne out by the fact that Carnac, in Breton, means "cemetery of the dead." But local legend relates perhaps the most romantic theory: Saint Cornély, when the village was threatened by advancing Roman troops, turned all of the soldiers into stone.

Delphi, Greece

Greek myth relates the story of the quest to find the center of the world. To solve this riddle, Zeus released two eagles from either end of the world and they met in the skies above Delphi, on the slopes of Mount Parnassus north of the Gulf of Corinth. To mark the spot, a stone, known as the *omphalos*, or navel, was laid.

As the center of the Greek world, Delphi was sacred. Throughout the seventh and sixth centuries B.C., it became a popular pilgrimage site. People flocked along the Sacred Way to visit the Temple of Apollo and to consult the oracle. Questions were asked on every subject from politics to marriage, fertility to money. Records indicate that answers could be straightforward or extremely ambiguous. The philosopher Socrates was told that he was the most intelligent man in Greece. But when Croesus of Lydia asked what would happen if he attacked Persia, he was told that he would destroy a great empire. He attacked, but in the war against the Persian Empire, he succeeded in destroying his own.

Delphi's influence lasted for more than 400 years and only began to decline with the emergence of the Roman Empire. Its final death knoll came when the site was officially closed by the Christian emperor Theodosius in 385 A.D.

Ephesus, Turkey

Home to the Temple of Artemis, one of the seven wonders of the ancient world, the city of Ephesus was one of the great metropolises of the Greco-Roman era. The site was first settled as early as 1000 B.C. by Ionian Greeks. The focus of their religion was Artemisia Ephesia, a hybrid deity associated with wild nature and fertility. A number of temples stood on the site, but the grandest was the last to be built, in 356 B.C. This impressive structure contained a forest of 127 marble columns that supported a roof 60 feet (18 m) above the ground, and its inner sanctuary was filled with marvelous statues.

Around the temple the city grew as a center for the Artemis cult, attracting, among others, practitioners of the magical arts such as fortune telling, astrology, and exorcism. Ephesus also became extremely wealthy, ideally situated as it was between the Near East and Greece and Rome. The city flourished for 500 years until 263 A.D., when it was razed by the Goths from northern Europe. In the sixth century A.D., the remaining temple columns were taken to Constantinople to be used in the construction of the Byzantine cathedrals. Today only the foundations of the Temple of Artemis remain.

Knossos, Greece

The Mediterranean island of Crete shelters the remains of the first major civilization of the Western world. The ancient Minoan people arrived on the island in around 7,000 B.C., and the extensive remains indicate that they rapidly became a wealthy culture. The preponderance of storehouses points to an emphasis on commerce.

Highly skilled artists, the Minoans were also famed for their carving, metalwork, jewelry-making, and pottery. Here, too, acording to mythology, lived the Minotaur. This half-man, half-bull stalked a labyrinth on the island and was eventually killed by the Greek prince Theseus.

The focal point of the ruins are the vast remains of the Palace at Knossos, which, according to legend, was home to King Midas. The palace is a vast collection of private apartments, public halls, storerooms, and baths grouped around a central courtyard. Grandest of the rooms is the throne room, which still contains the high-backed gypsum throne guarded by two painted griffins. Frescoes throughout the palace adorn the walls, depicting athletic events and dolphins, the Minoan symbol for joy.

Mycenae, Greece

The extensive ruins at Mycenae constitute the last remains of the oldest city on the Greek mainland. First excavated in the 1840s, Mycenae did not yield its greatest treasure until 1874, when the archaeologist Heinrich Schliemann made a spectacular find. He uncovered a series of five treasure-filled shaft tombs that contained 19 bodies. This hoard included a unique, magnificent golden death mask, which Schliemann attributed to Agamemnon, the Greek king who laid siege to the city of Troy in Homer's epic poem, the *Iliad*.

The site's other treasures are extremely ornate and reveal a culture of immense wealth which flourished for some 500 years between 1600 and 1100 B.C. But the site itself is also impressive. Huge battlements some 16 feet (5 m) thick, made from massive limestone blocks – according to legend built by the fabulously strong mythical Cyclops – surround the city. Strategically, Mycenae offered commanding views over the plain of Argos and the mountain passes up to the Gulf of Corinth. Yet despite its impressive wealth and strength, the

civilization inexplicably vanished, plunging Greece into a dark age from which it did not emerge for 600 years.

Stonehenge, England

The standing stones of Stonehenge on Salisbury Plain have, for centuries, remained shrouded in mystery. No one is certain why these massive chunks of rock were dragged here, some from as far away as Wales, and then erected in precise patterns. Suggestions vary from a ceremonial burial ground to an astronomical clock. The site was considered to be a Druid's temple, and until recently services were still held there.

What has been determined is that the stones were erected over a period of 1,500 years during the late Stone and early Bronze ages, but mainly between 1800 and 1400 B.C. The structure itself consists of an outer ring of some 30 huge sandstone monoliths, called sarsens. Inside this are two horseshoe-shaped formations. Considering the primitive nature of the tools available to these early builders, this feat of construction is truly astonishing, particularly the precision involved in the ball and socket joints that hold the vertical and horizontal stones together.

So incredible was this feat that folklore attributes the creation of Stonehenge to something more mystical. A medieval English chronicler tells the story of how Merlin, the wizard of Arthurian legend, transported the stones to Salisbury Plain and erected them using his magic.

Thera, Greece

Since the dawn of civilization, legends have told of a rich and powerful island continent, whose people were expert sailors and whose influence covered the known globe. The Greek philosopher Plato described the mythical country of Atlantis as "larger than Libya and Asia Minor together," and related that its inhabitants, descendants of the god Neptune and his mortal wife, Clerio, lived in harmony. But disaster befell Atlantis: according to Plato, the nation vanished beneath the waves without leaving a trace.

For generations, Westerners have tried to find the spot where this ancient civilization disappeared. Of more than 40 suggested sites, the favorite is on the island of Thera. Here the ruins of a Bronze Age civilization dating back nearly 3,000 years indicate a culture skilled in the art of sailing and with a strong influence throughout much of the Mediterranean. For nearly 1,500 years, the culture flourished, but it met with disaster when, in 1500 B.C., the volcano on the island exploded, destroying much of Thera and the cities on it. Today, from the rocky cliffs on which the new city of Thera has been built, all that is visible of the volcano is its rim.

Outposts of the Beyond

Faroe Islands

At the extreme western edge of the continent of Europe is a collection of 17 main islands, along with numerous small islets and reefs. Called the Faroe Islands, they are situated in the rolling waves of the Atlantic between Iceland and the Shetland Islands and offer a haven from the icy realms farther north.

The coastline here is marked by sheer perpendicular cliffs, including those at Slaettaratindur, which reach 2,894 feet (882 m) above the waves. Around these fly numerous seabirds, including puffins, which come here to nest on the sheer cliffs and rear their young. Inland, the flattened summits of the majestic peaks are separated by narrow ravines, and, where the land flattens out, a thin peat soil covers the hard volcanic rock beneath.

Despite their northerly latitude, the islands enjoy a relatively mild climate, since warm Atlantic currents keep the harbors and fjords that dot the coastline relatively free of ice. The islands are a self-governing outpost of the country of Denmark, whose people, descendants of the Vikings who first arrived here around 800 A.D., rely heavily on the bounty of the sea for their livelihood.

Lapland

Covering almost a quarter of Sweden, Lapland is Europe's most northerly region and marks the boundary between the icy wildernesses of the Arctic and the milder realms of the temperate world. From its peaks and snow fields, the region sweeps down into a broad slope that stretches to the Gulf of Bothnia, a northern stretch of the Baltic Sea.

Lapland encompasses glistening snow-covered summits, alpine tundra, deep carved valleys, lakes, peat bogs, and marshland in a countryside sculpted by the gigantic ice sheets that last retreated some 10,000 years ago. Humanity has yet to make an impression in this, the largest protected wilderness in Europe, which stretches over 1,292,850 acres (523,200 hectares). Sarek National Park alone contains 90 mountains whose summits are above 5,900 feet (1,800 m) and more than 100 glaciers. The region is home to an array of wildlife, including golden eagles, gyrfalcons, bears, elks, and lynxes. It is also the land of the Laplanders, or Sami, who lead a semi-nomadic life herding reindeer across the snowy countryside.

Surtsey, Iceland

On November 14,1964, the island of Surtsey was born out of the violence of a volcanic eruption from the floor of the Atlantic Ocean. Within two days of the initial eruption, a ridge of rock had appeared above the steaming waters, and by the end of two weeks, it stretched 130 feet (40 m) above the waves and was 1,800 feet (550 m) long. The plume of smoke towered nearly 50,000 feet (15,250 m) above the speck of rock as further explosions hurled chunks of cool lava into the air.

By the end of January 1964, the island covered 1 sq. mile (2.6 km²), and subsequent eruptions coated the ground with lava, protecting it from the battering waves of the Atlantic. Once the eruptions had ceased in 1967, the island was left a dark gray unworldly mass, reminiscent of a lunar landscape. Named after Surtur, the Norse god of fire, Surtsey has offered scientists a perfect chance to study how Nature claims apparently barren and infertile areas of land. Despite the violence of its birth, the island is, today, a peaceful place. Its dark rocks are broken by patches of greenery where mosses and grasses have obtained a toehold in the soil. Meanwhile, the skies above the island have started to fill with a variety of birds that have chosen Surtsey as their nesting site.

INDEX

FURTHER READING

The books in this list, which is not intended to be exhaustive, offer interested readers an opportunity to delve more deeply into the background and the treasures of the places featured in this title.

GENERAL
Automobile Association *Train Journeys of the World* AA Publications, 1993
BBC *Great Journeys* BBC Books, 1989
Branigan, Prof. K. (ed.) *The Atlas of Archaeology* Macdonald, London, 1982
Hawkes, Nigel *Man on the Move* Reader's Digest, 1992
Hindley, Geoffrey *Tourists, Travellers and Pilgrims* Hutchinson, London, 1983
Morris, Jan *Among the Cities* Viking, New York and London, 1985
Views from Abroad: The Spectator Book of Travel Writing, Paladin Books, London, 1989

CITIES OF ROMANCE AND CREATION
Allen, Alban *Andalusia* Nelson, London, 1974
Cookridge, E.H. *Orient Express* Allen Lane, London, 1979
Courthion, Pierre *Montmartre – The Taste of Our Time* Editions d'Art Albert Skira, Paris, 1956
Evans, Sarah Jane *Seville* Sinclair Stevenson, London, 1992
Facaros, Dana and Michael Pauls *The Cadogan Guide to Venice* Cadogan Books, London, 1991
Jullian, Philippe *Montmartre* Phaidon, Oxford, 1977
Morris, James *Venice* Faber and Faber, London, 1960
Sexton, Richard and Randolph Delehanty *New Orleans: Elegance and Decadence* Chronicle Books, San Francisco, 1993
Thubron, Colin *Among the Russians* Penguin Books, London, 1985
——— *Mirror to Damascus* Heinemann, London, 1967

ENTANGLED IN HISTORY
Dunlop, Ian *Versailles* Hamish Hamilton, London, 1956
Gibbon, Monk *Austria* Batsford, London, 1953
Haslip, Joan *Marie Antoinette* Weidenfeld and Nicolson, London, 1987
Mitford, Nancy *Madame de Pompadour* Hamish Hamilton, London, 1954
Musulin, Stella *Austria: People and Landscape* Faber and Faber, London, 1967
Naipaul, V.S. *A Turn in the South* Alfred A. Knopf, New York; Viking, London, 1989
Niscemi, Maita di *Manor Houses and Castles of Sweden* Scala Books, New York, 1988
Norton, Lucy *The Sun King and His Loves* Hamish Hamilton, London, 1983
Payne, Robert *The Crusades: A History* Robert Hale, London, 1994
Sharman, Tim *Poland* Columbus, 1988
Treece, Henry *The Crusades* Souvenir Press, London, 1978
Zamoyski, Adam *The Polish Way* John Murray, London, 1987

PARADISE FOUND
Black, Jeremy *The British Abroad: The Grand Tour in the Eighteenth Century* Alan Sutton, London, 1992
Buplin, T.V. *Southern Africa: Land of Beauty and Splendour* Reader's Digest, Cape Town, 1976
Collingwood, W.G. *The Lake Counties* 1902, revised by William Rollinson, J.M. Dent, London, 1988
Davies, Hunter *William Wordsworth* Weidenfeld and Nicolson, London, 1980
Johnson, Russell and Kerry Morgan *Kailas: On Pilgrimage to the Sacred Mountain of Tibet* Thames and Hudson, London, 1989
Knight, W.F.G. *Cumaean Gates* Blackwell, Oxford, 1936
Sculthess, Emil *Africa* Collins, London, 1959
Wainwright, A. *Wainwright's Tour in the Lake District* Michael Joseph, London, 1993
Wordsworth, Dorothy *Illustrated Lakeland Journals* Collins, London, 1987

FROM THE MISTS OF THE PAST
Baines, J. and J. Malek *Atlas of Ancient Egypt* Phaidon, Oxford, 1984
Baudez, Claude and Sydney Picasso *Lost Cities of the Maya* Thames and Hudson, London, 1987
Bingham, Hiram *Lost City of the Incas: The Story of Machu Picchu* Phoenix House, London, 1951
Bray, W.M., E.H. Swainson, and I.S. Farrington *The Ancient Americas* Phaidon, Oxford, 1989
Browning, I. *Petra* Chatto and Windus, London, 1973; Merrimack Pub. Corps, 1982
Burckhardt, J.L. *Travels in Syria and the Holy Land* John Murray, London, 1822
Coe, M.D. *The Maya* Penguin, Harmondsworth, 1971; Thames and Hudson, New York, 1980
Hemming, John *Conquest of the Incas* Penguin, London, 1983
Kamil, Jill *Luxor* London and New York, 1983
Moorehead, Alan *The White Nile* Penguin, Harmondsworth, 1973
Smithies, Michael *Borobodur* Oxford University Press (2nd ed.), 1991

OUTPOSTS OF THE BEYOND
Bowring, Richard and Peter Kornicki (eds.) *Cambridge Encyclopedia of Japan* Cambridge University Press, 1993
Collcutt, Martin, Marius Jansen, and Isao Kumajura *Cultural Atlas of Japan* Phaidon, Oxford, 1988
Kelly, Thomas and Patricia Roberts *Kathmandu: City at the Edge of the World* Weidenfeld and Nicolson, London, 1989
Nicol, Gladys *Thailand* Batsford Books, London; Hippocrene Books, New York, 1980
Papineau, Aristide J.G. *Guide to Bangkok: City of Enchantment* André, Paris, 1974
Sapieha, Nicholas *Old Havana, Cuba* Tauris Parke Books, London, 1990
Smithies, Michael *Old Bangkok* Oxford University Press, 1986

ACKNOWLEDGMENTS

l = left, *r* = right, *t* = top, *c* = center, *b* = bottom

1 Harald Sund/The Image Bank; 2–3 Tony Stone Images; 6–7 Andrew Errington/Tony Stone Images; 7 Tony Stone Images; 8 Robert Harding Picture Library; 8–9 C.A. Wilton/The Image Bank; 10–11 Michael J. Howell/Robert Harding Picture Library; 12–13 Zefa Picture Library; 14 Bob Krist/Colorific!/Telegraph Colour Library; 15*t* Zefa Picture Library; 15*b* Francesco Venturi/Kea Publishing Services; 16 Wojtek Buss/Rapho/Network; 17*t* Francesco Venturi/Kea Publishing Services; 17*b* Barry Lewis/Network; 18–19 Robert Harding Picture Library; 20 B. van Berg/The Image Bank; 21*t* Thomas Ernsting/Bilderberg/Network; 21*b* Coll. Crespi, Milan/Scala; 22–23 Michael J. Howell/Robert Harding Picture Library; 23 J. Hunter/The Image Bank; 24 La Vie du Rail; 26–27 Cesar Lucas/The Image Bank; 28–29 John Hatt/Hutchison Library; 29 Spectrum Colour Library; 30–31 Peter Charlesworth/Colorific!/Telegraph Colour Library; 31 Matthew Kneale; 32 Abbas/Magnum Photos; 33*t* British Museum/Michael Holford; 33*b* Rosemary Evans/Tony Stone Images; 34–35 Spectrum Colour Library; 36 T. Hoepker/Magnum Photos; 37*t* T. Hoepker/Magnum Photos; 37*b* J.M. Roberts/Zefa Picture Library; 38–39 Mark Segal/Tony Stone Images; 39 Peter Poulides/Tony Stone Images; 40–41 Bruno De Hogues/Tony Stone Images; 42 Zefa Picture Library; 43*t* Musée d'Orsay, Paris/Giraudon/The Bridgeman Art Library; 43*b* Tony Stone Images; 44 Zefa Picture Library; 47 Patrick Ingrand/Tony Stone Images; 48–49 John Miller/Robert Harding Picture Library; 50–51 Zefa Picture Library; 51 Michael J. Howell/Robert Harding Picture Library; 52 Blanca Trueba/Katz Pictures; 53*t* Terry Williams/Stockphotos; 53*b* Explorer/Robert Harding Picture Library; 54–55 Stephen Studd/Tony Stone Images; 56 Julian Nieman/Comstock; 57*t* Grant Faint/The Image Bank; 57*b* Joe Cornish/Tony Stone Images; 58 Michael Jenner/Robert Harding Picture Library; 59*t* Joe Cornish/Tony Stone Images; 59*b* Alena Vikova/Tony Stone Images; 60–61 Zefa Picture Library; 62–63 Robert Harding Picture Library; 64–65 Schulenburg/The Interior World; 65 E.T. Archive; 66–67 Obremski/The Image Bank; 68 Library of Congress; 69*t* David Muench; 69*b* Bob Krist/Tony Stone Images; 70–71 Superstock; 72–73 J. Allan Cash; 74 C.L. Schmitt/Britstock; 75*t* British Library/The Bridgeman Art Library; 75*b* Zefa Picture Library; 76 Tony Craddock/Tony Stone Images; 78–79 Doug Corrance/The Still Moving Picture Co.; 80 E.T. Archive; 81 John Freeman/The Royal Collection © Her Majesty Queen Elizabeth II; 82–83 Gerard Mathieu/The Image Bank; 84 Treasury of Wawel Cathedral, Cracow/The Bridgeman Art Library; 84–85 Christopher Rennie/Robert Harding Picture Library; 85 Christopher Rennie/Robert Harding Picture Library; 86–87 Robert Harding Picture Library; 88 Mary Evans Picture Library; 88–89 Lauros-Giraudon/The Bridgeman Art Library; 90 Philip Craven/Robert Harding Picture Library; 91*t* AKG London; 91*b* Marcel Isy-Schwart/The Image Bank; 92 Adam Woolfitt/Robert Harding Picture Library; 93*t* Explorer/Robert Harding Picture Library; 93*b* Richard Passmore/Tony Stone Images; 94–95 Nick Greaves/Planet Earth Pictures; 96–97 Images Colour Library; 98*t* The Mansell Collection; 98*b* David Lyons; 99*t* David Paterson; 99*b* David Lyons; 100–101 David Lyons; 102–103 Stephen Wilkes/The Image Bank; 104–105 Peter Pickford/NHPA; 105 *inset* Peter Newark's Historical Pictures; 106 Ian Murphy/Tony Stone Images; 108–109 Russell Johnson; 110–111 Russell Johnson; 112–113 R. Everts/Zefa Picture Library; 114–115*t* Scala; 114–115*b* Werner Forman Archive; 115 J. Allan Cash; 116–117 The Bridgeman Art Library; 117 Simeone Huber/Tony Stone Images; 118 Richard Ashworth/Robert Harding Picture Library; 119*t* Ronald Sheridan/Ancient Art & Architecture Collection; 119*b* Andrer Pistolesi/The Image Bank; 120 Joe Cornish; 122–123 Brian Kyles/The Still Moving Picture Co.; 124 G. Williams/Scotland in Focus; 125*tl* AKG London; 125*tr* AKG London; 125*b* R. Weir/Scotland in Focus; 126–127 Hugh Sitton/Tony Stone Images; 128–129 David Paterson; 130–131 David Paterson; 131 Robert Harding Picture Library; 132 Cecil Higgins Art Gallery/The Bridgeman Art Library; 133*t* Gerard Champlong/The Image Bank; 133*b* David Paterson; 134–135 Photobank Photolibrary; 136 Bernard Cox/National Archaeological Museum, Athens/The Bridgeman Art Library; 136–137 Images Colour Library; 138–139 Michael Mirecki/Impact Photos; 140–141 Mireille Vautier; 141 Thierry Cazabon/Tony Stone Images; 142–143 Mireille Vautier; 143–145 Francesco Venturi/Kea Publishing Services; 146–147 Bob Croxford/Zefa Picture Library; 148–149 Photobank Photolibrary; 149 Robert Harding Picture Library; 150–151 Fred Mayer/Magnum Photos; 151 Photobank Photolibrary; 152–153 W. Steinmetz/The Image Bank; 154–155 Hugh Sitton/Tony Stone Images; 155*t* Stephen Studd/Tony Stone Images; 155*b* Chris Haigh/Tony Stone Images; 156–157 Zefa Picture Library; 158–160 Mireille Vautier; 161*t* Robert Francis/South American Pictures; 161*b* Tony Stone Images; 162–163 Neil Beer/Tony Stone Images; 164–167 David Paterson; 168 Spectrum Colour Library; 169*t* Photobank Photolibrary; 169*b* Steve McCurry/Magnum Photos; 170–171 Christophe Bluntzer/Impact Photos; 172 Roland & Sabrina Michaud/The John Hillelson Agency; 173 James Strachan/Robert Harding Picture Library; 174 Roland & Sabrina Michaud/The John Hillelson Agency; 175*t* Francesco Venturi/Kea Publishing Services; 175*b* David Poole/Robert Harding Picture Library; 177 Roland Lewis; 178–179 Photobank Photolibrary; 180 Glen Allison/Tony Stone Images; 181*t* John Lamb/Tony Stone Images; 181*b* Robert Harding Picture Library; 182–183 R. Halin/Zefa Picture Library; 184–185 Photobank Photolibrary; 185 Michael Jenner/Robert Harding Picture Library; 186–187 Burt Glinn/Magnum Photos; 187*t* Francesco Venturi/Kea Publishing Services; 187*b* Zefa Picture Library; 189 John Massey Stewart; 190–191 Tony Waltham/Robert Harding Picture Library; 192*t* W. Louvet/Impact Photos; 192*b* Hiroji Kubota/Magnum Photos; 193 P. & G. Bowater/The Image Bank; 194–195 Nicolas Sapieha/Kea Publishing Services; 196 Francesco Venturi/Kea Publishing Services; 196–197 Christine Pemberton/Hutchison Library; 197 Francesco Venturi/Kea Publishing Services; 198 Range/Bettmann; 199*t* Range/Bettmann; 199*b* FrancescoVenturi/Kea Publishing Services